Collectables Manual

Published in April 2009

A catalogue record for this book is available from the British Library

ISBN 978 1 84425 682 2

Library of Congress control no. 2008939605

Published by Haynes Publishing, Sparkford, Yeovil, Somerset BA22 7JJ, UK

Tel: 01963 442030 Fax: 01963 440001
Int. tel: +44 1963 442030
Int. fax: +44 1963 440001
E-mail: sales@haynes.co.uk
Website: www.haynes.co.uk

Haynes North America, Inc., 861 Lawrence Drive
Newbury Park, California 91320, USA

Design and layout by Richard Parsons

Printed and bound in Great Britain

Acknowledgements

My most sincere and heartfelt thanks to:

Tina Weaver, Jill Main, Deidre O'Brien, Jane Kerr, Deborah Sherwood, Justine Naylan and all the Features and Picture Desk team at my paper, *The Sunday Mirror*.

This book would not have been possible without the continual opportunities that this superb Sunday newspaper has given me to reach readers far and wide, week in, week out via my column 'Treasure Hunters'. My Editor, Tina Weaver, has generously permitted me to reprint some updated information from columns gone by and I encourage you to keep an eye on the collectables market in 2009 and beyond by becoming a regular reader of the paper.

I would also like to offer thanks to Mark Hughes and Steve Rendle at Haynes Publishing, who have proved to be most supportive and flexible during my time preparing this book; John Hardaker, who spent his Christmas and New Year tidying up my words so effectively, and J Haynes, Group Vice Chairman and Managing Director of Haynes Publishing and his wife Valencia, who first put the idea in my head some years ago while in Cannes.

I would like to thank my friends Nicky Evans, Michelle Coss and Hanna Coss for supporting and encouraging me while I took the time to write *The Collectables Manual* and Martin Breese for his superb professional images.

I would like to express my enormous gratitude to my friends **Bronia Lee** and Nathan O'Driscoll from Cream and Chrome Collectables and Neo Belle Bizaar (Bronia's company) in Bristol who provided so many of the wonderful items you see in the images. This book would not have been possible without their expertise and generosity. Bronia now carries the title 'Special Picture Consultant to *The Collectables Manual*'!

Lorna Kaufman of Vectis Auctions (www.vectis.co.uk) has been on hand for the best part of six months to generously provide many superb images, and Hannah Schmidt of Christies (www.christies.com) has kindly made magic happen to help bring this book to life.

James Swyer of Fraser's has been very helpful (www.frasersautographs.com)

Other special thank yous are offered to:

Saxon Durrant of Metro Retro – www.metroretro.co.uk

Jon Gilbert of Adrian Harrington Rare Books – www.harringtonbooks.co.uk

Emily Johnston of Spink – www.spink.com

Andrew Stanistreet and Chloe Walker of Wedgwood/Royal Doulton – www.royaldoulton.com

Joanna Ling and Katherine Marshall of Sotheby's Picture Library – www.sothebys.com/picture-library

Ruth Ratcliffe of W.Moorcroft PLC – www.moorcroft.com

Michael Beatt of Mathmos – www.mathmos.com

Lynn Gray of The Doulton Lady – www.thedoultonlady.co.uk

Stephen Lane of The Prop Store of London – www.propstore.com

Colin P Ryan of Nicol Crests & Collectables – www.nicolcrests.co.uk

Teresa Wetton of Perfect Pieces – www.perfectpieces.co.uk

Robert Harrop and Dan Buckley of Robert Harrop Designs – www.robertharrop.com

Steve Harris of On The Air – www.vintageradio.co.uk

Jenny Wright of The Wade Collectors Club – www.wadecollectorsclub.co.uk

Paul Raeside whose pix appear in BBC Homes and Antiques Magazine – www.homesandantiques.com

Laura Mottram and Stuart Kerr of The Royal Bank of Scotland Group – www.natwest.com

Michael Rowe of World Rugby Museum,Twickenham – www.rfu.com/microsites/museum

Angela Metcalfe and Helen Scott of Enesco – www.enesco.co.uk

Sara Plimbley of Portmeirion Pottery – www.portmeirion.co.uk

Taya Pobjoy of Pobjoy Mint – www.pobjoy.com

Antony of Stylophone.com – www.stylophone.com

The SylvaC Collectors' Circle – www.sylvacclub.com

Pete Ferrary of Cornishware.biz – www.cornishware.biz

Chris Dickerson of Sheffield Railwayana Auctions Limited – www.sheffieldrailwayana.co.uk

Harper Collins/Michael Bond, Norman Huntley, Valerie Watson, Fred Woodward, Christine Nixon, Garry Johnson and Beryl Wrigley.

Getty Images, TopFoto and Rex Features

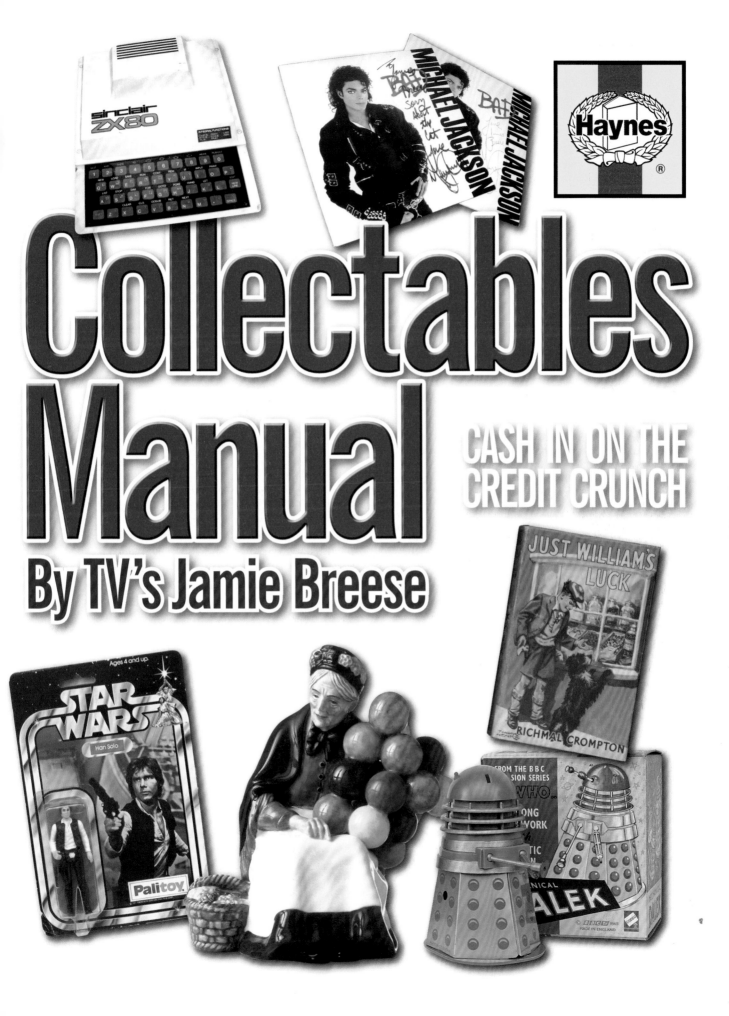

Collectables Manual

By TV's Jamie Breese

CASH IN ON THE CREDIT CRUNCH

Contents

Introduction

Welcome to *The Collectables Manual*. I have spent many, many years gathering this knowledge and I am delighted to be able to present it here, on paper, for you to both use and, I hope, enjoy.

I have also spent a good deal of my time helping to value and sell other people's collectables through my years with *The Sunday Mirror* and over the course of presenting or co-presenting several hundred television shows for the main UK network channels. I have written all sorts of articles, too, for many of the popular magazines: from *BBC Homes and Antiques* and *Woman's Weekly* to several years as a writer/expert for *Collect it!* and *The Daily Mail*'s 'Weekend Magazine'.

I say all this not to beat my chest, but to reassure you that the information is as accurate as I can make it. I have adopted my usual tone, which is non-fussy and reasonably snappy on the facts front.

The purpose of the manual is to shed light on some superb collectables, and to encourage you to take a look at what you might have lurking in boxes in the attic or elsewhere in your home. It is designed to be an informative A to Z of many of the key collectables of today, and in many cases I write in more detail in 'sidebars', giving a deeper insight into the subject. The suggested values are based on what collectables have sold for in the past – quite often very recently – to give you the best possible indication of whether you have an item that is worth looking into further.

Bow tie?

Antiques and collectables have, to a certain degree, still got a whiff of ultra-formality about them, but it doesn't have to be all pipe and slippers and Sunday evenings. There is, of course, an important place for such an approach, particularly with antiques – and there are many, many superb experts who have dedicated their professional lives to a certain pottery, designer, or collectable. I am just hoping that my *generalist* expertise will not be too 'bow-tie' but rather of practical help to you, whether you are looking to help beat the credit crunch with what you have unearthed at home, or fancy becoming an eBay buyer/seller, or want to develop a good collection and need inspiration, or are just looking for a good read and a bit of nostalgia to boot.

Enjoy the book. I hope it brings you good fortune in every sense of the word.

The author, Jamie Breese
(Photograph courtesy of Andre Regini/Kingbridge Photographic)

A very limited-edition reproduction of the first ever Corgi toy car – a Ford Consul – presented to the author at the Corgi 50th Anniversary party (Jamie Breese)

About the author

Jamie Breese has a reputation as a young and cheeky, antiques, collectables and 'de-clutter' presenter/expert. He has ten years of writing and TV presenting experience, including prime-time series such as *The Life Laundry* and *The Antiques Show* (BBC2), and ITV1's popular daytime shows *This Morning*, *GMTV*, and *Everything Must Go!*

Jamie's antiques background is with his family who operated from London's famous Portobello Road. As a teenager he set up on his own as a dealer at Camden Stables market.

After achieving a first class honours in Art and Design, his TV break came with BBC2's *The Antiques Show*. Jamie went on to present for Channel 4's *Collectors' Lot*, HTV/ Meridian's *Antiques Trail*, and *Trade-It*. He was the weekly collectables expert on Five's *Breakfast News*, and has enjoyed numerous other stints on popular shows, including BBC1's flagships *The Generation Game* and *Blue Peter*.

Jamie is perhaps best known for ITV1's *Everything Must Go!* This is presenter-led and features families selling up and moving on: Jamie hosts, values their worldly goods, and helps sell them in a madcap house sale and, later, an auction. Prior to this he co-presented BBC2's *The Life Laundry* and has added 'clutterbusting' to his skills. In this series Jamie helped individuals deal with hoarding issues. Jamie also co-devised and hosted the regular live slot – 'Cash or Trash' – on ITV1's *This Morning*. At the time of writing, Jamie is a regular antiques and collectables expert on *GMTV*.

For eight years Jamie has been penning the weekly antiques column 'Treasure Hunters' for *The Sunday Mirror*. He has written regularly for the BBC *Homes & Antiques*, for *Woman's Weekly*, and for *Collect it!* He also has written for *Antiques and Collectables* magazine, *Moneywise*, *Moneyweek*, *Prudential*, *Yours*, *Chat* and *Heyday* magazines, among others. In 2007 he judged Corgi's 50th Anniversary Ultimate Collector Competition and hosted eBay's 'eBay Your Streets', 'Hidden Treasures' and '2007 Xmas Investment Gifts' campaigns. Jamie is a 'generalist' expert with many special interests, including books, and rock, pop and film memorabilia. Jamie lives in the UK and counts filmmaking as one of his other passions.

Readers can find out more about Jamie and sign up on his mailing list at: www.jamie.breese.co.uk

Read this bit ...

Antique or collectable?

Some maintain that for an item to qualify as an antique it should be over 100 or so years old. Certainly, glass, jewellery, ceramics, furniture, and clocks from before 1900 are going to be tagged as antiques in almost all cases. Corkscrews straddle both descriptions – they are keenly collected (mostly by wealthy professionals in my experience) but are largely pre-1900. I include them anyway.

British guide prices

The vast majority of items featured in this manual are from the 20th century and from the UK, because these are what you are most likely to find in your own home. However, with the rise of Internet auction sites, such as eBay, the market is often a global one.

It is worth noting that in many categories of collectable a degree of serious specialist knowledge is required if you want to either build a fine collection or invest and make money. Take Thunderbirds collectables as an example. With just one model – the Thunderbird 2 craft – there are a number of manufacturers, many different versions based on the colour of the base, the colour of the legs, the colour of the craft itself, the condition of the toy, and the packing it came in! The true value will depend on these subtle differences that can affect the price by several hundred pounds. This is not said to put you off – far from it. It is just important to remember that other collectors have set standards, and that there's a definite need to research a subject well if you want the best chance of making a mint and/or developing a collection to be proud of.

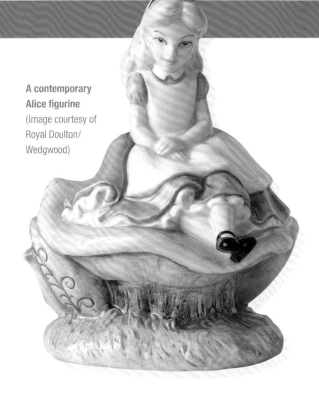

A contemporary Alice figurine (Image courtesy of Royal Doulton/ Wedgwood)

Condition can be everything

A practical example of how this can affect a sale is if you are looking to sell such a toy online – let's say eBay.co.uk. You'll need to describe the toy and any packaging in as much detail as possible and also provide good pictures. A seasoned collector, however, might just say 'good to very good in a near mint pictorial packaging'. Buyers will recognise that such a seller knows the deal and consequently they can probably be confident that the item is as it is described.

Having said all that, if you are a novice and perhaps a little stumped – then a good selection of pictures online will usually give potential buyers a good impression of what they can expect – and then the market will decide the value. It *can* be as simple as that.

This Jawa figure sold at Vectis Auctions in January 2004 for £320 (Image courtesy of Vectis Auctions)

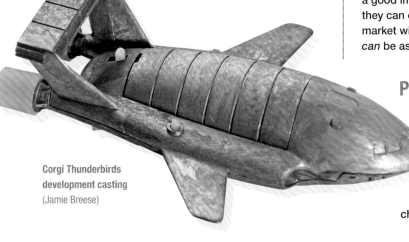

Corgi Thunderbirds development casting (Jamie Breese)

Prices?

This manual is not a definitive price guide. I see it more as a cross between a reference book, a good read with surprises, and some suggestions as to value that should be used as an *indication* only. At the time of writing (December 2008), the collectables market, like most others, is facing some challenges as a result of the worldwide credit crunch.

Maybe some prices will have dropped a little when you read this from March 2009 onwards. We got it into the shops as fast as possible, by the way!

It is important to realise that if you are looking to buy and sell items to make money, then just like the stock market the value of your items can fall as well as rise. There is inherent risk, of course. To make money if you are buying, you have to purchase the right collectables at the right time. Some say, of course, that when prices are low it's a good time to buy, but it depends on how long you have to wait for a recovery.

It is always worth checking online or looking at an auction catalogue or two before deciding exactly how much any finds or family items might be worth. If you have something really terrific and you need to seek clarification, you can always call your local auction house and take it in for an appraisal to throw more light on things. Ceramics and furniture are good examples of how an in-person inspection by a recognised expert can be valuable. Remember, though, the often-stated truth that ultimately something is only worth what somebody is prepared to pay for it on the day.

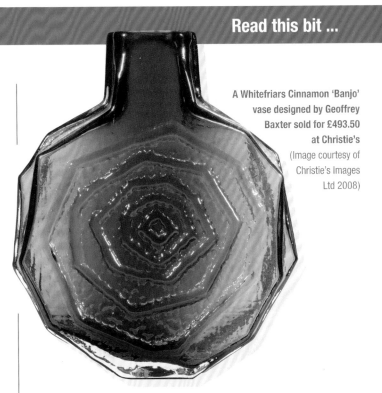

A Whitefriars Cinnamon 'Banjo' vase designed by Geoffrey Baxter sold for £493.50 at Christie's (Image courtesy of Christie's Images Ltd 2008)

The most popular type, made at the height of the Stylophone craze (Images courtesy of www.stylophone.com)

Auction, insurance, eBay, or high street?

The prices I have suggested are as realistic as possible. Unless specifically stated (e.g. this pen sold at Christie's in November 2008 for £1,250) then assume it is a guide price that *straddles* these three types of price/value – auction house, eBay.co.uk, insurance and dealer.

There is no hard and fast rule here – sometimes items can sell very cheaply on eBay as they have been listed in the wrong category, while dealers might sell it for a little more to cover their business costs. However, there are examples where a dealer might be a little cheaper (as you don't have the whole world able to bid on an item!) and you have that more personal contact/comeback, more often that not. A nice collectable figurine could be found very cheaply at a provincial auction house in a box of household items, sold without reserve perhaps, but then again, a large London house might sell the same piece for somewhat more as they have spent time promoting the sale across the globe, produced glossy catalogues, and have a huge list of existing clients.

Can't find a collectable?

I have done my best to feature a good selection of popular and surprising subjects here. In fact, I started off with a book twice as long! Of course, there are many, many thousands of different potential entries. If there is something you feel should be included in a later edition, why not write in and let me know?

Do visit my website and join my mailing group. Just click on www.jamiebreese.co.uk

The credit crunch

As the economy appears to be taking a bit of a pasting, there has been a renewed interest in all things collectable …

1 Go online! What makes this 'correction' so different from previous economic downturns is that now *anybody* with a computer and Internet access can research their possessions, to establish some idea of a value, and better still, sell them themselves!

■ **Research.** This is easy and here is my little tip – go to eBay.co.uk and search in the 'completed listings' section. Here you will find, in green, all the prices paid for the item you are searching for over the last few weeks. It's a free and bang-up-to-date price guide! Bear in mind that prices paid fluctuate, based on the number of bidders, luck, condition of item, etc., but you will get a 'feel' for values. Also bear in mind that 'eBay prices' are often said by experts to be the 'real world' price – sometimes a little cheaper than the guidebooks, etc.

■ **Sell.** In the early 1990s the Internet was in its infancy and online auction sites simply didn't exist. It was a more drawn out process to get valuations and sell your items. Today, if you need to realise some money and quickly, then do go online and sell your unwanted items. For the very first time, you can reach a global marketplace, and the marketplace decides the value. Other options include offering your wares to a dealer, going to an auction house, or setting up as a dealer yourself!

2 Do your very own *Life Laundry*. I used to present this iconic series for BBC2 a few years ago with Dawna Walter. We took an often troubled family and went through their entire house – the contents of which had been transported to a field or school gym – and we cleansed them of all their clutter in what we called

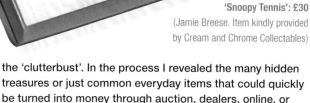

the 'clutterbust'. In the process I revealed the many hidden treasures or just common everyday items that could quickly be turned into money through auction, dealers, online, or car boot. Use the economic gloom to add some joy to your life. There is nothing better for the mind *and* the wallet than a de-cluttered home. Take the unwanted items which you can't or won't sell to your local charity, and recycle the rest.

3 Don't ignore the traditional ways of making money out of your possessions. The car boot is your best friend for a quick and fun way of getting rid of the day-to-day items and least valuable stuff. You do it in one fell swoop and you don't have to sit in front of a computer. You can easily net £200+ on a good day with a car-full of stuff. Be careful not to let any gems slip through your net though. This manual could be a useful read in that respect alone.

Car booting, with a bit of knowledge gained, can be great fun and, if you are buying, then a great way to find many collectables cheaply. There are pros and cons, as with any route to buying and selling. With car boots you have to work

Corgi Batmobile model 267. This can make hundreds of pounds if mint and boxed (Image courtesy of Vectis Auctions)

hard – early birds catch the worm here – and of course you have little comeback if you want to 'return' an item.

The car booting outdoor season is generally from Easter to early winter, but you can still find plenty of indoor fairs and hard-standing events (check with the organisers in advance). You might want to visit www.carbootcalendar.com or look in your local paper for listings.

Your local auction house can often be a great friend if you want to sell a bunch of items or a few gems which you feel are better suited for a specialist auction/collectors' market, e.g. rock and roll memorabilia, fine porcelain, works of art, etc. An auction house will often give you a free appraisal (cutting out the research time) and can sometimes handle the whole process, for a commission of course.

You can too opt to sell to, or even buy from, a specialist dealer. Clearly, they need to buy items to make a profit and to cover their business costs. Here, more often than not, you have the reassurance of face-to-face contact and the chance to talk about an item in detail, and many are members of professional associations. In some cases, a good dealer is the only place you can go to find what you are looking for as they have spent years developing contacts and knowledge, and working with suppliers around the world.

My advice, whether you are selling or buying, is to mix up all the different ways – live auctions, online auctions, dealers, car boots, and even charity shops. Some people still sell or find good items through classified ads in their local paper.

4 At the moment, the majority of antiques and collectables don't appear to be affected *too much* by the rumblings in the global markets. Again, antiques and collectables are often seen as an investment, but always remember prices can come down as well as go up! At the top end you have

'Mr Crockett' CG31 (Robert Harrop Designs)

A rare C-3PO hand, and signed cast photograph, which realised £22,100 at Christie's in 2007 (Image courtesy of Christie's Images Ltd 2008)

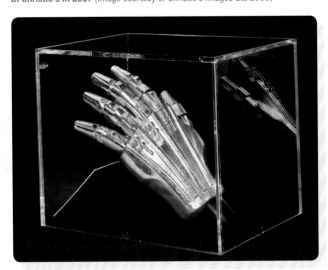

the extremes of antiques, such as fine wine, works of art, very fine porcelain, and furniture. Celebrity memorabilia seems as popular as ever, especially cult items connected to Hollywood legends or rock acts. Indeed, almost every week the top auction houses are reporting the smashing of world record prices paid for these more precious items. Damien Hirst's record-shredding, multi-million-pound auction in 2008 is a case in point.

5 I am not going to recommend either shedding your collection if you have one, or going wild in a hunt to start acquiring one – as this would be just fortune telling. If you are buying to speculate, perhaps the trick is to buy with your eye and heart. Buy things you enjoy yourself. With luck, over time (if you have the time), they will appreciate in value. However, it might be worth keeping an eye on the big auction houses and online auction sites to see the prices being paid. If you are a serious collector already, then you will probably be doing that each month anyway in the pursuit of your passion.

6 Lastly, if all goes horribly wrong with the economy I would imagine there's a chance we'll become a nation of small time dealers! I can see a time when we all start dabbling a little bit on the web – maybe buying something from somebody next door in a garage sale, and 'turning' it in a day for a profit online. Face-to-face trading used to be how most of us humans made money before the industrial revolution and, as I said, this time around we can reach not just our local community to buy and sell those little treasures, but a national or even international one.

Action Man

This legendary British toy has its origins in the US-made 'GI Joe'. In January 1966, toy firm Palitoy took the risk of launching a doll for boys in the UK and it proved to be an instant, award-winning hit. A few years ago, a new version appeared on shelves, renewing interest in the vast range of dolls, accessories, and vehicles of the vintage era of 1966–1983. The early and rare examples now make Action Man a true 12-inch soldier of fortune.

Collectors, not surprisingly, prefer boxed dolls: a real gem would be unopened. Accessories and clothing were mounted on to card: all items, however small, should be present. The vehicles never sold so well, thereby increasing their present desirability. Look for boxed tanks, racing cars, helicopters, and go-karts, among others. The earliest figures are more valuable: look for examples with flesh-coloured groin area (later ones wore blue pants!), hard plastic hands, and painted-on hair. Less well known models include the various footballer dolls (Chelsea, Man U, Wolves, etc.), Tom Stone the black Action Man, the Indian Brave and Chief figures, Captain Zargon the alien, and even Action Girl.

A 1970s Palitoy Action Man 'Talking Commander'. This realised £300 in December 2006 (Image courtesy of Vectis Auctions)

This 'Talking Commander' 2nd Issue doll sold in June 2005 for £120 (Image courtesy of Vectis Auctions)

This Palitoy Action Man Royal Engineers outfit made £45 at Vectis Auctions in November 2008 (Image courtesy of Vectis Auctions)

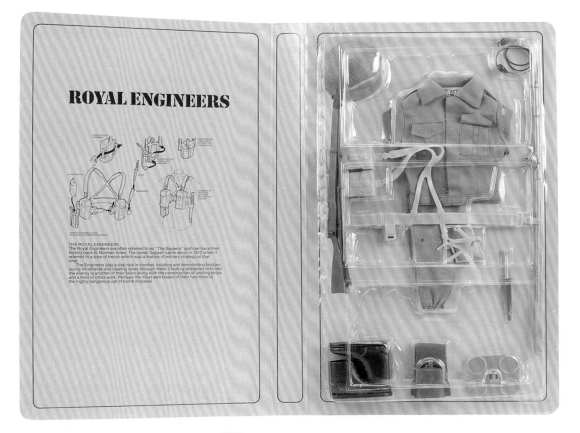

ACTION **man** Palitoy®

ROYAL HUSSAR

ROYAL HUSSAR
CONTENTS:
Jacket • Sword and Waist Belt •
Cross Belt and Pouch • Cap •
Trousers • Shoes • Spurs

Collect these Stars towards your Action Man gifts ★ ★ ★

A Palitoy Action Man Royal Hussar locker box
carded outfit of 1979. This made £220 at Vectis
in July 2008 (Image courtesy of Vectis Auctions)

How much?

It is fair to say that most models in very good condition
can be worth four times their original value; some will
make £100+. A mint condition, boxed 'Talking Commander'
from 1966 usually fetches around £300+. A version with
gripping hands, available in 1973 for one year only, wearing
officer's cap, scarf, and boots, sold at Vectis Auctions for
a mighty £460 in May 2004. A World Cup footballer doll
from 1970 in good condition will set you back around £240
from a dealer. A boxed helicopter could fetch £140 in top
nick and a rare, complete outfit can cost as much as
£300 to buy now. Single weapons strapped to the back
card may cost as much as £100.

There are a few highly-prized sentry box guards to
hunt down. The Royal Guard (wearing a blue and white
outfit) can make serious money if boxed and in mint
condition. Similarly, the Grenadier Guard (black hat and
red costume), also in a box, can fetch top dollar.

In the early 1990s, Hasbro breathed new life into this
classic toy. The newer ranges tend to avoid the overt
military theme. Instead you can find F1 racing cars and
mountain bikers, and so on. It could be wise to pick up
some models in the range and keep them aside and
unopened. Alternatively, take my advice, and scour car
boot sales for good-condition *early* dolls and vehicles.

Alfred Meakin

This well-known British pottery produced popular ranges of
ironstone china and many familiar tableware items, which
are fondly remembered. Though not a Clarice Cliff or Royal
Doulton in terms of secondary value or variety, some pieces
have stood the test of time and become collectable today.

The company was founded in Tunstall in 1875 and stayed
in Meakin/Johnson family hands until 1976. Famously,
they produced dinnerware for use on the legendary Flying
Scotsman and also made the world's biggest teapot in 1900
(enough tea for 480 people!). That gem has been lost in
time, but would be a very valuable find today.

How much?

Some of the art deco and art nouveau style items are quite
sought after, and the simple 1950s tableware is currently
affordable and quite classy. What is good news is that the
majority of Meakin is easy to find: a simple cup and saucer
with the elegant Tennessee pattern costs around £15 from
a dealer. For home decoration, a heavy white ironstone
chamber pot makes a superb planter or piece for the
washstand: these cost around £50. The popular cobalt blue,
Bleu de Roi, range is very pretty indeed, and a complete
six-piece place setting from around 1914 can be picked up
for as little as £50. If you look around you can find complete
coffee sets for £20–£50, especially on eBay.

Prices are higher in the USA where many of their wares
were exported via mail order quite early in the company's
history. In Britain, patterns such as Clifton and Hedgerow can
be found on large services and individual items: these can be
picked up at local auction houses or car boots – sometimes
very cheaply. My suggestion is that you buy because you like
the patterns you find, as long as there are no chips or cracks
– then maybe some day they will increase in value.

1950s/60s Alfred
Meakin plates. 'Bill and
Ben' large plate: £22.
'Cactus' small plate: £12.
'Brixham' small plate
£12 (Jamie Breese. Item
kindly provided by Cream
and Chrome Collectables)

Animation art

This is a comparatively new area of collecting which kicked off in the 1980s and offers the chance to own a truly unique item, which could remain valuable as long as people watch films! Very high sums have changed hands in some instances, but the market is also open to those on a budget, with original 'cels' from TV shows like *The Simpsons* being available for more modest sums. Cel is shorthand for celluloid acetate, which is the transparent film upon which animated characters are created. Often 24 single paintings are shot per one second of movie. Few survive, as they weren't seen as precious at the time and were destroyed, given to kids, or cleaned and re-used.

How much?

The value of a cel depends on several things: the movie (is it a classic?), the subject (is it a lead character, shown in full in a dynamic pose, the larger the better?), and expression (are they smiling with their eyes wide open?). A good original cel from *The Simpsons* can cost as little as £150. A fine cel from a cult movie like The Beatle's landmark *Yellow Submarine* would be much more desirable.

There are a handful of films, for example *Snow White* (1937), from which good, clear cels can be worth fabulous amounts. Cels of top characters like Bugs Bunny, Daffy Duck, and Mickey Mouse are also very collectable. In 1999 Steven Spielberg supposedly paid £70,000 for a cell from the Disney film *Aladdin*. More has been paid for single cels of Mickey Mouse.

Even limited edition reproduction cels are highly sought after. One such collectable was made by Disney in 1991. 500 reproductions of a single cel from *Alice in Wonderland* (1951) were made, and in November 2008 one sold on eBay for £425.

A great way to get going is to buy the very collectable serigraph cels (also known as sericels). These are cheap, beautiful reproductions made in limited numbers of 1,000–7,500. A much cheaper route is to buy original production drawings (rough sketches), which some see as the genesis of a character. These are unique.

A production cel from Disney's *Lady and The Tramp* (1955): £500–£800 (Martin Breese)

Star Trek, 2000AD, and other annuals (Jamie Breese. Item kindly provided by Cream and Chrome Collectables)

Annuals

Though they had been around during the war years (1914–1918), annuals first became truly popular in the 1920s. The 'Big Five' comics published by D. C. Thomson, which included *Adventure* and *Wizard*, were among the first to appear in annual form. The credit crunch has affected this area, as it has so many. At the time of writing, the prices on some cherished rare titles have dipped noticeably.

Always look for the signs which devalue an annual: see if the corner price tag has been cut out; if there is a large and scrawled-on dedication or child's name; if the crosswords have been filled in or crayon drawn on the pictures. Finally, look to see if the spine is damaged. All these serve to reduce the value. A number one issue is always the golden egg.

How much?

The massive figure of £4,200 was paid in 1995 at Comic Book Postal Auctions for a *Beano Book* number one from 1938. The *Dandy* number one (called *The Dandy Monster Comic*) once made £3,970 at auction. In late 2008 a fine copy made £2,000. Look out for *Oor Wullie* and *The Broons* – these are two titles which have continued to grow in popularity, and, as of late 2008, continued to sell well in very good or fine condition. A fine+ condition first *Oor Wullie* book made a superb £4,405 in early 2008.

Some years ago, a Rupert Bear annual from 1973 achieved an astonishing £16,500 at auction. It was one of a handful mysteriously produced with a brown-faced Rupert on the cover, but a white one inside. However, a second identical book failed to sell three months later. It is *just* that year when this anomaly occurred and no other.

The annuals to look out for which have become collectable include titles such as the *Doctor Who Annual* (early editions), those relating to any of the Anderson shows such as *Thunderbirds*, *Captain Scarlet*, *Stingray*, and so on. An excellent condition *Doctor Who* number one makes around £70–£100 right now.

Aston Martin

It's the 40th anniversary of the world's greatest secret agent. As recognisable as 'Shaken not stirred' and his PPK pistol, 007's Aston Martin DB5 car has been indelibly ingrained on the cinemagoer's mind. Corgi brought out their first version of the car in 1965 and received a 'Toy of the Year' award from the Toy Retailers' Association. It is now widely considered to be one of the best movie tie-in toys ever.

Corgi sold three million of them and they were just 8/6d [42 ½p] when new. It is unusual to find one boxed and in good nick – especially with the unopened 'Secret Instructions' and the concertina-like 'Model car makers to James Bond' leaflet which is often lost. This toy car has a retractable bullet shield and an ejector seat complete with a Korean agent.

How much?

Prices vary according to the condition of the car, the box, and the colour. There are gold and silver versions to hunt down. A Corgi No. 270 silver DB5 with tyre slashers, a first-issue wing flap, and bubble pack is worth £300–£400 at present.

A computer entrepreneur once paid over £157,000 at Christie's the auctioneers for a real silver 1965 Aston Martin DB5 car, which was used in the film *GoldenEye* and driven by Pierce Brosnan.

A few years ago, Corgi released an accurate reproduction of the original 1965 classic for a more affordable £7.49. It was part of a collection of 21 models made to capitalise on the resurgence of interest in the Bond phenomenon before *Die Another Day*.

The original 1960s Corgi Aston Martin DB5 diecast car (Image courtesy of Vectis Auctions)

A silver 1965 Aston Martin DB5 that was used in the film *GoldenEye* and driven by Pierce Brosnan (Images courtesy of Christie's Images Ltd 2008)

Atari 2600 games console

This breakthrough home console is now over 30 years old. In the 1980s-themed parties of today you may see this iconic machine hooked up to the TV and being enjoyed all over again. They are suddenly in demand and some of the original games and accessories are now seen as both cool and collectable.

This classic retro computer games machine arrived in 1977 in the US, and came to the UK in 1978. It was first called the Atari VCS, and later picked up the title 2600. The distinctive black plastic and mock wood design is now known as 'Woody'. It was hugely popular and effectively started the console war that has lasted to this day. A few of the games are more desirable than the console itself, and those such as 'Pac Man', 'Combat', and 'Pole Position' have all become classics.

How much?

The earliest US and UK version is known by collectors as the 'Heavy Sixer' on account of its weight. It also had chrome switches rather than later aluminium releases. It was made in Sunnydale, California, while all later machines were from Hong Kong. A mint, complete, boxed 'Heavy Sixer' has recently sold on eBay for £175. It had a few extra games and paddles with it. £50–80 will secure you a later 2600 with a few games and in OK condition.

The rarest cartridges include obscure, long-forgotten but extremely desirable titles such as 'Alien', 'Obelix', 'Pepsi Invaders', 'Demon Attack', and 'BMX Airmaster'. More popular cartridges such as 'Pac Man' sell for £2–£6.

An Atari 2600 games console with cartridges – 'Pac Man' and 'Space Invaders'
(Jamie Breese. Item kindly provided by Cream & Chrome Collectables)

An Arsenal jersey signed by 23 of the 2004/05 squad, including Thierry Henry and Patrick Vieira: £750 (Image courtesy of Fraser's Autographs)

Autographs

The collecting of autographs is called philography. Prices have steadily increased over the years, but the market is prone to supply and demand, fashions, and the unexpected. Top sports stars, screen idols, rock bands, and important historical figures dominate the upper ranks price-wise. Diana Princess of Wales is one of the most cherished autographs now.

There are many factors that affect values. Bear in mind that an autograph on a scrap of paper/album is worth less than one on a handwritten letter (top end) or photograph (medium end). However, if that scrap of paper was the back of, say, an early concert handbill, then it's worth a bit more. A signature in ink is better than pencil. A personal inscription to a fan with signature is usually worth less than a good, clear signature on its own. Bigger photos are better. A simple drawing, e.g. a caricature, together with a signature is always interesting. Lastly, condition and authenticity is of the utmost importance. Direct sunlight and damp should be avoided when storing or displaying.

How much?

Popular entertainers are considered the most exciting autographs and often the most valuable. Garbo hardly ever signed anything and is thought to be one of the more sought-after screen icons. Nelson weighs in at up to a mind-boggling £9,000, Bruce Lee is valued at £9,500 and the Apollo 11 crew are valued at £9,950 for a signed photo. The most precious signature is almost certainly that of William Shakespeare. There are six known and authenticated signatures on documents, including his will. Figures of several million pounds are mentioned should a signed document come up for sale, and a proven manuscript, if one ever appeared, would be truly priceless.

Experts, dealers, and collectors use authentic scanned signatures for close comparison. Some established dealers will offer a guarantee to protect you against the many fakes in circulation. Research if you can: many photographs are signed by stars' secretaries, or even by bands' roadies, and some celebrities, including presidents, often use a signature machine called an Autopen.

Autographs of icons

Winston Churchill's signature

Winston Spencer Churchill (1874–1965) is one of the most popular subjects for autograph collectors around the world. You often find the shortened signature of W. S. Churchill. He used this from time to time when out and about in the 1930s and in his later life. It is quite often the case that, if the content is not that historically interesting, a signed letter can be worth less than a good, clear full signature in pen on a photograph.

How much?

Top autograph specialists Fraser's include Churchill's signature in the top five of their top-100 investment index. They have established that the average growth in value from 1997 to 2008 has been 178 per cent. They suggest a valuation of £6,950 for a good signed photograph. In 2008 they had several letters available to buy: one was a simple thank you note, and the price tag was £4,500. You can pick up cheaper items which still give an insight into this great man's life. Online you can purchase a photocopy of Churchill's will from October 1961. This will cost about £20.

A set of Beatles signatures in blue ink that sold at a Christie's auction in May 2003 (Images courtesy of Christie's Images Ltd 2008)

A typed letter signed at the close as 'Winston S. Churchill', dated 8 December 1956: £4,500 (Images courtesy of Fraser's Autographs)

> 8 December, 1956.
>
> My dear Willy Sax,
>
> Thank you very much for your letter and for your good wishes on my Birthday.
>
> I am so much obliged to you for the most acceptable present you have sent me. It was indeed kind of you.
>
> Yours very sincerely,
>
> Winston S. Churchill

A signed drawing of Winston Churchill (Images courtesy of Fraser's Autographs)

Fab Four autographs

The Beatles have proved themselves to be timeless both in terms of their music and their memorabilia. None is more cherished than a good, clear set of authenticated autographs. Only a handful of other personalities – including the crew of Apollo 11, Napoleon, and Harry Houdini – have experienced a growth in autograph value stronger than the Fab Four.

If you have their autographs, did you get the item in person? Around 70% of signatures from after 1963 were signed on behalf of the band by two assistants. Before 1963, the band would usually do the honours. The most money will get spent on a set of signatures which all appear on one page, the larger the better. Single autographs are still worth an awful lot: Lennon alone can make up to £3,500+.

How much?

Currently, a respectable dealer will sell an album page with four very clear signatures for £9,500 or so. A signed photograph can vary considerably. Autograph dealers Fraser's produce a useful autograph index: according to their figures, a signed photo of the Beatles has risen to an astonishing £24,500.

As there is so much money at stake, experts have developed an good eye and can usually tell if the signature is authentic or not, even from a photocopy. I used to present *Everything Must Go!* on ITV1, and in one episode, tragically, our house owner, a few weeks before we turned up, had incinerated a full set of signatures believing they were of no value!

Avengers

The Avengers was the cult hit TV series of the 1960s. It was huge in Britain and the US and is keenly collected today. The original merchandise was quite thin on the ground at the time, making rare pieces valuable today.

The Avengers first burst on to the scene in 1961. It proved so popular that a stage play was made, and it was brought back again in 1976 as *The New Avengers*. The big screen version of 1998, starring Ralph Fiennes and Uma Thurman, sadly flopped.

How much?

Copies of the TV guide *The Viewer* attract £100 each if featuring Avengers cover stories. The original 'Shooting Game' made by Merit is very rare, while the later 'New Avengers' shooting game by Denys Fisher makes £125. The crudely made Emma Peel dolls by the Fairylite Company are much sought after. Echo made 'Avengers' stockings in the 1960s (£50) to cash in on the sexy look of the leading lady: Diana Rigg. If you are on a budget, the superb, modern Strictly Ink trading cards are worth looking out for.

One of most cherished collectables must be the famous Corgi Avengers Gift Set (number GS40). It features both Steed's Bentley and Emma's Lotus and was expensive at the time: in 1967 it sold for 16/11d [85p]. The box itself is a classic of groovy graphic design, and really epitomises both the show and the 'Swinging Sixties'. Keep your eyes peeled: in 2008 a few mint and boxed examples sold in the region of £300–£350. Purdey's TR7 by Dinky from the 1970s makes £50 boxed.

'The Avengers' Gift Set from Corgi Toys: £300-£350 (Image courtesy of Vectis Auctions)

Six Babycham table mats: £24 (Jamie Breese. Item kindly provided by Cream and Chrome Collectables)

Babycham

'Hey, I'd lurvvv a Babycham!' One of the most familiar drinks brands in the UK is enjoying a bit of a retro revival, and you could find that those Babycham promotional items lingering in the cabinet may well be collectable.

The West Country based Showering brothers discovered the original perry (fermented pear juice) sparkling drink in the 1940s. In the 1950s it started to develop as a brand and was known as Champagne de la Pomme. Babycham proper was launched in 1953, aimed at women only. It was quite a revolution for its day as it was the first ever alcoholic drink to be advertised on telly! The deer logo and the famous glasses all made their debut in that decade.

How much?

The classic Babycham glass stands 11cm tall, features the little yellow 'Flying' Bambi-like character below the rim and has the name written in blue around the base of the glass. If you have a set, depending on condition, you should be able to command between £6 and £10 a glass as there is little difference in value between the 50s and 70s versions. A plastic deer with the blue scarf was used as a pub promotional item and today sells for up to £35. The blue Beswick ashtrays, melamine trays, and beermats are all collectable too.

Carlton Ware and Beswick, too, made special ceramic figurines that are both worth more than a few quid today. The first Beswick figurine (model number 1615A) was handpainted and designed by Albert Hallam – one of their top designers. It was in production between 1960 and 1975 and is worth £50+ at auction.

Babycham is undergoing a bit of a marketing boost with a number of accessories and garments, all sporting the little deer and funky colours. Time will tell whether the special trainers, handbags, socks, underwear, and shades will become collectable 'Breweriana' (drinking antiques). Readers can take a look at www.babycham.com for details.

Bagpuss figurine (Model BG01) (Image courtesy of Robert Harrop Designs)

Babycham glasses: £30 (Jamie Breese. Item kindly provided by Cream and Chrome Collectables)

Bagpuss

The saggy cloth cat has become a figure of almost cult proportions. Perhaps the crowning moment for his creators was the BBC poll that named him the favourite children's programme in 1999. Not surprisingly, there is quite a bit of merchandise out there and his timeless appeal may well make some of these items 'ones to watch'.

Bagpuss was created in a barn by Peter Firmin and Oliver Postgate (who died in December 2008 at 83) and was first broadcast in 1974 as part of *Watch with Mother*. The duo were also behind *The Clangers* and *Ivor the Engine*. Bagpuss's appeal lies in the fairly crude animation, appealing oddball characters, and a liberal dose of cat magic. Strange facts: Emily was played by Peter's daughter and Bagpuss was meant to have been orange: his famous pink fur came as a result of a dyeing error.

How much?

There are all sorts of collectables to look out for. A set of great Bagpuss coasters costs around £4.50. Bookmarks cost £1.95 each, and there is even a 30th anniversary limited-edition stamp cover that is signed and costs £25+. There is also a special limited edition Carlton Ware ceramic Bagpuss that currently sells for around £45. The first 100 have special gold back stamps and are already more collectable. Sugarlump Studios, too, have made a few lovely Bagpuss collectables in the past.

'The Marvellous Mechanical Mouse Organ' was released as part of the wares created by Robert Harrop. They were not limited editions, so may not jump in price quickly, but are charming nonetheless. They play music from the show and cost £39.95. The Bagpuss figurine is another gem to look out for.

Banjolele

George Formby's most cherished banjolele was sold at auction in 2008. The entertainer was one of the biggest names in British showbiz for decades and starred in numerous films. His trademark was a cheeky chappie style, and he had a song for all occasions.

The Abbott 'Monarch' banjolele, or 'Little Strad' as Formby referred to it, was played extensively by the entertainer for both concert and studio work, including the recording of his most famous song 'When I'm Cleaning Windows'. For any collector of the great man, this must be the Holy Grail.

How much?

The instrument in the Bonhams Entertainment auction in June went for a whopping £72,000, more than three times its estimate, to a UK private buyer in the room. This particular banjolele is believed to have been George Formby's favourite instrument. Formby's gold-plated Dallas E banjolele, which he used during his live performances, fetched £21,600.

Banknotes

There is money in old money! What's great about the collecting of banknotes as a hobby – known as notaphily – is that you can pick up notes, even if your pockets aren't that big. Lots of people will have old bank notes lying around and there are collectors all over the world.

The single most important factor is the condition, and after that, as collectors admire the engraver's work, comes the visual appeal. Most enthusiasts see their displays as an art collection. Examples should really be mint and preferably not folded. Tears or writing on the note have a major adverse effect on the value. 'Uncirculated' is the term used to describe the perfect condition. For in-depth information, seek out the three-volume *Standard Catalogue of World Paper Money*.

How much?

All notes are effectively limited editions and, in general, most sought-after banknotes tend to rise in value over time. Historical events affect demand too: some Hong Kong notes doubled in value at the time of the Chinese takeover. The first £1 note printed was in 1797. A second print of one of these once fetched £57,000 – somebody out there will probably have a priceless number one!

The record-breaking note from the USA is called the $1,000 'Grand Watermelon' because of the shape of the zeros on the reverse. Grand is slang for thousand, of course. From 1890, it is one of three known to exist. It recently made over a million dollars.

The original 1694 British pound notes were written by hand and were issued with odd amounts. The trusty printed one-pound note was withdrawn in 1984. There are several things that can make a note rather special – for instance, if it's showing part of the next note on the sheet, or there is overprinting, it starts to become a little more exciting, as such errors are rare.

A million pound banknote from the Bank of England (Image courtesy of Spink)

Banknotes for charity

In 1696, The Bank of Scotland became the first commercial bank in Europe to successfully issue banknotes. In September 2007, the Bank organised a very special auction in Edinburgh. Up for grabs was a selection of brand-new, ultra-rare banknotes and sheets.

The date of the sale was special as it was also the day the new 'Bridges' banknotes went into general circulation around Scotland. This was the 47th new design in the 312-year history of the Bank. The notes featured a portrait of Sir Walter Scott and various well-known bridges, including Brig o' Doon, Glenfinnan Viaduct, and the Forth Bridge.

£50 and £100 banknotes sold at special auction in Edinburgh in September 2007 (Images courtesy of Spink)

How much?

The sale was conducted by Spink, and the first lot was a set of the new banknotes – £5, £10, £20, £50 and £100 – all with the ultra-desirable number AA000001. The lot was conservatively estimated to fetch £4,000–£5,000. There was also a sheet of 28 x £100 notes, all dated 17 September 2007 with serial number AA000000, and with SPECIMEN overprint, estimated to fetch £2,000–£2,500. All proceeds from the sale went to the British Heart Foundation.

Million pound note

A £1,000,000 note came up for auction in late 2008. This incredibly rare banknote was believed to be one of only two of this high value in existence. Banknotes are a very specialised and quite sophisticated collectable, and the best examples can command tens of thousands of pounds.

The million pound note was issued in connection with the Marshall Aid Plan (an American scheme to help rebuild Europe after the Second World War). The note was intended for internal use as 'records of movement' for a period of six weeks only. It is believed that nine examples were produced and that only two, Nos. 7 and 8, survived. This No. 8 note is dated 30 August 1948. It bears the signature of E. E. Bridges in the lower right-hand corner and is cancelled over the signature and stamped 6 October 1948, Bank of England.

How much?

The sale took place at Spink's in Bloomsbury, London, in October 2008. The same lot previously sold at auction at Christie's in October 1990, where it made £21,000. Spink placed an estimate on it of £40,000 and it realised a pleasing £78,300 on the day. Spink (www.spink.com) is probably the best-known auctioneer of coins, stamps, medals, and banknotes in the world. They were founded in 1666 and have offices in London, Singapore, New York, and Dallas. They are also holders of three royal warrants and plenty of records for prices achieved at auction.

Barbie

As well as being a toy, Barbie has become the most collectable doll, largely because of the numerous collector and limited-edition dolls designed specifically for the adult collector. Arguably, mainstream interest began with the first Barbie national convention back in 1980.

The very first doll was displayed by Mattel's founders, Ruth and Elliot Handler, at the New York Toy Fair in 1959. It was a new idea to have a teenage doll for young girls to play with, and it took off quickly. The best-selling Barbie of all time was the Totally Hair Barbie – she is worth less, therefore, than the majority of specially produced limited-edition dolls. Each one is sold with showcase packaging that includes a Certificate of Authenticity. A Barbie is classed as vintage if she was made between 1959 and 1972.

The first Barbie, sporting a black-and-white striped swimsuit, cost just $3 back in 1959. There are five of these 'ponytail' Barbies which collectors look for, made between 1959 and 1961, and each one features subtle improvements. The very first featured white irises, and had holes in her feet. There were 23 outfits for Barbie in 1959, including her original swimsuit.

Mattel 'ponytail' Barbie doll, 1960s, together with early Mattel Ken, 1961: £45 (Image courtesy of Vectis Auctions)

This rare, near-mint Mattel Barbie Debutante Ball outfit from 1966/67 fetched £130 at auction in December 2008 (Image courtesy of Vectis Auctions)

How much?

The early dolls are very hard to locate in a box. Without one, a fine condition number one could still cost £2,000–£3,000 at auction. A far more valuable one-off Barbie was created for her 40th anniversary and featured actual diamonds.

Over 4,000 Barbies were auctioned at Christie's in London in September 2006. It was a complete collection and made a total of £111,384. One doll went for an amazing £9,000.

Barbie.com is an official site designed primarily for children's entertainment. Barbiecollectibles.com is orientated more towards adult collectors and features a year-by-year history. There is an awesome array of pricing guides available to help collectors and newcomers to identify and value their acquisitions. Searching the auction results on internet auction sites is a good way to assess the current market. It's hard to imagine that the collecting of Barbie will ever slow down.

the only car designed for the *Barbie* and *Ken* teenage dolls

A Barbie and Ken plastic Austin-Healey sports car, in its original but re-cellophaned box, realised £420 when sold in September 2006 (Image courtesy of Vectis Auctions)

Ty Beanie Baby 'Pinky
the Flamingo' (1995): £5
and below Ty Beanie Baby
'India the Tiger' (2000): £5
(Jamie Breese. Items kindly
provided by Cream and
Chrome Collectables)

Beanie Babies

The market for the Beanie toys reached a peak in the mid-to-late '90s. Since then prices have dropped, even on the rare items. However, many still passionately collect them.

Created by the elusive Ty Warner, Beanie Babies first appeared in 1994 and were an immediate smash hit. It is also the adults who have created the sensational demand through the years. The most important items were traded privately by wealthy professionals. The number of bears made is unknown – once the company produces a new design, existing models are 'retired' and not sold again.

How much?
The famous 'Britannia the Bear' (one of two special British releases) has dropped from £200+ to around £10 or so, showing that the collectables market can fluctuate wildly.

The rarest bear could be the No. 1 bear, of which only 253 were ever made and given only to Ty sales reps to mark sales over $1 billion in 1998. Each one is scarlet and has a signed label on the ear. Look for the hash sign and the number 1 embroidered on the front. At its peak, the market value was between £5,000 and £9,000! It is worth considerably less today. The dark blue version of 'Peanut the Elephant' was one of the rarest commercially available Beanie Babies. The swing and tush tags need to be in place for a Baby to hold its value. In January 2008, Ty introduced a new line called Beanie Babies 2.0, declared as the next generation of the beanbag toys.

Beatles

Given that the Fab Four were possibly the most important icons of the 20th century, it's hardly surprising that their memorabilia is so popular. However, it wasn't until the late '80s that the market really began. Prices have spiralled since and it's become a truly international collecting phenomenon.

An awful lot of merchandise was made at the peak of the band's popularity. Much of it was cheaply made, some of it highly bizarre, but as each year passes, it becomes increasingly valuable. Beatles wigs are classic, so are plates, rugs, bed linen, stockings, and masks. High-end items include instruments belonging to the boys, any awards and gold/platinum discs are prized. Look also for handbills and early concert programmes and posters. These can make hundreds, occasionally thousands, of pounds at auction.

How much?
Obviously autographs are now highly sought after (see under 'A'). However, there are surprises – a cashmere overcoat which belonged to Lennon with an estimate of tens of thousands was once sold at auction for a knock-down figure of £4,023! Top merchandise includes the 'Bobbing Head' dolls (like nodding dogs) and the Selcol plastic Beatles guitar (with printed signatures they make £600+ in packaging).

A great treasure would be any handwritten lyrics to a song. Almost any example would probably be priceless, and especially if from a classic. But owning a 'personal' item needn't break the bank: a library book with young John's signature once cropped up with a price tag of £300–£500.

Washington
Potteries 'Beatles'
small plate (1960s): £22 (Jamie Breese.
Item kindly provided by Cream and Chrome Collectables)

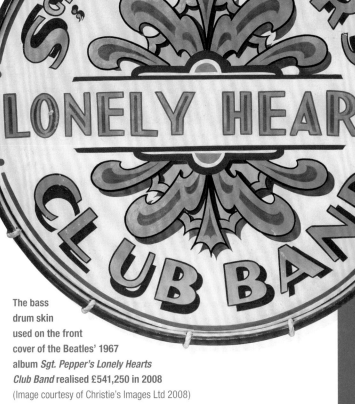

The bass
drum skin
used on the front
cover of the Beatles' 1967
album *Sgt. Pepper's Lonely Hearts
Club Band* realised £541,250 in 2008
(Image courtesy of Christie's Images Ltd 2008)

Jaws dropped in July 2008 when the legendary handpainted bass drum skin, used on the front cover of the Beatles' groundbreaking album *Sgt. Pepper's Lonely Hearts Club Band*, sold at Christie's for £541,250.

Good condition toys are a good start. The Yellow Submarine by Corgi is affordable, but ensure you have the box. Even Cavern Club memorabilia is becoming popular, with bags and other gift items now coming up for sale at auction. Lots of the singles are still affordable and can be collected easily.

**A trio of
Beatles trays**
(Jamie Breese)

Lennon's lyrics

John Lennon's lyrics for 'Give Peace a Chance' from the legendary Montreal Bed-In of 1969, along with personal photos which had never been seen in public before, came up for sale in 2008.

Give Peace a Chance was the first hit record to be made by an individual band member while still in The Beatles. When John saw TV clips of nearly half a million anti-Vietnam war protestors singing his song outside the White House in November 1969 he said it was one of the biggest moments of his life.

How much?

This important item was the highlight at Christie's Rock and Pop Memorabilia sale in July 2008. The estimate was a mighty £200,000–£300,000 but the lot made £416,827 on the day. Twenty lines of incomplete lyrics to *I Am The Walrus*, written by John Lennon on a single page, went for £78,500 at Christie's many years ago.

The lyrics and photos were offered from the collection of UK-based comedy writer and presenter Gail Renard. Just 16 and living in Montreal at the time of the Bed-In, Gail and a friend sneaked into the Queen Elizabeth Hotel, via the drainpipe, where John and Yoko were holding their protest for peace and became friends with the recently married Lennons. John gave Gail a few mementos at the time, including the lyrics, telling her: '… one day they will be worth something …' and she has had them ever since.

John Lennon's lyric sheet sold in July 2008 for £416,827 (Image courtesy of Christie's Images Ltd 2008)

Beatrix Potter gems

One of our most cherished children's authors, Beatrix Potter was born in 1866. She wrote around 35 books in total, some of which are almost priceless today. Collectors also seek a whole host of other gems – from figurines to board games – and the market shows little sign of letting up.

Potter's first book was called *A Happy Pair* and was published a whole nine years before the first *Peter Rabbit* book appeared, and only a handful of known copies exist today. All her early books, especially the first editions, are sought after. You need to have a beady eye to spot them – as most bookshelves in the land have a storybook by her. A general rule for spotting 'firsts' with Potter is to look for the date of publication on the front of the title page. If a book says F. Warne Ltd, then it will be a later copy from the 1920s onwards.

How much?

Her first book, *The Tale of Peter Rabbit* from 1901, was a self-published effort and only 250 copies were originally printed. These can be identified as they featured pale boards and did not mention her soon-to-be publisher – Frederick Warne. Top nick copies can fetch over £20,000. Signed or inscribed copies would probably make much more. First editions of the second issue of *Peter Rabbit* – which was limited to 200 copies in 1902 make around the £15,000 mark.

The absolute Holy Grails are Potter's original artwork and drawings. Potter would usually sign them with three letters – B.H.P. For collectors, Beswick have made their famous Beatrix Potter figures since 1948. Over 100 characters have been created and are keenly sought after. Some have made several thousands of pounds in the past.

Beswick Beatrix Potter Figurines

These famous peices were originally designed by Arthur Gredington for Beswick in 1948, under license. Beswick was founded back in 1894 and these gems proved to be one of its most timeless collectables. They proved a smash hit and many are still made today by Royal Doulton.

A whole series of these charming miniature figurines has been made - over 100 characters have been released. How valuable each piece is varies according to the age and how delicate it is. The earliest examples have a patina, or feel, to the actual backstamp, while the later versions have a glazed print. The presence of the early gold backstamp and a box improves value.

How much?

The slightest variation can affect desirability: 'Mr Benjamin Bunny' is a good example – he was modelled by Gredington. There are several different versions. It all depends on whether he has a pipe in his mouth, whether his ears are in or not, and the colour of his coat. One of the rarest pieces is the Mr Bunny holding a pipe in his hand with a gold, oval backstamp. He is valued at around £180 or so. If you had the version with a brown jacket, green beret and orange pompoms, you would be looking at even more.

'Duchess with Flowers' with the Gold Oval Backstamp (actually a Black dog, bearing multicolored flowers) was issued between 1955 and 1967 and wasn't a big seller. Incredibly, at one point several years ago, this tiny piece which cost just 5 shillings, was worth over £2000! Today, the value has fallen quite dramatically, and depending on backstamp, age and condition, she can fetch around £1500–£2000. She has been spotted in the States recently (2009) offered for $3,600.00. The 'Duchess with Pie' (BP3, 1979 to 1982) is often fetching £200–£300. Many of the pieces fall into the £100–£150 price band. 'Mrs Tiittlemouse' (BP1, gold circle backstamp) is worth £120–£140 currently. 'Mr Jeremy Fisher Digging' (BP6, brown backstamp) is worth £110–£130.

Five Beswick 'Beatrix Potter' porcelain figures and display stand: £250
(Image courtesy of Vectis Auctions)

Beatrix Potter's record watercolour

The colour of her stories was matched only by the superb illustrations that she created to accompany them all. Over the years, any original artwork by her has become extremely sought after, and this goes for anything from a drawing she made in a letter to the best illustrations used in her books.

A UK-based private collector recently paid a record amount to secure a piece of literary history. Her watercolour was one of 20 original illustrations, books, unpublished Christmas cards, and letters by Potter that originated from the collection of the artist's brother, Bertram.

How much?

This superb lot was sold in the July 2008 English Literature and History sale at Sotheby's. 'The Rabbits' Christmas Party: The Departure' sold for the extraordinary figure of £289,250. This was nearly five times its high pre-sale estimate of £40,000–60,000. It set a new record for any book illustration sold at auction. A princely £121,250 was also paid for another Beatrix Potter watercolour entitled 'The Rabbits' Christmas Party: The Arrival'.

One of just 250 special first editions of *The Tale of Peter Rabbit* sold for £41,825 in July 2002 (Image courtesy of Sotheby's Picture Library)

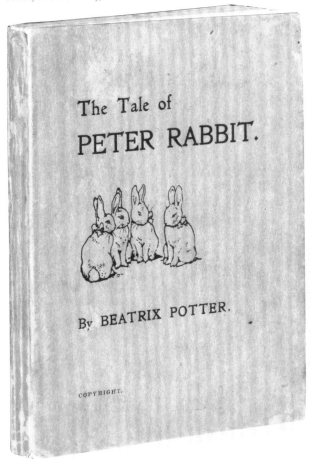

A Belleek set (Norman Huntley)

Belleek

One of Ireland's oldest and most famous potteries, Belleek wares have become very collectable, particularly in North America. Founded in 1857 by David McBirney in Co. Fermanagh, the popular organic and leafy designs were widely copied, though the prices for original wares have managed to remain steady.

The earliest wares were usually marked just with the name 'Belleek'. A little later the mark of 'Co. Fermanagh, Ireland' was used as well. The more standard marking features the Irish wolfhound, harp, and round tower. The firm is famous to this day for not letting defective items leave the factories, and the standards remain extremely high. Perhaps their most famous output was the lustrous, pearl-like 'Parian' wares, and the famous Shamrock items. You can't miss the elegant shell lines either: these use real seashells and sea urchins to decorate vases and other sets.

How much?

A complete 'Cabaret' tableware set can make several thousand pounds at auction. Individual teapots, depending on age and condition, make several hundred pounds upwards if of any rarity. The famous Belleek baskets are delicate and highly sought after: individual pieces can make thousands of pounds. A superb Belleek 'Celtic' coffee set from the 3rd Black Mark period would sell today for about £1,000+.

There are a great number of extremely valuable gems to seek out. Some busts and statues are at the top of collectors' wish lists (e.g. The 'Prisoner of Love' creation can be worth a small fortune, and the 'Figure of Erin' has made over £6,000). A set of top 'Minstrels' paperweights could be £4,000+, while the rare 'Deer' candelabra was valued at around £7,000 in the mid-2000s prior to the crunch.

If starting out, learn how to identify the various markings that appear in several key colours: black, green, gold, and blue. As with almost any ceramic object, the condition is absolutely vital: Belleek is known for its very fine edges. The Belleek Collectors' Society was founded in 1979 and now has 7,500 members in 29 localised chapters. You can visit www.belleek.ie for more information.

Beswick

John Beswick set up this famous pottery in Stoke-on-Trent in 1894. Their factory was one of the most prolific of the 20th century. The Royal Doulton Group bought Beswick in 1969, and with the original Beswick factory ceasing to exist, interest in their many series began to grow.

Beswick are perhaps best known for their recreations of animals. Horses top the popularity list, with dogs and cattle coming next. 'Red Rum' (Model No. 2511) was designed by their master craftsman Graham Tongue and issued in 1975 as part of the Connoisseur Horses Series. 'Nijinsky' (Model No. 2352) was issued in 1971 and was designed by their other master craftsman Albert Hallam. Both stand around 30cm tall with a lovely matt finish and are likenesses of two of the world's most famous horses. These are rare, incredibly detailed studies worth £550–650+ and £450–£550+ respectively.

One of my favourites is the Beswick 'Dulux' dog which is now thought to be very rare. Beswick created mantelpiece dogs of the Staffordshire variety from 1898. The Old English Sheepdog has become synonymous with the 'Dulux' brand through advertising. The ceramic version was made between 1964 and 1970 and was prone to damage, partly because they were produced for paint shops only. It is known as Model No. 1990. I know of one having sold for up to £700 at auction. Today most go for a low of £250 to a high of £500 in top nick.

The Beswick 'Dulux' dog: £250–£500
(Image courtesy of Christine Nixon)

Beswick Top Cat

There were seven pieces made in this great series from 1996–1999. They were designed by Andy Moss and based on the animated characters in the Hanna-Barbera early 1960s TV series. The title of the show often confused viewers as it was for a time broadcast here as *Boss Cat*. Nevertheless, the cheeky alley cats made a mark and eventually became immortalised as collectable figurines.

The seven pieces are 'Officer Dibble', 'Top Cat', 'Benny', 'Fancy Fancy', 'Brain', 'Choo Choo', and 'Spook'. Apart from 'Officer Dibble' and the diminutive 'Benny', the pieces were 4 ½in in height, and they all came with a special certificate.

How much?

Each character was a limited edition of 2,000, which is reasonably low. Between £200 and £300 will bag you the whole collection currently at auction. They should be boxed and in very good to mint condition for that kind of money. TC is one of the lesser-known Beswick ranges and could be a good bet for the future with a lowish current value.

Beswick Rupert

Rupert the Bear is one of their later star series, and was first introduced by the pottery in 1980. He was part of a small range called Rupert and His Friends. The production period was relatively short and all figures were withdrawn in 1986. Today, these colourful figures are quite rare and sought after by collectors of Rupert memorabilia.

The set featured five characters, ranging from 7cm to nearly 11cm in height: 'Rupert Snowballing'; 'Algy Pug'; 'Rupert the Bear'; 'Bill Badger', and 'Pong Ping'.

How much?

Figures in boxes and in pristine shape sell on the high street for premium prices. Chips, crazing, and cracks reduce value. The basic Rupert figure (Model No. 2694 with arms behind back) was frequently traded for around £250, but today an auction price would be around £50–£80. 'Rupert Bear Snowballing' (Model No. 2779) is one of the true rarities, and such an example sold for £260 in June 2007. 'Bill Badger' at auction might cost £120–£150.

Occasionally, complete sets of five come up for grabs and can sometimes be picked up cheaper than buying individual pieces separately. A few years ago, one auction saw such a set make just under £900, though a similar set sold for just £528 at Bonhams in Cheshire in August 2007. If these are beyond your budget, then there is a whole world of affordable Rupert collectables out there, most of which are available on line.

Alice series

Inspired by Lewis Carroll's well-known children's book *Alice's Adventures in Wonderland*, published in 1865, Beswick (the pottery founded in 1894 and known the world over for great collectables) made a superb series of figures between 1973 and 1983. Having had a good deal of success with the Beatrix Potter range, Alice's friends are lurking nearby and have stolen some of the limelight in recent years. Maybe you have one from the series?

A Rupert figurine by Beswick (1980s): £50–£80 (Martin Breese)

All the figures are easily identifiable as they are marked 'Beswick made in England' and this is usually accompanied by 'Royal Doulton Tableware Ltd'. Alice herself was made in several different styles. The figures have a great deal of detail for small items – 'The Mad Hatter', created by Albert Hallam, is just as you imagine him from the book – all colour and wackiness!

How much?

The prices paid have varied a lot in recent years. Condition is a really big factor with these pieces. 'Alice' (Model No. 2476) is worth around £90–£120 at present. The best find would be the sleeping 'Cheshire Cat' who commands a little more on the tree stump display stand. 'The Mad Hatter' did occupy the middle ground in the desirability stakes at about £250, but one sold at Clevedon Salerooms near Bristol in October 2008 for just £50. The cheaper pieces are characters like 'The Fish Footman' and 'The King of Hearts'. An unboxed but complete set of 11 figures sold in 2007 for just £580.

I have seen much cheaper and undamaged figures at auction recently. If you know where to go, you at least get a chance to buy before a dealer or someone else gets their paws on them. 'Winnie-the-Pooh' characters are also made by Beswick and they, too, are worth keeping an eye out for. The better money is perhaps in the harder-to-find Beatrix Potter series pieces. You need to know your stuff when looking at these, as there are different back stamps and different values – sometimes, big values! Royal Doulton/Wedgwood were recently still producing some superb Alice pieces.

A contemporary 'Mad Hatter's Tea Party' study (Image courtesy of Royal Doulton/ Wedgwood)

SylvaC flying mallard (1950s/60s). **A full set costs £125** (Jamie Breese. Item kindly provided by Cream and Chrome Collectables)

Flying mallards

Ever since Coronation Street's Hilda Ogden first hung a set of these classic decorative plaques on her wall in 1976, these kitsch gems have been considered the height of good/poor taste! Today, there are many variations of flying birds to seek out, and some have a surprisingly high collectability factor.

The famous flying mallards, with their distinctive rich colour and high gloss, were designed by Mr Watkins and made by Beswick (now owned by Royal Doulton) between 1938 and 1973. They have come to be associated mainly with the 1950s. Their Beswick design number was 596 and there were five different sizes available. Today they have a great kitsch appeal and make a fine retro decoration. There were two different colour choices – one was brown, teal green, and white, the other was white with yellow beaks. Other manufacturers, such as SylvaC, also made these types of wall plaques.

How much?

These days a set of five mallards will make £100–£180, if tidy. They were worth an extra hundred or so in the early 2000s. Beswick made a number of other winged wall decorations. There are sets of partridges, seagulls, and even swallows. All of these gems can make good money if in good nick – the swallows fetch around £300, the seagulls maybe £400–£500. The most elusive set of three pink-legged partridges can pull down over £800.

The most popular flying birds are actually the Guinness Toucans made by the legendary British pottery, Carlton Ware. First produced in the 1950s, like all the Guinness items, they have steadily been increasing in value. The original set of three from around 1957 can make anywhere from £200–£300 if truly mint. Beware the dreaded fakes: the orange on the beaks of the originals is far richer and graduated than the lighter orange of the fakes. The feet are also painted with more detail on the originals.

Betty Boop

Betty is one of those icons that no one can quite remember how exactly she came to be so popular. It's hardly surprising when you discover that she is over 75 years old. Oddly, Betty evolved from a cartoon dog in the early 1930s and was the creation of Dave and Max Fleischer. Her popularity waned with the US morals sweep-up known as the Hay's Code: Betty was forced to wear longer skirts, and so forth. Today, like many classic characters, she is enjoying a revival, which is good news for collectors.

There were only 100 or so cartoons and these were made primarily in the 1930s, yet somehow her cutesy sweetheart image had an enormous impact around the world. Almost as enduring as Marilyn Monroe, Betty's image appears on everything from collectors' plates to ladies' underwear; from salt and pepper shakers to mobile phone covers. I'd imagine you could spend your life collecting her and never amass it all!

How much?

Some of the more affordable contemporary collectables are the limited-edition Wade figurines from C&S Collectables. There have been numerous models released through the years, many of which have risen in value, and there are quite a few to collect (for more information go to www.wadecollectorsclub.co.uk). The Betty hatpins and lapel badges are good quality and can be picked up for around £5–£6 each on the web.

There are an incredible 7,000+ Betty Boop related items currently for sale on pretty much any given day on the Internet auction site eBay.com. These range in price from a few pounds for a pillowcase, to many hundreds for original animation art (or cels as they are known). For further information, readers could get *The Definitive Guide to Betty Boop Memorabilia* by Leonard Ellis (Hobby House Press).

A Wade Betty Boop 9in 'Halloween' figurine
(Image courtesy of Wade)

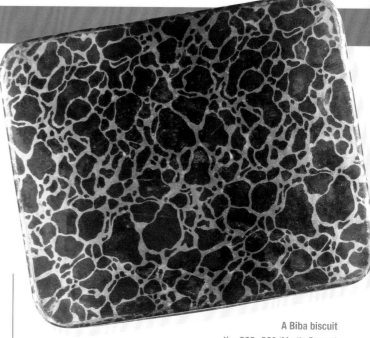

A Biba biscuit tin: £20–£30 (Martin Breese)

BIBA

Biba was of one of the most iconic British businesses of the 1960s and '70s. In its heyday, the total fashion experience that was Biba attracted 100,000 customers a week to the flagship art deco store in trendy Kensington, London. The label became a must-have for the trendy set. Today, the clothing and accessories are considered chic and retro, and a new book hit the stores in 2004 celebrating the revolutionary brand.

In the mid '60s, Polish-born Barbara Hulanicki turned her tiny mail order fashion firm and boutique into a bustling business occupying a huge department store that was the old Derry & Toms in London. It was THE place to shop for food and fashion, attracting swinging-sixties celebs from Twiggy and Brigitte Bardot to Jean Shrimpton and the Stones. It was a complete shopping theme park with everything from soap flakes to furnishings, and was made distinctive by the beautiful black and gold packing. The big store lasted just two years, but the influence has remained strong.

How much?

Original vintage Biba clothes are becoming increasingly collectable today. The swirling early themed get-ups are not cheap now: £500 to £1,000 is the price for good condition trouser suits, two pieces, and velvet jackets, for example. I have seen an original pendant for sale recently for £89 and a Biba Baked Beans tin sell for £20. Knee-high boots sell for around £80–£100 and the wallpaper for upwards of £50 a roll.

September 2004 was the 40th anniversary of the first Biba shop, and a book crammed full of pictures and info on Hulanicki's collectables and story was released. Interested readers can learn more about Biba in *Biba: The Biba Experience* published by Antique Collectors' Club.

Bicycles

Much like vintage cars and motorbikes, many of the most famous names of the past, such as Parr & Co, Elswick, Royal Sunbeam, and the famous Rudge have long been forgotten. As you might expect, vintage bicycles are passionately collected by cycle buffs. From the vintage lightweight 'racers' (where a few components alone can cost thousands) to the iconic bikes of the 1970s, big money changes hands for the best examples of the rarest machines.

Some of the earliest bicycles make the eyes pop out: Baron von Drais created one of the first in 1816. It was called 'The Draisienne' and looked more like a crossbow! Wacky designs weren't restricted to the early days – the Bowden 'Spacelander' from 1960s America was an incredible sight.

How much?

A fairly standard sprung seat, vintage Post Office bike, if restored, will cost around £100. The Raleigh 'Chopper' was the bike for a whole generation of kids (see below). Philips the auctioneers sold some amazing examples including an 'Otto Safety Bicycle' (from 1882) for over £30,000 once. The Lotus bike used by Chris Boardman on his record-breaking Olympic ride in 1992 was once sold by the same auctioneers for £25,000! Ordinary pushbikes are always popular on the secondary market.

Cheaper finds to search out include antique prints, magazine covers, and cartoons from the late 1800s. These are collected avidly and are usually in the £20 to £50 bracket. A great place to find out more or look at pictures of the earliest examples is www.bicyclemuseum.com. In Britain, the Veteran Cycle Club has a strong presence – www.v-cc.org.uk. They publish a journal called *The Boneshaker*.

The Raleigh 'Chopper'

This two-wheeled wonder bike was a throwback to the 'Easy Rider' cool of the late 1960s. The 'Chopper' sold very well at the time and is one of the most enduring youthful icons of the 1970s with early, original condition models starting to become collectors' pieces.

This legendary kids' dream machine was designed by Alan Oakley and first appeared in 1970. It cost around £32 for the standard model, or around £55 for the DeLuxe, had funky drop-handlebars, three gears and came out first in a few standard colours, including red and yellow. More exotic colours appeared later. There was even a 'racing bike' version with different, curved handlebars called 'The Sprint' (very rare today).

How much?

If your 'Chopper' has the circular knob on the famous central gearshift instead of the later 'T-Bar' and one-piece solid rubber pedals, then you'll probably have one of the early Mark 1 models. A lot of these frames were recalled over strength issues (apparently prone to snapping!). Look out also for those with the optional windshield. Today, very fine condition examples are changing hands in smart shops for around £450–£600. The rarest bike of all is USA-only, ten-speed model DL560 of 1970/71. This is worth considerably more. Currently, a collector might pay £2,500 for an ultra-rare 1979 Mark 2 Prismatic in original order.

The famous elongated seat encouraged two-up cruising and wheelies, and led to untold accidents. This, coupled with a big surge in collectability of anything 1970s, means top condition models are far harder to come by. Collectors have travelled from abroad to seek out pristine bikes. Why not have a look in your garage today!

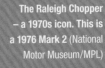

The Raleigh Chopper – a 1970s icon. This is a 1976 Mark 2 (National Motor Museum/MPL)

A selection of 'Noddy' books
(Jamie Breese. Items kindly provided
by Cream and Chrome Collectables)

Blue Peter collectables

Blue Peter is one of the world's longest-running children's TV programmes, and ever since 1958 there has been a flow of collectable items, from key fobs and stickers, from aprons to the famous badges. You may be surprised at the relatively high values of those *Blue Peter* items tucked away as keepsakes.

It wasn't until 1964 that the first *Blue Peter* Annual appeared on shelves. Finding one in fine condition is nearly impossible today. A value of between £75–£100 is not unreasonable. Look for copies without the puzzles completed and the price tag intact. The first three are the rarest.

First introduced in 1963, *Blue Peter* badges are a must for a collector. The basic badge is the fairly common Blue badge. The Green and Silver examples make a little more. The ultimate accolade is the Gold Badge, of which only 850 or so have been awarded thus far, to those who save a life or represent our country, etc. This would be a sought-after item, though selling them is naturally and understandably frowned on by the show.

How much?

Bleep and Booster were two space age characters introduced to the show. As well as the books and other related items, they were made into puppets by the famous Pelham Puppet Company. Today they are very rare, but the third alien character is rarer still. A set of all three, boxed, could make £300–£500+.

Look out for the annuals and books at car boot sales and charity shops. You can usually pick them up for a few pence. You might find one of the first three. Look for signed publicity cards, photographs, and even the *Blue Peter* sponge: this would expand permanently when placed in water.

A *Blue Peter* badge
(Jamie Breese)

Enid Blyton

A recent survey revealed that Enid Blyton was top of the charts with adult readers. Commissioned by the Cartoon Network and the Prince of Wales Arts and Kids Foundation, the survey threw a spotlight on the legendary children's author, and this can only be good news for collectors.

Enid, one of this country's best-sellers, was born in London in 1897 and died in 1968. She made a huge impact on children everywhere, with 700 books and sales topping 400 million copies worldwide. Most famous were her 'Famous Five', 'Noddy' and 'Secret Seven' tales. The surge in interest began in wartime Britain with the very first title *Five on a Treasure Island* (1942).

How much?

The early 'Famous Five' titles, books one to seven, are the ones to look out for. In good condition, complete with dust jackets, they will always be worth good money, and they show signs of continuing to increase in value. Rare and valuable titles include first editions of *The Island of Adventure* (Macmillan) 1944. This can make over £1,000 in good shape. The good news is that almost all her titles are 'affordable', compared to first editions by Rowling or Tolkien.

A first edition of *The Circus of Adventure* (1950s) (Martin Breese)

An early book from any of the popular series with its wrapper should always be snapped up if offered on the cheap. A fine first edition copy of *Five Go Down to the Sea* (Hodder & Stoughton) from 1953 can command over £200 today, so keep a look out for the pre-1960 titles. First editions of some of the early 'Noddy' books, such as *Noddy Goes to Toyland* (1949), *Well Done Noddy* (1952) and *Hurrah for Little Noddy* (1950), can also fetch figures that can easily pass the £100 mark if the condition is fine and the dust jacket is present and tidy.

Box Brownie

The Kodak 'Box Brownie' camera conjures up so many memories for so many people. It was usually their first camera and as a result they are enthusiastically collected. The simple operation and ease of use made it a true revolution. Don't forget, this humble device was one of the first mass-produced objects and brought photography to everyone. They were actually intended for children and named after the popular characters by author Palmer Cox.

The most famous camera of all time was first introduced in February 1900. Designed by Frank A. Brownell and called simply 'Brownie', it sold 245,000 units in the US and the UK before the first model was discontinued in October 1901. The picture size was 2 ¼in x 2 ¼in and they cost only one dollar, which was five shillings in the UK, and used film that sold for 15 cents a roll.

How much?

Most 'Brownies' which you find, whether plastic or board, tend to be worth around the £5–£25 mark. So many different models were released (125) during the 'Brownie's' lifetime (70 years), that some have inevitably become far harder to find today. For example, there was a special 'Baby Brownie' camera made only for the New York World's Fair in April 1939: then costing $1.25, it now makes up to £200. Similarly, in 1932 a model was released featuring an American Boy Scout emblem: this makes around £150–£200 in olive green casing today.

As a general rule, any of the models with a colour body tend to be more sought-after today. For example, the 'Beau Brownie' of the early 1930s came in five different colours and was designed by design guru Walter Dorwin Teague. It had a metal body and featured an elegant geometric art deco motif. The Rose-coloured version is the rarest and worth around £120 today.

A 'Box Brownie' camera
(1950s): £15–£20 (Jamie Breese)

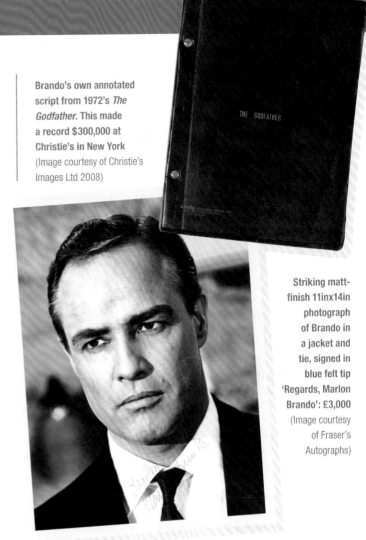

Brando's own annotated script from 1972's *The Godfather*. This made a record $300,000 at Christie's in New York
(Image courtesy of Christie's Images Ltd 2008)

Striking matt-finish 11inx14in photograph of Brando in a jacket and tie, signed in blue felt tip 'Regards, Marlon Brando': £3,000
(Image courtesy of Fraser's Autographs)

Marlon Brando

This iconic screen heavyweight passed away a few years ago. Considered by many to be the most important Hollywood actor of his time, it is not surprising that memorabilia connected to him is highly sought after.

Brando (1924–2004) was the reclusive star of hits like *On the Waterfront* and *Apocalypse Now*. An auction of 250 of his personal items following his death proved that the film memorabilia market is very much alive.

How much?

The auctioneers Christie's of New York recently sold the Holy Grail: Brando's own annotated script from 1972's *The Godfather*. It made a stunning $300,000, the highest amount ever paid for a film script and ten times the estimate. Among the other gems was a telegram from Brando to Marilyn Monroe from 1961, which sold for $36,000.

More affordable will be a simple signature by the great man. Currently a top autograph dealer will value a good signed photograph at £3,000. This has a chance of increasing in value as time passes.

A Watneys home pump: £39 (Jamie Breese. Item kindly provided by Cream and Chrome Collectables)

Breweriana

The term refers to the collecting of pub and drink-related items. This is a comparatively new field, with many objects easily found and surprisingly affordable. Many of the important British potteries made such items – Carlton Ware, Royal Doulton, Wade, and Beswick. Prices have steadily been increasing over the years and there are several specialist dealers and auction houses to visit.

There is a vast and diverse selection of objects to hunt down – from actual bottles to advertising figures, from stoneware jugs to pub mirrors. At the top end of the market, collectors look for whisky-related objects. Breweriana manufactured between 1880 and 1925, particularly items which relate to the short-lived breweries, are good starting points. Corkscrews are highly sought-after – some rare concertina-style examples may make as much as £800. Novelty corkscrews are also desirable and can be worth over £300. See below for more information.

Look also for ashtrays, copper, leather, or pewter measuring jugs (£100 upwards), pocket watches, books, bottle holders, and pamphlets by the breweries. Classic examples of posters and show cards can be worth anywhere from £50 to £500. All prices vary according to age, condition, and material used.

How much?

Guinness collectables are perhaps the most colourful and also valuable. A 'Guinness is Good For You' lamp, featuring the famous Seal made by Carlton Ware, has fetched over £400. The famous set of three flying toucans from the 1950s usually command £500+ in top nick, and ornaments are even hotter. The very rare flat toucan plaque goes for £1,100+.

There is no one specific Holy Grail item. However, sets of ceramic spirit barrels dating from the 19th century, which feature colourful decoration and mini taps, fetch up to £2,000. They measure around 30cm in height, are made by several potteries, and are usually found in sets of four or eight.

Whisky and beer mats are very popular to collect as they can be bought for a few pence, yet feature long-forgotten drinks. Keep aside modern promotional items for the future.

Corkscrews

The mixture of innovation and novelty makes these good collectables. The Reverend Samuel Henshall invented the 'Button Screw' corkscrew in 1795, which was superseded in 1802 by Edward Thomason's 'draw' type, which pulled the cork automatically from the bottle. Another popular model was the 'King's Screw' which had a smaller handle fixed at right angles to the main handle which extracted the cork when turned.

The common feature of the Thomason and the King's Screw was that both had a small brush fitted to the side of the handle, and the existence of the original brush will add to the value of these corkscrews today. There are hundreds of different styles of corkscrews and many 19th-century examples have survived, but novelty 20th-century corkscrews are also sought after.

How much?

A standard Thomason design corkscrew will cost anything up to £1,000. A German novelty corkscrew by Steinfeld and Reimer in the shape of a pair of lady's legs wearing coloured stockings and boots would cost £200–£300 at auction.

One of the rarest corkscrews, a Celestin Durand 19th-century rack and pinion corkscrew, sold at auction some years ago for over £10,000. More recently a rare Shrapnel example, with its nickel closed barrel engraved with two crests, sold at Christie's, South Kensington, for £17,625.

You do not have to be rich to start an interesting corkscrew collection. Straightforward T-shape pull corkscrews can be bought for a few pounds, but the price soon goes up for anything a bit more unusual. A dog with the screw as its tail could cost £20–£30. A cast silver-handled corkscrew in the shape of a fish could fetch £500. Look around at car boot fairs or flea markets for the best bargains!

A rare Shrapnel (I) corkscrew (H. N. S. Shrapnel 1839 Patent No. 8224) sold at Christie's, London, for £17,625 in May 2003 (Image courtesy of Christie's Images Ltd 2008)

Britains farm figures

Everyone and their auntie has heard of Britains. They have been in existence since 1893 and are perhaps best known for their legendary military figures and vehicles. The farm series has also captivated hordes of collectors, both young and old, who appreciate the often idyllic representation of country life.

The farm range was first launched in 1921 with 30 individually collectable 1/32 scale figures. This expanded over the years to include such gems as the collectable 'Village Idiot', vehicles of every description, and even a clergyman.

How much?

The carthorses were always popular – in a box most make around £35 each. 'Worzel Gummidge' from 1980, complete with 'Aunt Sally' and some 'swop-over' heads, was one of the more unusual figures the company produced. It is quite sought after today and, if complete with packaging, it could realise £30–40 at auction. In May 2008, a very tidy 'Model Farm' set (No. 120F) sold for a respectable £130. At the same sale, a boxed but incomplete farm lorry (No. 61F) from 1936 made £280.

Back in 2004, a Britains tractor from 1965, with an original price of 15/- [75p], reached nearly £1,700 on an Internet auction. A full-size tractor of the same era was recently advertised in a tractor mag for a similar price! The rare 'Village Idiot' figure, produced from 1926, frequently makes over £100. In November 2007, Vectis Auctions sold a version in a light blue smock for £260.

In 1948, the first tractor was introduced and this has become the biggest seller to this day. The 'Massey Ferguson Combine' was the most celebrated toy in the series and was awarded 'Toy of the Year 1978' by the National Association of Toy Retailers. Britains remains a leading name in the business.

Britains Farm People (No. 587) 'Village Idiot' in light blue smock with dark blue trousers: £260 (Image courtesy of Vectis Auctions)

British Bikers in 1950s attire with two Café Racers at The Goodwood Revival (Jamie Breese)

British motorcycles

The first motorbike was produced by the Germans in 1885, but for most collectors and enthusiasts around the world, the British produced the very best machines. There were dozens of marques prior to the 1960s, most of which are prized today.

The market is less volatile, perhaps, than that for classic cars. Pre-war British bikes are most popular. Of importance to collectors are actual competition machines (used by key racers), the rarity and originality of a model, and its condition. There's also the nostalgia of tracking down their favourite machine from their youth.

How much?

Among the most popular names in British bikes are BSA (Birmingham Small Arms), Triumph (making machines once again), Vincent (the stunning 'Black Shadow' featured in Hollywood movies), Matchless, and Norton. Many of these manufacturers' models now start at a few grand and go up from there.

For many, the Rolls-Royce of bikes was considered to have been the Brough Superior. An SS100 model was famously owned by T. E. Lawrence. Prices can easily stretch to £20,000 for great examples of top models.

It's a good idea to look at a few of the specialist classic bike magazines. The International Classic Motorcycle Show is probably the biggest classic motorcycle show in the world and takes place at the Stafford County Showground, Staffordshire, in April each year. There are a number of specialist dealers and clubs around the country to consider. Sotheby's and other key auction houses have sold vintage bikes too.

Bugatti

We all know the name Bugatti – it conjures up images of vintage Grand Prix and masterful, passionate design, but how much do you know about this sought-after marque? This is a slight departure from the general 'collectables' theme of this manual, but I couldn't resist giving a name check to the one marque that is possibly the most desirable in the world.

The work of Ettore Bugatti is considered the last word in both early motor racing and design. Just 8,000 cars left the factory, and only around a quarter are known to remain in running order. He designed planes, boats, limos, tools, and even trains! Bugatti was the son of a well-known designer, and art was in the family. The company was set up in France in 1909 and produced extraordinary designs for over 30 years. Possibly the most famous car was the Type 35 Grand Prix car, made from 1924 to 1931. It was credited with over 2,000 race wins!

How much?

Bugattis were also available to the man – albeit the rich man – in the street. The Type 41 Royale model is the yardstick, and in the mid-1980s the auction world was knocked for six when one was sold for over $8 million! Only six were ever built. In 1990 the record was broken when a model changed hands for $15 million in Japan!

I suspect it's unlikely you have one of these gems hiding in your garage, and you may not have millions to spend, but you can still get close to the action with the popular market in Bugatti automobilia. A few years ago, for example, ten fine photographs of various models were sold for £450 at the Goodwood Revival auction held by Bonhams. A superb original poster advertising Bugatti cars and trains made £690. A Bugatti wristwatch by Jean Perret, in its box, made nearly £600.

A rare Bugatti Type 35B Grand Prix two-seater for sale in the Bonhams enclosure at the Goodwood Revival (Jamie Breese)

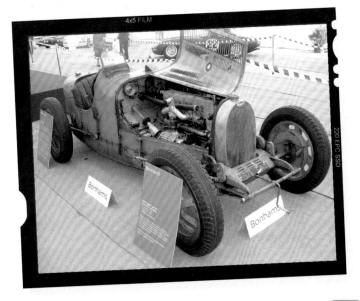

Bunnykins

The inspiration for these famous rabbits came from the drawings of the daughter of the managing director of Royal Doulton in the late 1920s and early '30s. Barbara Vernon Bailey was a nun who was teaching children at the time, and her pictures started the craze for some of the most popular mugs, plates, bowls, and figurine designs ever produced.

The earliest items date back to 1934 and are classed as nursery ware. Because of their use in nurseries, many pieces became damaged, and those left intact are quite expensive to buy today. It wasn't until 1939 that the first six figures were released. There was a hold on production during the Second World War until the early 1970s, and these figurines were still made until recently.

A Royal Doulton Bunnykins 'Happy Birthday' figurine (DB21). Designed by Harry Sales and issued between 1983 and 1997: £15–£20 (Martin Breese)

With so many different characters now available, the collectors' market has boomed. Most of these figures fall within the £20 to £50 price bracket. A special 'Golden Jubilee Celebration' Bunnykins was introduced with a Jubilee back stamp in 1984 – these are worth picking up if found cheap.

How much?

Barbara's printed signature ('Barbara Vernon' – Bailey was not used) was dropped from the ranges in the early 1950s, so collectors tend to look for this and pay a premium. The earliest figurines, such as 'Freddie' or 'Reggie Bunnykins', can make as much as £1,500 or more at auction. There are plenty of more modern limited editions to look out for: the hard to come by 'Trick or Treat' figure from 1995 was a run of 1,500 and can now make £400. New figures, such as 'Girl Guide' from 2007, will cost around £30.

In late 2008, a rare pair of figures – 'Mr & Mrs Bunnykins at the Easter Parade' (DB51 and DB52) – made in limited edition for special events in 1986, achieved a mighty £1,000 at Potteries Specialist Auctions.

Because they are so small, these figurines are ideal for display: buy an old printers' font tray from a car boot sale for a tenner; hang the tray on the wall and place the figures in the spaces once used for holding old letter blocks.

Cabbage Patch Kids

Over 80 million Cabbage Patch Kids have been 'adopted' since their first mass-produced appearance in 1983. Their development goes back to the late '70s when their 21-year-old inventor, Xavier Roberts (who made the original dolls called Little People) founded a company called Original Appalachian Artworks. These early dolls were so popular that US toy giant Coleco bought the firm and changed the name to Cabbage Patch Kids, and the craze took off, leading to near riots and then an international collecting market. The success of the firm took them to the front cover of *Newsweek* in 1983.

The majority of Coleco-made kids in mint condition are only worth tens of pounds. It is generally true that no two dolls are the same, and elaborate computers were used to ensure this. In a way, this is a collector's dream as each toy is effectively unique. In terms of value, it is the earlier or limited-edition kids that are most desirable. The first doll, limited to 1,000, was named 'Mai-Ling', and was a soft sculpture ceramic. There are two other very early dolls, and after that fabric was used. The original Coleco mass-produced dolls come with adoption papers and birth certificate. Identifying is easy, with a black Xavier signature (without date) appearing on the 1983 kids.

The exceptions to the rule are numerous when it comes to value. Eye colour, the shape of the head, and the year of manufacture all affect price, as does condition. In the mid-1980s, a number of 'speciality' dolls were made (astronauts, twins, etc.): these are very popular and often fetch hundreds of pounds. A doll called 'Kelly Marie' from 1984, MIB (mint and boxed), was on sale on eBay in 2008 for £140.

How much?

It depends on how much a collector is prepared to pay on the day. Some years ago, Xavier Roberts claimed in an interview that one doll was 're-adopted' for over £15,000. Certainly, some of the very early soft-sculpture Little People can go for a fair bit, and a 'Mai-Ling' would be a star find. Values are often changing, and some research before starting a collection is advised.

In the late 1990s, Mattel issued a mass recall of their Cabbage Patch 'Snacktime' dolls. These clever toys simulated eating with battery-powered mouths, but complaints that they ended up eating some children's hair led to the recall. Those who didn't send them back and kept them boxed and mint are possibly sitting on a mini-treasure for the future.

This one-off Donald Trump Cabbage Patch Kid doll, autographed by Trump, was sold on eBay for $6,200 in December 2004 to raise money for a US children's research hospital (Getty Images)

Three Cabbage Patch Kid dolls: £80 (Image courtesy of Vectis Auctions)

'The Jogger'
CGQ02 – another
Quaker Oats TV
advert tie-in
(Robert Harrop
Designs)

'Molly's Car' CGQ01
– one of the Quaker
Oats TV advert tie-ins
(Robert Harrop Designs)

Camberwick Green

Who doesn't remember this cult children's TV series, created in the 1960s by Gordon Murray? It's been many years since Brian Cant uttered those immortal words: 'Here is a box, a musical box …' In more recent times a fine range of figurines has been released into the very human world of collectors.

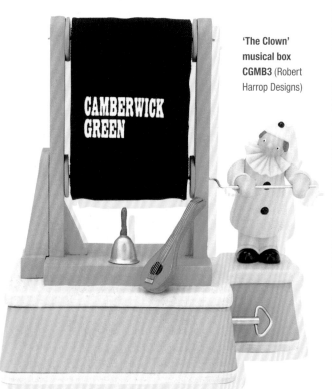

'The Clown'
musical box
CGMB3 (Robert
Harrop Designs)

The actual puppets were created using ping-pong balls for heads and polyurethane foam for the bodies. Stories abound of the entire collection of puppets being chucked on to a bonfire by their maker. Happily, Robert Harrop designs started to produce the figurines in 1998. Over 100 different designs of small figures have now been released and many limited and Collectors' Club editions, together with buildings, are also available.

Beswick have also produced a series of Camberwick Green ceramic figurines, including 'Dr Mopp' and 'Windy Miller'.

How much?

The top find will be the Music Box from 2001. This was a Robert Harrop limited edition of 2,000 and cost £34.95. It now sells for around £300–£500+. A few years ago, one sold for nearly £1,000. The miniature and also the large versions of 'Trumpton Fire Station' from 1999 and 2000 are now making good money. On the figures front, keep an eye out for the Robert Harrop 'Mr Crocket' with the petrol pump – he's retired now, but sells for £50+ (he sold for £16 new a few years ago). The first figure from 1998 – 'Windy Miller' (Model No. CG01) – is also retired, and is making £20 or more. The rare pewter version was an event piece from 2003 and is estimated to be worth £200+.

Pieces to watch out for include the limited editions of the 'Townhall Clock' musical box. The Large as Life figures have been available for a few years and are usually limited editions of 2,500. There are some special signed ones around and these can make several hundred. There is a Robert Harrop Collectors' Club which can be contacted on 01952 462721.

Carlton Ware

The legendary Staffordshire pottery has produced a magnificent variety of ceramic pieces for over a hundred years: everything from floral embossed ware, promotional items (such as Guinness), luxury boxed coffee sets, splendid vases, and even the novelty ranges such as Walking Ware (with feet on – see elsewhere). Since the late '90s, prices on many examples have been going up, and consistently so.

Carlton Ware pottery was started at the Carlton Works in Stoke-on-Trent in 1894 and sprang from the Wiltshaw and Robinson firm. Though it closed in 1992, it left a legacy of fantastically collectable, and often quite masterful, objects. They became best known, perhaps, for their now valuable lustre ware vases and dishes, which came in a variety of electric colours. The Carlton Ware name, and some of the moulds, were acquired by Francis Joseph in 1997.

A 'Mephistopheles' jug sold at Christie's, South Kensington, in April 2007 for £2,400 (Image courtesy of Christie's Images Ltd 2008)

A Carlton Ware Guinness Toucan lamp, inscribed 'How grand to be a toucan, just think what toucan do', sold at Neales the auctioneers for just over £200 in June 2008. A stunning 'Mephistopheles' jug painted with the devilish character and his shadow on a turquoise ground (and painted pattern No. 3765) sold at Christie's, South Kensington, in April 2007 for £2,400.

Carlton Ware can be picked up at boot fairs and flea markets, charity shops, and specialist art deco fairs and centres. Dating is considerably easier than other Staffordshire names, as the back stamps are added to with the shape numbers moulded into the underside. Nothing can beat a good handbook, though! If you are on a budget, look out for the distinctive Rogue Royal wares – these are from the '50s and feature striking colours on dishes and other pieces of crockery.

How much?

Carlton Ware often goes into the thousands. My favourites are a musical tankard called 'Last Drop' featuring a grinning devil as a handle (it's from the 1930s and makes £100–£180 at auction), and a bride-and-groom ashtray pair from the late '20s (they make about the same at auction).

Top of the collector's wish list must be the superb 'Guinness is Good For You' collectables from the 1950s. The set of three 'Flying Toucans' usually fetch £250–£300 at auction. Each one is balancing two pints on their beaks. The 'Zoo' series of animal figures are extremely popular and can sell for several hundred each!

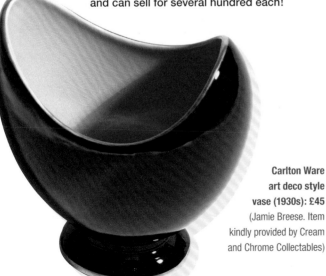
Carlton Ware art deco style vase (1930s): £45 (Jamie Breese. Item kindly provided by Cream and Chrome Collectables)

Walking Ware

Walking Ware is a type of novelty ware that Carlton Ware started to produce in the early 1970s. It is instantly recognisable. They are usually white table items such as teapots, plates and mugs, but they feature feet! The feet are sporting stripy socks too. Bigger feet are better. Make sure the pieces have the familiar 'Carlton Ware' back stamp for authentication purposes.

How much?

One of the most popular items is the standard egg cup, which makes around £10–£15 a time. A standard teapot fetches about £50–£75 at the moment, while a soap dish gets around £50. Look, too, for the two-handled loving cup and the creamer – both sell for around £45 at antiques fairs.

There are a few rare pieces that make more money: the blue-shoed 'Biscuit Barrel' is valued at over £200 at present. The miniature teapot is sought after and makes up to £150 today. A large plate can come in at around £100, and the mug made for the Moscow Olympics makes anywhere from £300 to £400+, depending on condition. Carlton Ware also produced a Jubilee Walking Ware mug with buckled shoes back in 1977 – it's a collectors' piece too.

A Walking Ware eggcup: £8–£10 (Jamie Breese)

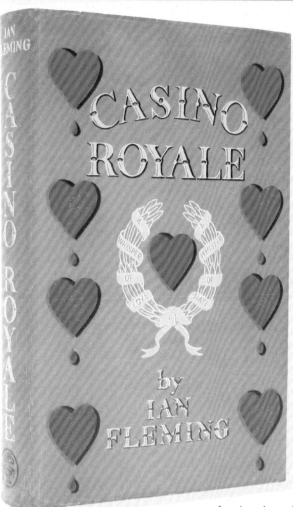

An extremely rare first edition copy of Casino Royale
(Adrian Harrington Rare Books)

Chitty Chitty Bang Bang

This toy car made by Corgi Toys is seen by many collectors as one of the very finest pieces of movie merchandise ever.

Corgi released the model in 1968 to tie in with the British-made film, based on the book by James Bond's creator, Ian Fleming. Three quarters of a million of these wonderful toys were originally sold in the distinctive yellow boxes with windows after the film came out, though this is nothing when compared with the five million Batmobiles that Corgi sold!

How much?

There are two main models to hunt down, and remember that condition is very important to top collectors. These are Model No. 1006 with yellow main wings and orange front and rear wings, worth £75–£100 tidy and boxed; and Model No. 266, a 1/42nd scale version, with spring-out red and yellow striped wings, which makes up to £240–£300 today. Look out for the plastic kit made by Aurora (Model No. 828), also released in 1968 – it is rare.

Four actual cars were produced for the film and all have survived. The last I knew, one was in a museum in the UK and another is available for private hire. They feature the distinctive 'GEN 11' number plate, which was the closest the filmmakers were allowed by the authorities to get to the word GENIE.

If you are lucky enough to own an original of the toy, check that all four characters are present, as missing parts massively devalue this gem. More recently, Corgi re-released a slightly modified version of this classic toy and it retailed for around £19.99.

A superb 'Chitty Chitty Bang Bang' Corgi toy like this can make several hundred pounds
(Image courtesy of Vectis Auctions)

Casino Royale

Casino Royale was the first James Bond novel created by Ian Fleming back in 1953. Fleming was himself an insider when it came to espionage and all things Bond-like, and some have described his first work as his best. Anyway, it is by far the rarest title. It features the 'bleeding hearts' dust jacket designed by the author.

How much?

Prices vary tremendously. True first editions of *Casino Royale* are sometimes seen up for sale by fine book dealers for £25,000+ in excellent condition. Why not have a look on your shelves at home: look for first editions of any of the Bond books. They all have a value, especially if in good condition and complete with dust jacket. *Thunderball* from 1961 is worth about £500, for example.

If you are a Bond fan and fancy living the dream, there is a fun website called www.jamesbondlifestyle.com dedicated to the watches, cufflinks, and cars.

Clarice Cliff

Clarice Cliff – also
affectionately known
as 'The Sunshine
Girl' – was one of the
greatest and most
prolific designers Britain
has ever produced. What
makes this accolade
greater still is the simple
fact that she was a woman
in a then male-dominated
industry. Today, Clarice
Cliff is the last word in
collectables and has
developed an almost cult-like following in the biz.

Young Clarice started work in the potteries of Stoke-
on-Trent in her early teens. She attended the seminal and
crucial 'Exposition Internationale des Arts Décoratifs et
Industriels Modernes' which took place in 1925 in Paris
– this started the art deco movement. By this time Clarice
was already working for the Wilkinson pottery and her lucky
break came with the release of her famous 'Bizarre' range
of painted wares in 1927. Her work is familiar to many on
account of the bright, bold, and often geometric or floral
style patterns and colours. The classic deco look! For some,
Clarice has proved to be a fine designer to invest in too.

A superb Clarice Cliff teapot in
typical bold and bright colours (Image
courtesy of Sotheby's Picture Library)

How much?

Her golden era really was the '20s through to the late
'30s. During her lifetime, Clarice managed to create a
whopping 2,000 different patterns – many of which were
groundbreaking for their time – and over 500 different
shapes. You really will find it hard to find many pieces for
under £50 today. Anything brightly painted, as opposed
to her later plain wares, makes north of £100. The norm is
hundreds, if not thousands, for complete art deco coffee
and tea sets. A single conical 'House and Bridge' cup and
saucer, circa 1930, made £744 at Bonhams in London in
September 2008. Get a guide book and get hunting at car
boots and charity shops – but beware, as most folks now
realise that Cliff = cash!

Sadly, Clarice passed away in 1972, just as her work
received its first major exhibition. The real boom in prices
took off in the late '80s and '90s, but even in the 2000s
the odd record is being broken. In May 2003, a stunning
1932/33 'May Avenue' charger went under the hammer at
Christie's in London: the estimate was between £10,000
and £15,000 and it sold for an astonishing £39,950, a world
record price for an item by Clarice Cliff at auction. An
Inspiration 'Morning Glory' Meiping vase, circa 1930,
sold for £1,800 at a Bonhams auction in London in
September 2008.

'Age of Jazz' figures

These classic figures are now regarded by
some to be the most significant ceramic
designs of the entire art deco era. Created
by the 'Sunshine Girl', Clarice Cliff, they have
become extremely sought after and have made
astonishing amounts at international auctions of
her work. Have you got one?

The figures were designed in 1930 as table
centrepieces, or for placing upon the wireless.
Though they are only a few inches high, and flat sided,
they are noted for their colour and boldness. However, when
introduced during the depression years, they failed to sell
that well – an ideal element for the collector of rare things.

How much?

Prices vary according to the actual design and condition.
There were only five designs made in different shapes,
including a pair of dancing figures, and a banjo player and
pianist combined. Because they are so thin, they'd snap or
crack easily. Christie's have sold quite a few. An oboe and
drummer example made nearly £14,000 in 1997. Another
sold for £15,525, a record price, in February 2000. Not bad
for an example from a range of which many ended up being
disposed of because of poor sales. More recently, Keys
Auctions in Norfolk sold a dancing couple (with signs of
repair to the arms) for £6,700.

In 1996, Wedgwood produced 150 limited-edition
reproductions of these fabulous figures. They were
handpainted and of a very fine standard. Today,
boxed, even these sell for around £100–
£150+. Tracking one of them
down could be the
next best thing.

A Wedgwood 'Age of Jazz'
reproduction, along with
another figurine, made £329
at Christie's a few years ago
(Image courtesy of Christie's
Images Ltd 2008)

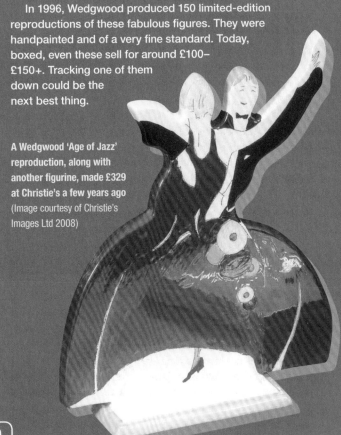

Coca-Cola memorabilia

This world-famous soft drink was created by Dr John Pemberton, an American pharmacist, in 1886. Coca-Cola was sold first for 5 cents a go as a fountain drink at Jacob's Pharmacy, Atlanta, Georgia. The success of the drink was heavily based on the remarkable volume and quality of advertising and merchandising. Coca-Cola is sold in over 200 different countries around the world, so collecting is now global.

There's a wealth of fantastic, colourful items to look out for: Coke calendars first appearing in 1891; magazine adverts dating back to 1904; the famous Buddy Lee and Santa Claus dolls which appeared in the 1950s – while the high end tends to feature the metal trays (can make many hundreds of pounds depending on age and condition); large cooler cabinets; and early letters from the inventor. Items produced for internal use within the Coca-Cola business are usually more valuable than those sold in shops. Smaller pockets are catered for by the wide variety of clocks, yo-yos, cans, bottles, cards, toy cars, and trains – and even educational items such as pencils and blotters.

A superb Coca-Cola World Cup glass and box: £15 (Jamie Breese. Item kindly provided by Cream and Chrome Collectables)

Coca-Cola tray: £15 (Jamie Breese. Item kindly provided by Cream and Chrome Collectables)

How much?

A simple item such as the 1930 Coca-Cola sandwich plate could still set you back several hundred pounds, while a Coca-Cola advertising calendar from 1918 once sold for £4,500. A Coca-Cola calendar in A1 condition from 1907 has changed hands for over £11,000. A Victorian tray from 1897 featuring an elegant lady is one of the true Holy Grails and was once valued in the thousands.

There are plenty of extremely rare items. The early 1950s 'Vendolator' vertical vending machines are particularly iconic: designs such as the 5 cent Model 44 start at around £1,500 as of 2008. Other rare models were made by Jacobs, Mills, Westinghouse, and Glascock Brothers.

In the early 1970s, the Coca-Cola Company picked up on the memorabilia market and started to make reproductions of vintage Coke items. These are usually different in shape and are obviously worth far less. There are also some fakes in circulation. In the 1980s, the Coke trademark was offered to companies producing a wide range of licensed goods. These are numerous and are already collectable, especially if kept in their original packaging. The peak in collecting may well have been the late '80s to late '90s. As for the future, they aren't going anywhere, so I suspect there will still be a demand for these colourful and collectable items.

Coins

Rare coins are easy to store and can represent a good long-term investment if chosen wisely. The market has gone up and down like many specialist collectables, but there is no denying that this is one of the most classic and classy areas in which to hunt for treasure.

Coins come in all shapes and sizes. Some are rare because they were trial coins, made to test a design, or they could be proof strikes. Others can be 'survivors' which began as one of many but were withdrawn and melted. Remember that scarcity is not connected to the age of a coin: some Chinese coins that are over 1,000 years old are only worth a few pounds! Collectors seek uncirculated, perfect coins where possible. The tiniest sign of rubbing can mean a massive price drop.

In 2006 a new world record was created for a British coin. It was an Edward III Double Leopard Florin at £460,000 (Image courtesy of Spink)

How much?

A few years ago a new world record price of over $17 million dollars was paid for a $20 US gold coin from 1933. The British Grail must be the famous George V Penny, also of 1933. There were enough pennies in circulation in that year so none was made, except for a few that were ordered to be buried under the foundation stones of new buildings of the time (a tradition). There is clear evidence for six specimens, but there could be others. If a genuine penny surfaced, it would be very, very valuable indeed. Spink's, with its headquarters in London, holds over 35 auctions a year around the world. In June 2006 they shattered the world record for a British coin sold at auction with the sale of the Double Leopard Gold Coin for a mighty £460,000.

Do not be tempted to clean a scarce coin. It can literally destroy the value. Bear in mind that the market for rare coins, as with so many other categories of collectables, can be volatile.

Collectable coins produced by the Pobjoy Mint to tie in with *Harry Potter and the Prisoner of Azkaban* (Image courtesy of Pobjoy Mint)

Record-breaking coins

One of the best-known established coin specialists is Spink. Spink was founded back in 1666 and is a specialist auctioneer known for its expertise with coins, stamps, medals, banknotes, bonds, share certificates and even autographs.

One of its most widely reported auctions took place in May 2003 during the sale of the Slaney Collection of English Coins. This collection had been created in the first half of the twentieth century and, according to Spink: "was possibly the last of the truly great coin collections". All 285 lots were sold, and the auction raised over £1million. A new record was set for an English silver coin known as the 'Petition' Crown of 1663. This realised a mighty £138,000. Another star was the Charles I Exeter Mint half crown (£40,250). This coin had previously remained off the auction block for exactly a century.

The Coinex sale in October 2004 saw the sale of the only known purpose-made Anglo-Saxon gold penny, of clearly regal design, fetch a record-breaking price of £230,000. The auctioneers claim it was the most important discovery in British numismatics for many years, and was the first Anglo-Saxon gold penny to come to light for almost a century.

April 2005, saw the sale of the final part of the Louis E. Eliasberg, Sr. Collection of World Gold Coins and Medals. The sale saw 3,600 lots sold and made a total of $10,118,246. A Korean 5 Won of 1908 sold for $287,500.

The English coin known as the 'Petition' Crown of 1663. This realised £138,000 in the Slaney Collection of English Coins in May 2003 (Image courtesy of Spink)

The Coinex sale in October 2004 saw the sale of the only known purpose-made Anglo-Saxon gold penny of clearly regal design fetch a record-breaking price of £230,000 (Image courtesy of Spink)

Eagle comic, complete Volume One,
Nos1 to 52 inclusive – 14 April 1950/6 April
1951: **£480** (Image courtesy of Vectis Auctions)

Comics

Comic collectors have divided the market into several different areas of interest that include the Platinum Age (1897–1932), Golden Age, Silver Age, Bronze Age, Horror, Western, and Sci-Fi. It is the first appearance of a popular character which creates the most interest, but collectors also look out for comics with such characters' final appearance.

Classic British comics have found a great niche and have proved to be an area to collect in themselves. Values are usually far less than US gems, but they're easier to find. *Funny Folks* (1874–1894) is regarded as the first true British comic, while Ally Sloper of *Ally Sloper's Half-Holiday* (1884–1916) was the first British comic strip hero.

A comic which features the first appearance of a US Superhero is wildly collectable. For example, the first Batman comic was published in 1940, but Batman actually appeared a year before in the comic book *Detective Comics* No. 27 of May 1939. This is worth tens of thousands of pounds, and fewer than 100 copies are known to exist. The first issue of *Whiz Comics* in 1940 unveiled Captain Marvel (at one point worth over £26,000). The famous girls' comics, such as *Bunty*, are not particularly sought after, as the majority of collectors tend to be fellas. The same goes for popular nursery titles.

How much?

A real find would be a No. 1 comic with its free give-away gift. The first issue of *The Beezer*, a British comic that appeared on 21 January 1956, came with a 'Whizz Bang' toy and is worth £500+. Many rare and popular comics can be bought for much less – *Chips*, *Comic Cuts* and issues of the *Eagle* can all be found for £2–£6. Spider-Man's debut was in *Amazing Fantasy* issue No. 15 which can be bought for a more modest £200.

A copy of *The Beano* No. 1 from 1938 recently created a world record price for a British comic when it sold for over £12,000. The most valuable American comic, and the true Holy Grail is *Action Comics* No. 1 from 1938, which features the first ever Superman.

The secret to unearthing a gem is perseverance: keep sifting through boxes at car boot sales, and check out your attic. Condition, however, is crucial and a standardised grading system has been established by collectors and dealers. The market is always changing as kids grow up and start collecting the comics they read as a child.

If you are just starting out as a collector, try to find the very best condition comics. Remember to handle them carefully, as fingerprints easily show up on dark covers. If you find a classic gem, contact your local dealer and ask for professional bags and backing. Auctions often sell issues bound in years, and these can be picked up quite cheaply.

Action Comics No. 1

There have been over 800 issues of this classic comic book since it all began in the 1930s, and the great attraction of the No. 1 issue, apart from it being the first, is that it contains the debut of Superman and marks the beginning of the comic book fantasy genre, the notion of the superhero and the 'Golden Age of Comic Books'.

Superman's creators were Joe Shuster and Jerry Siegel – Shuster produced the drawings and Siegel did the writing. Surprisingly, the idea was turned down by a lot of publishers at first, but DC Comics eventually took them on. Initially tagged 'Man of Tomorrow', the man of steel's alter ego worked for *The Daily Star*. It was an instant hit and was followed up with the Superman comic book series a year later, going on to spawn endless other costumed action characters.

The cover of Action Comics No. 1,
from June 1938, featuring the
debut of Superman (Getty Images)

How much?

There's good incentive to have a rummage in the attic for a copy. Around 75 are known to exist, and a mint condition example will command many thousands. Oscar-winning actor Nicolas Cage sold his personal copy a few years ago for $86,250.

Sadly, both creators of Superman lived out their lives in near poverty working as a clerk and a blind messenger. After a legal battle in the '70s, the men were awarded a small pension by the then owners of the copyright. Their legacy includes several movies, numerous TV spin-offs, and there is even a Museum in Metropolis, Illinois, with the largest collection of memorabilia in the world.

The Eagle

The first edition of this classic boys' comic appeared on 14 April 1950. The comic was put together by Frank Hampson and Reverend Marcus Morris and quickly became one of the most popular comics of the era selling three-quarters of a million every week. Star feature, Dan Dare (originally meant to be a 'Space Chaplain'), became one of the most worshipped heroes and there was a hoard of merchandise produced as tie-ins.

Interest in Dan's adventures and his collectables has been rekindled recently by the successful creation of a computer-generated animated series on Channel 5. A whole new audience has been introduced and this must be good news for collectors. Smaller items, such as badges and bedcovers, can be picked up cheaply at car boot fairs if you know what to look out for.

How much?

Most of the key toy manufacturers produced various Dan Dare wares – Merit and Waddingtons included. Items to look out for include the Ingersoll pocket watch (worth around £400 if boxed), the classy space-age toy laser called 'The Planet Gun', made of tin and plastic (£200+), and the Dan Dare pinball set made by top toymakers Chad Valley. There are board games and jigsaws, all of which are more affordable.

Though some toys are worth more, the first ever comic, in mint condition, must be the collector's dream! A complete Volume One 1950–1951, Nos.1 to 52, sold for £480 in January 2008 at Vectis Auctions. The No 1 wasn't great, hence the price. Four original artwork boards by Frank Hampson sold at Christie's, South Kensington, in October 1997 for £633.

Eagle annuals are an easier place to begin if you wish to collect (the first one landed on planet earth in September 1951 and they are far easier to hunt down) – prices go from £50 to £100+ depending on condition. Later editions also make great reading and can cost as little as a few pounds.

Dan Dare collectables

Colonel Daniel McGregor Dare is a charming toy range to collect. He first appeared in the *Eagle*, tagged as 'the pilot of the future'. Dan was the big pull for that legendary boys' comic. Interestingly, the *Eagle* was co-created by Reverend Marcus Morris, and Dan was actually meant to be a 'Space Chaplain'! The comic quickly became one of the most popular of the era, selling nearly a million copies a week, and with the popularity came the merchandise – and lots of it.

The very first issue featured hero Dan on the cover and was published back in 1950. Interest in his adventures, and therefore his collectability, has been rekindled in recent years with the creation of the computer-generated animated series on British TV.

How much?

A Dan Dare fob watch, made by Ingersoll, can make £300–£400 at auction if boxed. A first issue *Eagle* in fair condition will set you back £100 at present, but If in truly mint condition, then it'll be many times more: perhaps £600–£800+. A tin Dan Dare ray gun complete with fantastic lithographed graphics and real sparks, made by Merit Toys, can be worth up to £1,200 in a box. A boxed set called 'Electronic Space Control Radio Station', also made by Merit, can make £100. A Wallis Rigby designed Dan Dare 'Anastasia' Jet Plane model from 1955 was sold originally as a press-out book, and if in perfect condition can fetch £100–£150 at auction.

Look out for the various board games and other puzzles. The Dan Dare wooden pinball game by Chad Valley can command £200, and the standard Waddingtons jigsaws, boxed and complete, make £30–£50 or so.

This British 1950s DCMT Crescent rare 'Genuine Dan Dare Atomic Jet Gun' made £800 in May 2008 (Image courtesy of Vectis Auctions)

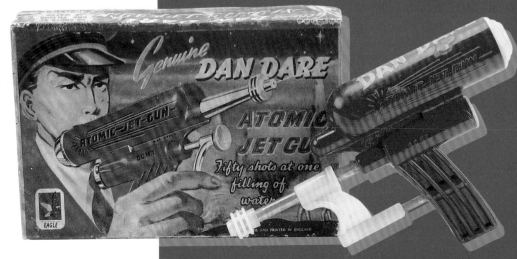

The Sinclair ZX81 may be a future collectable if kept in good shape and boxed (iStockphoto)

Sinclair ZX80 computer

Did you know that your humble little Sinclair computer, up there in the attic, could be worth a mint? We all remember the groundbreaking, record-selling black box called the ZX81, but did you buy its little predecessor – and keep it safe? Designed by British inventor extraordinaire Sir Clive Sinclair, the ZX80 was one of a number of world firsts for the great man: pocket calculators (1972), digital watches (1976), pocket televisions (1977), and mass-produced electric cars (1985). Sinclair was made Chairman of British Mensa in 1980 (he has an IQ of 159!) and is still working on amazing devices to this day.

The computer went on sale in the spring of 1980 in kit and ready-made form. The language used was BASIC, and basic it was. Though highly limited compared to today's machines, with only one kilobyte of RAM (many PCs today have several gigabytes!), it still sold in numbers between 50,000 and 70,000.

How much?

The highest price I've seen paid for a boxed machine, complete with the manual, has been £900 on the Internet a few years back. You should expect less than half that for a machine on its own if tidy. There were some cloned models made, and they may make less. These figures are incredible when you consider the high street price of £100 originally. A ZX80 is on display at London's Science Museum.

You may still have the much-loved ZX81, which followed. It was around £30 cheaper to buy, though noticeably more powerful, and Sinclair sold around 500,000 units in the first year of release: 1981. Keep these machines in good shape and in their box and they might appreciate in price. The ZX Spectrum came along next in April 1982 and really put Sinclair on the map. It became a games machine for most owners and spawned the industry as we know it today.

Computers

Who would've thought that these dull plastic boxes would appear in a book about collectables! Much like early mobiles, the first home computers have already caught collectors' imaginations. Remember, the humble US/UK-made machines, in a way, were as important and revolutionary as the car, the telephone, or the loom!

Though it was the Intel Corporation that started the home computer gold rush with the very first microprocessor in 1971, it was the Apple Company that seized the new technologies and released the Apple II personal computer in 1977. A host of other small plastic boxes appeared in the late '70s and early '80s, all of which, to varying degrees and dependent on condition, would be considered rare and quite collectable today.

How much?

The Apple II is now so rare that prices really do vary. If mint and boxed, you might have to pay hundreds of pounds to become a lucky owner. Most won't know the true value as they were so basic. Look for more obscure early home computers, boxed, with names like 'Oric 1' or 'Oric Atmos'; Jupiter 'Ace'; 'Dragon 32'; 'Commodore Vic20', and so forth.

One of the most sought-after gems would probably be an Apple I personal computer designed by Steve Wozniak and Steve Jobs in July 1976. This will *one day*, along with the kit-form Altair 8800 and Scelbi 8H, be viewed as one of the most significant creations of the last millennium. It helped start the revolution which changed everybody's life beyond recognition. Also elusive are the Tandy TRS-80 and the Commodore Pet, both from 1977.

Looking to the future, it is quite clear that Apple's stunning iMac from 1998 will be a Holy Grail of sorts one day (see below). The net, not surprisingly, offers plenty of info for those interested in starting a collection of vintage home computers.

Sinclair ZX80 personal computer (1980), boxed with manuals: £600–£800 (Jamie Breese)

The Apple iMac

Many design and computer experts would probably now agree that the revolutionary iMac computer was one of the most important products made at the close of the 20th century. Now, looking back, one has to wonder why designers and manufacturers had never previously considered making a personal computer a bit more personal, colourful, and fun.

Several million iMacs have been sold since they were first introduced back in August 1998. It is well known that the all-in-one personal computer saved the beleaguered Apple Computer Company from some problems. Not only was it an instant smash hit worldwide, but it was also designed by Brit Jonathan Ives. The teardrop shape, translucent plastic case, built-in monitor and modem, and ease of use made this an instant classic.

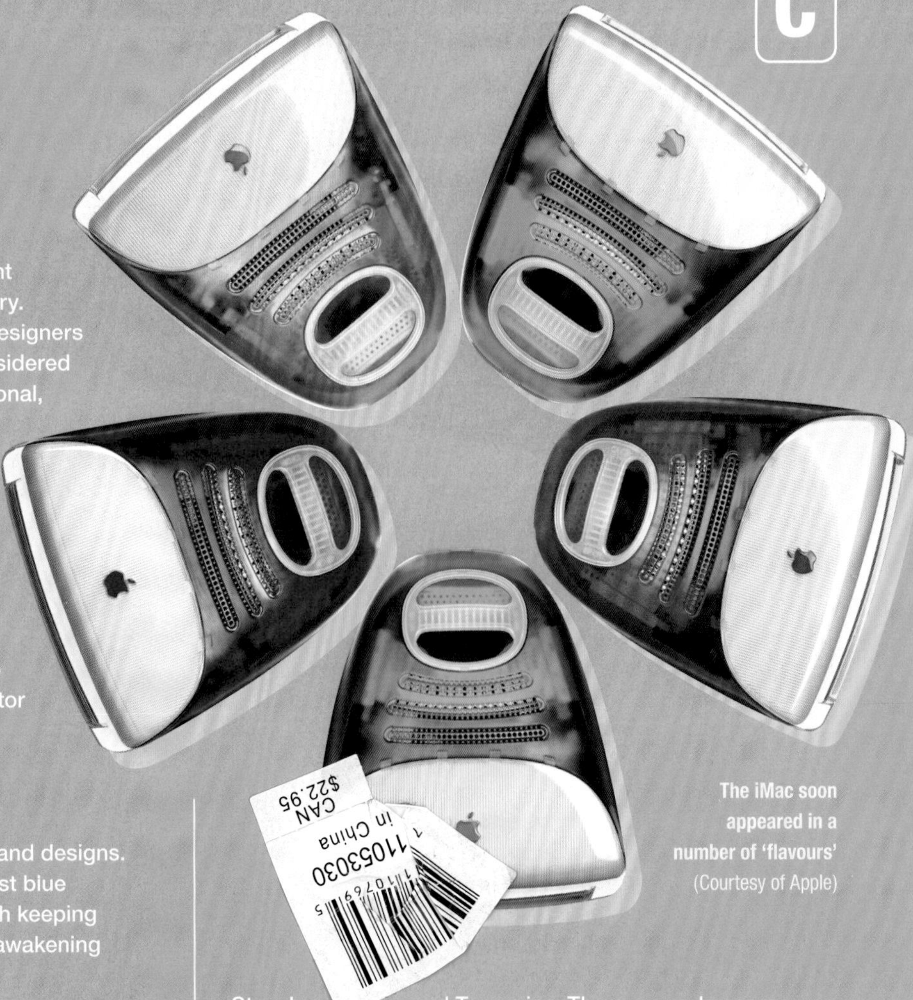

How much?

The early iMacs came in a variety of colours and designs. The five 'fruity' colours which followed the first blue machine are not sold any more, and are worth keeping aside: these included the outrageous office-awakening

The iMac soon
appeared in a
number of 'flavours'
(Courtesy of Apple)

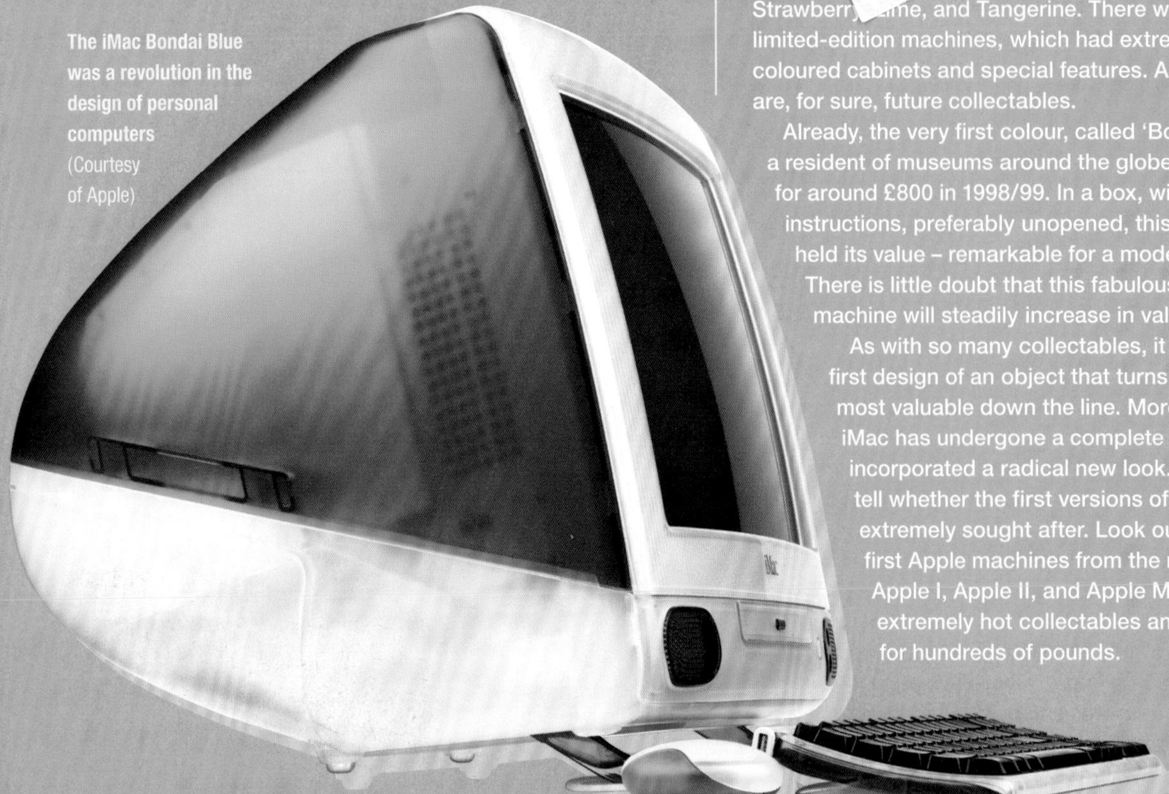

The iMac Bondai Blue
was a revolution in the
design of personal
computers
(Courtesy
of Apple)

Strawberry, Lime, and Tangerine. There were also some limited-edition machines, which had extremely innovative coloured cabinets and special features. All these iMacs are, for sure, future collectables.

Already, the very first colour, called 'Bondi Blue' is a resident of museums around the globe. This sold for around £800 in 1998/99. In a box, with original instructions, preferably unopened, this may well have held its value – remarkable for a modern computer. There is little doubt that this fabulous-looking machine will steadily increase in value.

As with so many collectables, it is so often the first design of an object that turns out to be the most valuable down the line. More recently, the iMac has undergone a complete facelift and again incorporated a radical new look. Only time will tell whether the first versions of this will become extremely sought after. Look out for the very first Apple machines from the mid-1970s. The Apple I, Apple II, and Apple Macintosh are now extremely hot collectables and change hands for hundreds of pounds.

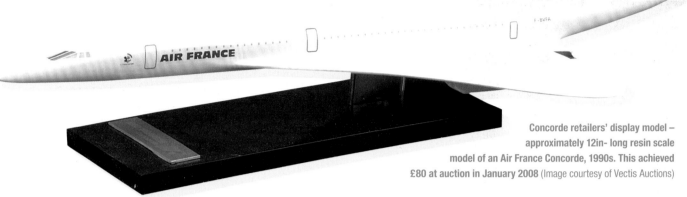

Concorde retailers' display model –
approximately 12in- long resin scale
model of an Air France Concorde, 1990s. This achieved
£80 at auction in January 2008 (Image courtesy of Vectis Auctions)

The Holy Grail? This Concorde nose cone was sold at a
Christie's sale in Paris in 2003 (Getty Images)

Concorde collectables

Concorde made its first flight back in March 1969.
Amazingly, only 20 aircraft were ever built. Perhaps its most
memorable impression was left during the finale of the
Queen's Golden Jubilee on 4 June 2002 with a jaw-dropping
fly past. Collectors of Concorde memorabilia exist, and
interest is likely to increase.

There are three or four different ways to make a collection.
If on a budget, you can opt for the limited number of items
made available to the general public (such as the more recent
commemorative range from British Airways); you can go for
pictures of the craft which cost upwards of £20 or much more
if signed by important figures such as Captains; you can go
for in-flight items such as the flight certificates, brochures
or luxury presentation items given to VIPs; or very specific
rarities such as fittings from an actual plane.

How much?

Concorde blankets are currently traded for around the £40
mark, whereas you can pick up a genuine, used metal galley
container for around £35 upwards. One of the most elegant
pieces is a specially-produced British Airways Concorde pen
that was given to VIP passengers. These were recently being
sold on the secondary market for around £200. Other great
pieces, such as candle snuffers, plates by Royal Doulton,
and even bespoke VIP napkin rings, can all be found on
Internet collectors' sites.

Air France held an auction of memorabilia, including
pilots' seats and a nose cone (the Holy Grail?) at a Christie's
sale in Paris in 2003. There were no reserves and all the
money raised went to a children's charity. About 1,300
people watched, and a few key lots exceeded their estimates
by more than ten times.

On 2 May 2002, The Royal Mail celebrated Concorde
with a special stamp. These are obviously going to be worth
keeping an eye on in the future. If you have more money to
spend, the most curious items to own would have to be a
pair of passenger seats, or a nose cone. Take a look at
www.concordecollectables.com.

This winged pig by artist Damien Hirst sold for just over half-a-million pounds in late 2008 (Rex Features)

Contemporary art

Where is the money at right now? It seems that London is becoming top dog when it comes to prices paid on the international contemporary art market. You may not have heard of most of the artists, but they are setting international auction rooms on fire, as a recent Sotheby's sale demonstrated. Do you have an early work by a struggling artist in their early years or at school?

British artists are making big waves at the moment. Tim Noble and Sue Webster's flashing light work of a bleeding heart, entitled 'Toxic Schizophrenia', gained for the pair a new world record at auction of £356,000 recently. Other more established European and American names are on the up too, including Gerhard Richter, Roy Lichtenstein, Jean-Michel Basquiat, and Andy Warhol (of course).

How much?

Sotheby's recently held the most successful Contemporary Art sale ever staged in Europe. The final total was a spectacular £45,762,000, well in excess of the pre-sale estimate. British artists fared brilliantly, attracting bids from international buyers. A new world record was achieved for Peter Doig, whose early masterpiece 'White Canoe' from 1990/91 made a whopping £5.7 million against a pre-sale estimate of just £800,000–£1,200,000.

If paintings aren't your bag and you have a few million to spare, you could invest in a seriously desirable photograph. One lucky punter walked away at the same sale with Andreas Gursky's powerful '99 cent II Diptychon', from 2001. At £1,700,000, this was a record for a photograph at auction.

Banksy

Britain's brightest urban star and graffiti artist icon has made it into the international art auction market. Famous for his spray-painted works on walls across the country, Banksy and his anti-war, anti-capitalism, and anti-establishment stance is now fetching serious money.

Banksy first came to the fore as more than a graffiti artist in 2003, with his first exhibition, Turf War. His best-selling book *Wall and Peace* can be found in bookshops across the country. He is a master of clever PR stunts, such as smuggling his doctored oil paintings into famous museums, yet his identity remains a mystery.

He is appreciated internationally and by collectors of all ages and walks of life, and his works have opened up art to a whole new audience. In early February 2008, the auctioneers Sotheby's held two sales – at Olympia and New Bond Street. Time will tell if the recent Banksy excitement will weather the recession.

How much?

'Bombing Middle England', a work of acrylic and spray-paint on canvas which was commissioned directly by the vendor in 2001, soared above its estimate of £30,000–£50,000. The unique piece sold to an anonymous telephone bidder for a whopping £102,000 – a then world auction record for the urban artist. 'Ballerina with Action Man Parts' sold for a mighty £96,000 with a pre-sale estimate of £15,000–£20,000. Over the two days, the Banksy pieces fetched a combined total of £372,000.

Banksy is one of the most exciting contemporary artists and he has attracted attention from the best dealers and Hollywood A-listers (Wikimedia Commons)

Corgi

2006 marked the 50th anniversary of one of the most fondly regarded and long-lasting names in toy history. Corgi has endured more changeovers than most, and survived both a huge business-destroying fire in 1969 and the dip in the die-cast market in the late '70s and '80s, to remain a player in the collectables market. Today they are owned by another great toy institution – Hornby.

Of course, it is the gems of the past that grab the headlines. 'The Yellow Submarine', 'The Magic Roundabout', 'Chitty Chitty Bang Bang', and the 'Batmobile' are but a few of the icons from the '60s alone. It all started in July 1956 with the release of ten models – the first being a Ford Consul – hardly a Bond car, but it was a huge hit. Just lately they have added to their collectability with a top-end range of gold-plated classic models from the 50th anniversary editions.

A Corgi Chevrolet Impala in mint condition, in its original box sold for £90 in January 2009 (Image courtesy of Vectis Auctions)

How much?

Recently a special Corgi Aston Martin 007 toy (made originally for VIPs only) went for an astonishing £1,300! The best-selling die-cast toy was the 'Batmobile', which makes £300 to £450 in top shape today. The newer limited-edition 50th anniversary gold-plated Spitfire could be one to watch in the future.

Corgi produced a range of 50th anniversary limited-edition replicas of some of the landmarks from their history. These look like the real thing in authentic retro boxes and come with certificates and a special stamp. If you can't afford the original toys, this could be the next best thing – at least you can guarantee they will be 'mint and boxed'! Included is the very first toy – the Ford Consul.

Corgi Ford Consul

The first model went on the market in July 1956. Within three months the initial production of 100,000 had sold out and another 250,000 had quickly to be made. It was a revolution back then as it had a metal chassis, turned wheels, and windows. A collectors' club was set up that very year.

How much?

The Consul cost 2/9d (14p) – a bargain compared to the £663 that the actual car cost. In four months Corgi had produced

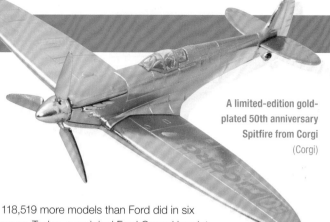

A limited-edition gold-plated 50th anniversary Spitfire from Corgi (Corgi)

118,519 more models than Ford did in six years. Today, an original Ford Consul in mint condition and boxed is worth £200–£300. Vectis Auctions sold the first ever Ford Consul (this belonged to the key Corgi designer Marcel R. Van Cleemput) and it made a princely £950. Another identical model made £1,100.

To mark the anniversary, Corgi produced a limited edition of just 300 worldwide of an unpainted exact replica in special packaging. These were given away, not sold. They also made a Consul that came with a book (limited to 1,000 and costing £69.00), a Brown Consul (limited to 5,000), and a Gold-Plated Consul (limited to 500).

Batmobile

This classic comic strip legend turned TV hero has been seen again on the silver screen in recent years. Rarely leaving the limelight, the collectability of the Gotham City crime fighter has not often dipped.

The ultimate toy for any BatFan must be the legendary Batmobile. The first version by Corgi is the Holy Grail. Known as model 267, the original toy came with some important extras, such as 12 firing rockets, a flame-throwing rear exhaust, and a chain slasher. Also important to have are the badge and secret instructions pack (such things came with Corgi's Bond toys too).

How much?

A near mint condition boxed toy with all the paperwork and missiles included (but not on the sprue), will currently cost you around £300 to £450. However, one near mint but wholly complete example sold in March 2008 at Vectis Auctions for a mighty £850. What made this so special was that it was signed in felt pen on the rear of its box by Adam West, the original Batman. This is naturally hard to come by, and being a cult collectable, most likely represents a good bet for future appreciation. The condition of the box, as well as the toy, is vital.

One of the limited-edition Corgi Ford Consuls (Jamie Breese)

Cornish kitchenware

Inspired (allegedly) by the blue skies and white-crested waves of the Cornish coast, Cornish kitchenware has never been anywhere near Cornwall – it has always been made by T. G. Green at Church Gresley, Derbyshire. Widely imitated but never bettered, Cornish kitchenware has filled kitchen shelves across the land since 1926, and still looks fresh today.

Every piece of Cornish Ware was turned on a lathe in order to create the sharp-edged blue and white bands that made the brand a design classic. Each storage jar had one of over 100 different ingredient names emblazoned on their sides, or you could have your own made to order.

How much?

Cornish Ware can be bought new today, but look out for older pieces at markets and antiques centres that bear the green or black shield mark on the base. Standard storage jars will cost up to £100 each – while the whole range goes from pudding basins (common) to egg separators (rare).

Storage jars with uncommon ingredient names have sometimes pushed their way up to bigger figures. A 'Boracic Crystals' jar sold for £585 at auction in 1998. Recent finds have included 'Carb Soda' and 'Parsley Seasoning'. A 'Dripping' jar was recently listed by a dealer at £250.

Beware of fakes. Unscrupulous people have tried to add rare names to ordinary jars. A genuine named jar should have a black shield mark, not a green one. These are great collectables and have a timeless style that should last and last.

A Cornish Ware Melior Cafetiere from the 1950s would be expected to sell for £250–£300 (Courtesy of cornishware.biz)

Bold, dark fountain pen ink signature 'W. G. Grace' on a sheet of plain notepaper: £1,250
(Image courtesy of Fraser's Autographs)

Cricket collectables

This great game, along with football and golf, has been doing quite well on the collectables market over the last decade or so. It is a quite specific field that appeals to collectors of different age groups across the world. As with music and film, it is the personal items that are connected in some way to the greatest names of the past, for example W. G. Grace, that command the biggest figures today.

Like footballs, signed bats have become a must-have for the enthusiast. Match-used balls are great finds, and genuine match bails even better. However, it is the memorabilia that dates from the dawn of the test match in the late 1800s that are currently the most valuable items.

How much?

Fledgling collectors should dig around the attic for the famous Wisden Cricketers' Almanacs. They date back to 1864 and are hugely collectable if you have the original editions, which haven't been rebound. Even facsimile editions make hundreds! A rebound edition from 1916 usually makes £300+. Ceramics are big too: a Coalport plate created in 1895 to commemorate W. G. Grace's Century of Centuries sells for over £500 today. Bats are best: in October 2000, Garfield Sobers's bat, which he used to hit six consecutive sixes in a single over, was sold for a record £54,257 at an auction in Australia. Another bat, used to score a then world record in 1958, was also sold for an amazing £47,476 at the same time.

Any genuine signatures of the great cricketing legends are timeless and valuable: look for autographs of Donald Bradman, Garfield Sobers, Ian Botham, W. G. Grace and others. As of late 2008, autograph dealers Fraser's Autographs (www.Fraser'sautographs.com) were offering a good signature of W. G. Grace on notepaper for £1,250. There are quite a few rare books to track down too: look for *The Noblest Game: a Book of Fine Cricket* by Neville Cardus, published in 1969. This can make £25+ if it is a first edition.

Cadbury's Christmas
confectionery tin (1950s): £15 (Jamie
Breese. Item kindly provided by Neo Belle Bizaar)

Christmas collectables

Christmas started to become collectable from the late 1970s. It was the Victorians who created the annual craze, although the modern image of Santa Claus has perhaps closer links to a Christmas advertisement for Coca-Cola in 1931. The popular belief is that Prince Albert brought the idea of the Christmas tree to our shores in around 1840, yet it was a Brit who took the idea to Germany first. The first Christmas card was produced in the mid-1800s for the founder of what was to become the V&A museum, and mass production of cards, along with crackers and decorations, followed suit. In 1846, sweet-maker Tom Smith produced the first sweet-filled 'cracker'.

The main collectors are American. They look for several different types of memorabilia: lights (e.g. the Mazda Disney set from the late '20s, featuring bell-shaped bulbs and painted characters and in a box, fetches £50); Bon-Boniers – large, cardboard, sweet-filled Santas (which fetch from £100, even up to £2,000 if they are the large 2ft varieties); cards, the most desirable being those featuring Santa, which are either able to move (with a lever), or have a concertina element. The lithographed, embossed cards featuring angels are also sought after, and items featuring Santa in Blue are popular as well. The first Pirelli calendars were special Christmas gifts, and these too are collected widely.

How much?

'Snow babies' are possibly the most collectable items. These are Edwardian cake and table decorations that come in a vast array of designs. Look out for the unusual examples, such as a baby on top of a tank, or riding a motorcycle. Makers included Kestner, Hertwig and Heubach. A group of six sold at one of the Bonham's annual sales for £590. Four in ultra-rare colour variations sold at Christie's in London for £576 in December 2005. Beswick produced a superb 'Ebenezer Scrooge' character jug from 1939 to 1973. A large version makes up to £100 today.

Other Christmas items, with a more sombre connection, are the small brass gift tins from 1914 that were sent by Princess Mary as part of a Christmas Fund for soldiers serving in the trenches of France. Over two million were distributed, and they sell for around £30 today.

Prices are never really astronomical, though collectors have paid up to £2,000 for the very rare Tipp & Co. 'Father Christmas' toy car. This was a tin plate, wind-up and battery-operated toy that was around 12in long. The elaborate lithographed images featured a tree sticking out of the boot and a variety of toys. Bonhams sold a blue-clad Santa shop display (clockwork, circa 1900) for £3,000 in 1998.

Christmas biscuit tins from
Huntley & Palmers and
Peek Frean (1960s):
£8–£12 each (Jamie
Breese. Item kindly
provided by Neo
Belle Bizaar)

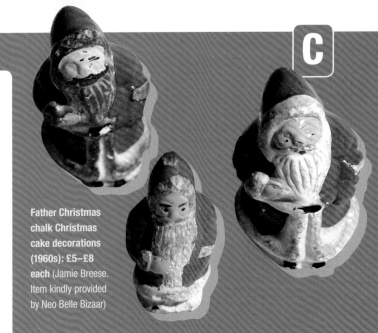

Father Christmas chalk Christmas cake decorations (1960s): £5–£8 each (Jamie Breese. Item kindly provided by Neo Belle Bizaar)

Rowntrees Christmas Club advert. 1950s. £28 (Jamie Breese. Item kindly provided by Neo Belle Bizaar)

At the very top end you could always seek a first-edition copy of *A Christmas Carol* by Charles Dickens (Bradbury and Evans, 1846). One inscribed copy sold at Christie's New York in April 2008 for $91,000. Possibly more valuable would be a complete and clean copy of the most sought-after magazine in the world: *Beeton's Christmas Annual* of 1887 featured the first Sherlock Holmes story by Sir Arthur Conan Doyle: *A Study in Scarlet*. A complete and tidy copy would be worth tens of thousands of pounds.

Cheaper finds now would include biscuit tins from the well-known firms, such as Huntley & Palmers, decorative plates, and also the tin tree decorations which acted as candle-holders. Turn of the last century postcards were a cheaper alternative to the elaborate greetings card and are still cheap to collect today (£2–£150).

Christmas decorations

The notion of decorating a Christmas tree was not popular until the mid-19th century. Initially sweets and other edible items were used, but it was the fabulous glass ornaments produced in Lauscha, Germany, and sold in Britain from the 1880s, that really made it fashionable. These original 'kugels' are very collectable today and can be worth £100s per item.

How much?

During the Soviet era in Russia, many non-Christian decorations were produced using scraps and papier-mâché. Some of these figures are very rare and quite valuable today (a rare Grandfather Frost figure can make £400+). The Fontanini family's handpainted 'heirloom' nativity sets are legendary, collectable, and still made today after nearly 100 years. Some of their hard-to-find nativity figures, such as the Gloria Angel, can make good money.

After the Second World War, the German grip on the market was replaced by the Americans. They are considered the best when it comes to Christmas tree lights, while the Japanese prevailed with ornaments. These are much cheaper to pick up today (£20-£60+). It is still possible to unearth valuable German antique glass items, as families keep them boxed and only bring them out once a year.

A Christmas issue of *Woman* magazine (1950s): £5 (Jamie Breese. Item kindly provided by Neo Belle Bizaar)

Plastic Christmas cake decoration (1960s): £3–£5 (Jamie Breese. Item kindly provided by Neo Belle Bizaar)

James Dean

For millions of fans, James Dean remains one of the most enduring icons of Hollywood. Although he appeared in less than a handful of movies, he established himself as the face of angst-ridden teenage America. Much like Monroe, Dean has never wavered as a hugely collectable and sometimes very valuable subject for movie fans.

Despite his sudden and tragic death in 1955, his memory lives on. There have been tons of small gift items, from calendars to lighters, all branded with his image or name in some way. These are collectable but rarely that valuable. The real money lies with the original owned items, much sought after by serious collectors and museums.

How much?

His movie posters can be really popular. A US 'one sheet' from the seminal 1955 classic *Rebel Without a Cause* could set you back £3,000–£4,000 if in good condition. An auto museum in the US was at one stage offering $1 million to anybody who might have the wreck of his 1955 Porsche 550 Spyder in which he died. James Dean's autograph is extremely rare, resulting from his premature passing, and examples rarely appear on the open market – they fetch thousands when they do. Well-respected autograph specialists Fraser's in 2008 suggested a valuation of £9,500 for a signed photograph in fine condition.

One of the key places to visit is his hometown of Fairmount, Indiana. Each year there is a special festival celebrating his life. You can see items such as awards, clothing, and motorbikes owned by Dean at the Fairmount museum. The James Dean Gallery, also in Fairmount, houses the world's largest collection of memorabilia.

Denby Pottery

One thing I really love about the antiques and collectables business is the way in which fashions change – often dramatically. Not so long ago I would wander around car boot fairs and find tables full of stuff like this – and it was cheap. However, Denby is now creeping back into fashion.

The company opened its doors in 1809 following the discovery of a seam of clay in Denby during the construction of a road. Local entrepreneur William Bourne found the clay had extraordinary qualities and established the pottery, originally known as Joseph Bourne, for his son. Bottles and jars were their mainstay and later, under Danesby Ware, they became famous for decorative and gift ware. From the 1950s, their tableware took off, with best-sellers including 'Greenwheat' and 'Studio'.

How much?

After nearly 200 years, the firm still produces popular wares in Derbyshire under the name of The Denby Pottery Company. Some of the most popular Denby pieces are the animals from the 1940s: the delicate giraffe makes about £60, and the popular solid rabbits begin with prices from £20. Some of the attractive designs from the 1930s, such as 'Orient ware' and 'Electric Blue' are well liked by collectors today. A 62-piece Luxor Dinner Service was sold on eBay.co.uk in November 2008 for a respectable £313. A rare wounded Bulldog from the Second World War attracted six bids and made £114 on the same site in the same month.

It's not a reflection of the quality of the pieces, but the fact remains that Denby is still easy to pick up very cheaply if you know where to look. Car boot sales and charity shops are great, as many folk don't realise that the subdued colours – brown in particular – and many designs from the 1970s make Denby quite fashionable in today's modern, funky homes. Denby may not have the glamour of Clarice Cliff, but it is durable and popular, and some of the best designers have made pieces for the firm through the years.

A Denby Studio
Set (1970s): £35
(Jamie Breese. Item kindly
provided by Cream and Chrome Collectables)

Dinky Toys

The first Dinky Toys appeared in late 1934 as a spin-off from the Hornby railway sets. Both brands were actually owned by Meccano Ltd. Within a year, the cheap, durable, and colourful toys proved so popular that over 100 models had been created. These days, the name is very much alive among collectors, and rare mint, boxed, and early, models can make thousands of pounds.

The famous Supertoys appeared from 1947 and helped seal Dinky's dominance in the toy business. Fewer of these larger models (such as trucks and planes) were made, so they command high prices these days – the Supertoy advertising lorries being particularly sought after. Dinky faced stiff competition from both Corgi and Matchbox in the 1960s, and the company finally reached the end of the road in 1974 when the Liverpool factory was closed for good.

How much?

There are Dinky Toys to match every pocket. A medium-priced example would be Lady Penelope's FAB1, Model No. 100 (1967–75). This was a Rolls-Royce that fired harpoons and missiles and was one of their most popular cars. In top condition and boxed it can make up to £300. As a rule of thumb, the pre-war vehicles are worth more – these usually feature white tyres and metal wheel hubs. Boxed sets of early vehicles have been known to sell for many, many thousands of pounds.

In October 1994 a superb price was achieved at Christie's for a Dinky van. This was possibly the only known example of the Pickfords van to feature the Bentalls department store livery, and it made an amazing £12,650. It had cost 6d (2 ½p) originally.

For those who are starting out and have a smaller budget, why not consider collecting the toys produced from 1954? The numbering of Dinky models became a simple three-digit code and started at 001, and though not as desirable as earlier vehicles, they are far cheaper.

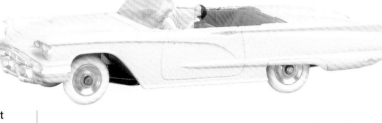

A Dinky South African issue cream Ford Thunderbird in original box made £2,820 at Christie's in London (Image courtesy of Christie's Images Ltd 2008)

Dinky 'Holy Grail'

To most, this toy car and damaged pictorial window box (below) would look like any other toy in the attic. It is John Steed's Jaguar XJ 5.3 Coupé from the popular '70s hit TV series *The New Avengers*, and comes complete with plastic figures of both John Steed and an unlucky 'fly off' assailant whom he has just run over. However, it is almost certainly the only example ever to surface at auction and it generated a lot of interest.

This supremely rare toy was the property of Mr Eric Moody who worked for Meccano in Liverpool. He started out as an apprentice in 1939 and was there supervising the shutdown of the plant in November 1979, just prior to its sale and change of ownership.

How much?

The model was not released for sale to the general public, and only a small number had been shipped from the Hong Kong manufacturer before the closure of the factory. This makes it ultra desirable today. The estimate at Vectis Auctions for the 2007 sale was a whopping £2,000–£3,000. It realised £5,400.

Dinky No. 113 *The New Avengers* John Steed's Jaguar XJ 5.3 Coupé – metallic turquoise: £5,400 (Image courtesy of Vectis Auctions)

Dinky No. 157 Jaguar XK120 Coupé manufactured between 1954 and 1962. This made £260 in June 2008 (Image courtesy of Vectis Auctions)

A Royal Doulton 'Simba' figurine. This is a current piece, No. DM10: £25 (Image courtesy of Royal Doulton/Wedgwood)

Disneyana

Uncle Walt (1901–1966) set up his own animation studio in 1923 in Hollywood. The first Mickey Mouse cartoons were *Plane Crazy* and *Steamboat Willie*. The resulting success and universal appeal of the movies that followed spawned an array of merchandise that has led to a vast, often quite serious, collectors' market. Prices range from a few pounds to tens of thousands.

Collecting heated up in the 1970s – first in the USA, then in Japan and Europe. America is still the greatest market, as, to many, Disney is American culture and part of their heritage. The timeless toys have a pull on kids and adults alike. The market is divided into many areas: pins, plates, toys, comics, and animation cels, to name but a few. This is further divided into pre-war and post-war (Second World War, that is). The most desirable items come from the late 1920s to the late 1930s. Toy production more or less ceased during the war, and the look of the characters changed to more 'rounded' or 'cuddly' when production resumed afterwards.

A tin plate 'Mickey Mouse' mechanical money bank by the German company Saalheimer & Strauss is a real gem. Made in the late '20s, a penny placed on his tongue would disappear inside. Four different ones were made, and they have fetched £10,000 each in good order. Another tin toy, featuring Mickey as an organ grinder, made by Distler (with Minnie on the top) is very elusive. Made around 1930, one such example sold for over £25,000 at auction in Maine, USA, in June 2008. The 'Disneyland 45th Anniversary' pin made for press visitors and given away in February 2000 is already changing hands for around £200–£250. At the other extreme, a 'Donald Duck' ceramic money box from the '60s can cost as little as £15.

How much?

The sale in the US of a tin plate Mickey and Minnie on a motorcycle, in a box, for nearly £70,000 reflects the seriousness of the market, as does the sale by Bonhams and Brooks of a single design of a Disney tricycle toy for the Tri-ang company (which never went into production) for nearly £700. The colourful WDCC (Walt Disney Classics Collection) 'Snow White and the Seven Dwarfs' collection from the 1990s is highly prized. £1,500+ is about right for a good collection of 14 pieces.

Merchandise and toys from the 1950s and '60s, if in good condition, is starting to become sought after. The collectors' items produced in the '80s and '90s solely for collecting (plates, toys, etc.) are perhaps less desirable. Walt Disney autographs are popular. A top dealer will look to get £3,000–£4,000 for a strong signature on a very good photograph today. Disney's signature has increased in value by 900% in just ten years, according to some experts.

Some people invest in animation art (actual cels from the movies), which can change hands for thousands of pounds. An animation cel featuring Mickey Mouse from the Disney classic *Fantasia* sold for over £26,000 at auction in 1999. A poster of *Touchdown Mickey* from 1932 has made over fifty grand too, but the most money by far is now paid for early production drawings. The first ever drawing of Mickey was valued a few years ago at $3.2 million!

More affordable gems include the early lunchboxes, annuals, comics, and soft toys (including lots of Beanie versions). Tea sets and train sets are also desirable. The famous 'Mickey Mouse' telephone made by Plessey in 1978 is now worth over £100. The Internet provides thousands of swap boards, collectors' forums, and clubs for Mickey memorabilia. Any fairly modern Mickey item, if kept mint and unopened in packaging, has a chance of keeping or improving in value.

A Royal Doulton 'Jiminy Cricket' figurine. This is a current piece, No. DM2: £20 (Image courtesy of Royal Doulton/Wedgwood)

Disney favourites

Doulton Dalmatians

In the mid-1990s, Royal Doulton produced a superb series of 11 studies from the Disney classic *101 Dalmatians*. Production ran from 1997 to 2001 and three of their finest designers created these little gems. They are bright and fun collectables, some showing moderate increases in value.

Some are single characters, some come in the form of a tableau. Each piece is marked with a design number: DM1 being the first in the series. They should all come with a clear back stamp which says 'Royal Doulton. Disney's *101 Dalmatians*', and should carry an inspection sticker too. My favourite is Martyn Alcock's version of Cruella.

How much?

'Lucky and Freckles on Ice' (Model DM10) makes around £40 at auction. The infamous 'Cruella De Vil' is a great piece too. 'Pups in Armchair' (DM11) was made for a time-limited period of 101 days in 1999. The one to snap up quickly if you spot it is 'Patch, Rolly and Freckles' (DM5). This was limited to 3,500 and came with a numbered certificate and base.

The Disney Showcase range of Alice was wonderful – there were five pieces in total. 'Cheshire Cat' and 'Mad Hatter' were charming. Other Doulton Disney Showcase series include the 'Little Mermaid', for example. 'Sebastian the Crab' is great fun, as are 'Peter Pan' and 'Winnie-the-Pooh', among others.

'Cruella de Vil' is perhaps the strongest character from the One Hundred and One Dalmations series by Royal Doulton. Currently, a good dealer will offer her for around £80
(Image courtesy of The Doulton Lady)

'Pups in Chair' is a popular piece amongst the colourful One Hundred and One Dalmations series
(Image courtesy of The Doulton Lady)

A group of six 'Mickey Mouse' wristwatches. These sold at auction in June 2003 for £420
(Image courtesy of Sotheby's Picture Library)

Mickey and Minnie

This lovable duo are part of the American identity: President Carter once said, 'Mickey Mouse is the symbol of goodwill, surpassing all languages and cultures. When one sees Mickey Mouse, they see happiness.' Mouse Power is set to become even stronger as the years pass. Mickey and Minnie dominate the international Disney secondary market. The Golden Age is the 1930s, but later pieces from your youth are also sought after.

Mickey was created by Walt Disney and his chief animator Ub Iwerks in 1928. A vast quantity of collectables centred on the duo has been produced since the very start when Mickey and Minnie first appeared together in 1928 in *Plane Crazy*. Toy production followed immediately, with almost overnight success.

How much?

Hagen-Renaker made plenty of early Disney ceramics, including Mickey as a conductor – which in the mid-2000s was valued at around £100. Original posters can be very hot: Mickey Mouse in *Lonesome Ghosts* is a true rarity. At the top end, you have the incredibly rare tin toys and animation art. One such gem had Mickey and Minnie riding a clockwork motorbike: it eventually sold for over £50,000. Later, another example with its box sold for £70,000!

The Mickey Mouse Club was first set up in 1929. By 1932 the national club in the US had over a million members, with over 800 chapters! Collectables from this period are really scarce and worth hunting down (hundreds of pounds), with badges, manuals, and newsletters being very desirable. The second wave came in 1955, and the final launch was in 1977.

Doctor Who collectables

Dr Who began life in 1963 with the first of the cult BBC TV series. Since then there has been a wealth of toys, comics, books, replica props, and games produced, totalling over 3,500 items. The market was given a boost with the show's airing in the US, and the collecting fever is supported by groups worldwide, dedicated swap meets, conventions, and endless websites.

With so much merchandise collectors have a broad base from which to begin. Increasingly rare authentic props and costumes occupy the high end, and these are more likely to appear at international auction rooms these days and can easily make several thousand pounds. Smaller props, such as phasers and gloves, can be found for a few hundred. With the toys, condition and the presence of a box are paramount.

How much?

The Berwick Dalek playsuit from 1965 sells for £250–£300 in a box. Smaller items for under £20 include the Viewmaster 3D toy, the majority of later action dolls, the Waddingtons 200-piece

A Codeg Dalek: £440
(Image courtesy of Vectis Auctions)

jigsaws, issues of *Radio Times* (with The Doctor on the cover), or the various anniversary calendars. There were Dalek balloons, kites, and even nursery ware.

The 'Bendy Dalek', coated in foam rubber and made by Newfield Ltd in 1965, tended to disintegrate. Consequently, remaining examples are quite rare, and have become sought after today. The annuals can make £10–£60 depending on year and whether or not the puzzles have been filled in. The 1965 edition of the *Dalek Outer Space Book* published by Purnell and Sons is now very rare and can cost over £100.

Autographed items are always hot: there are many events, collectors' fairs, as well as in-store signings – even the signatures of forgotten Doctor's assistants can fetch good money today, especially if they don't make appearances often. Not everything increases in price – many collectors kept vast and collectable video libraries, which have now been devalued by DVD releases.

If you haven't got a few grand for an authentic prop, why not look out for the various board games? Prices are creeping ever on up for early games such as the 'Dalek Shooting Game' from the '60s, now worth several hundred in top condition. A real modern gem to look out for in the

A Doctor Who Snowstorm and book. These made £560 at Vectis Auctions in February 2006 (Image courtesy of Vectis Auctions)

A Marx Doctor Who and the Daleks Bagatelle game from c.1965 sold at auction for £110 in January 2008 (Image courtesy of Vectis Auctions)

Daleks

The Daleks (the mechanical monsters of the small and, occasionally, big screen) were first made for the show by the Shawcraft Company based on the designs of Ray Cusick. Legend says that BBC executives objected to their look – but it was their appearance in 1964 that really boosted the show's popularity. In the 1960s, Sugar Puffs did a cross-promotional tie-in with the film and gave a couple of actual Daleks away to some lucky, lucky winners! If you look closely at one of the films you can see Sugar Puffs posters on the walls several times!

Dalek gift set (Image courtesy of Vectis Auctions)

world of comics is a special one-off title by Marvel called *Dr Who: The Age Of Chaos* from 1994. This was written by and featured Doctor No. 6 – Colin Baker. This will probably increase in value. Early copies of the *Doctor Who Weekly* that started in 1979 are now valuable too. Don't forget the huge variety of collectable Doctor badges and even rare postage stamps (1999 Dalek stamp for example), and for the future, look out for products that are produced under licence by the smaller firms, as these are often short-run editions. There is buoyant trading which can be daily observed by the novice on Internet auction sites.

How much?

If you have managed not to run for cover behind the sofa, then you'll be amazed at how much good condition original toys and actual costumes can cost today. It would be definitely worthwhile to invest in a time machine of your own to go back and snap up loads of the Dalek collectables when they were being sold as new! A Talking Dalek toy can be worth £150. The very first Doctor Who toys were the battery-powered Daleks made by Louis Marx in 1964: these command over £200 in top condition today.

An original Dalek used in a film or on TV is the Holy Grail: for example, a later, authentic Dalek from *Revelation of the Daleks* (1985) sold for £6,800 in 1991 at Bonhams the auctioneers. Earlier examples would cost double if complete. The ultimate burglar deterrent: officially-licensed full-size reproduction Daleks can be bought today for as little as £1,895.

Cheaper Dalek toys include colourful Dalek board games. The 'War of the Daleks Game' was produced by Strawberry Fayre in 1975: it makes £80–£100. The 'Dalek Bagatelle Game' by Denys Fisher in 1976 makes around £100. Lastly, the 'Daleks Oracle Question and Answer Game' from 1965 makes over £190 in good condition on a good day.

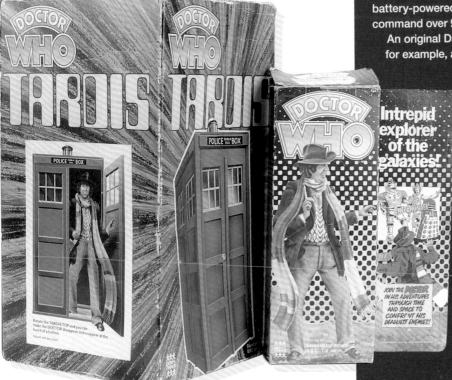

A Denys Fisher Doctor Who Tom Baker figure and Tardis, from 1976, sold for £50 at auction in November 2008 (Image courtesy of Vectis Auctions)

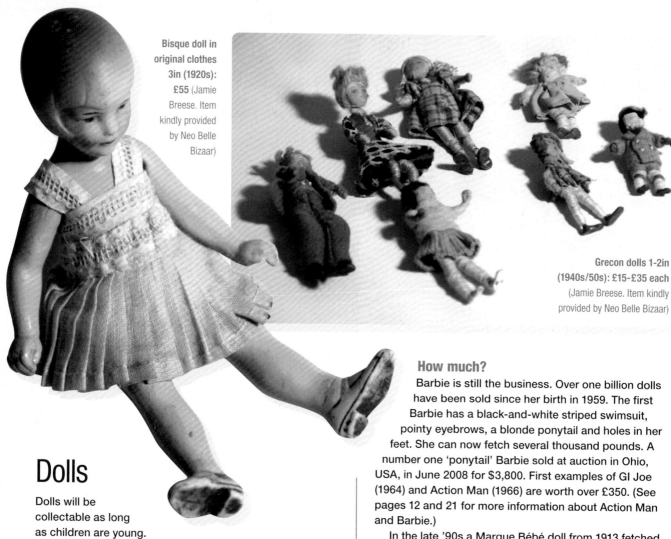

Bisque doll in original clothes 3in (1920s): £55 (Jamie Breese. Item kindly provided by Neo Belle Bizaar)

Grecon dolls 1-2in (1940s/50s): £15-£35 each (Jamie Breese. Item kindly provided by Neo Belle Bizaar)

Dolls

Dolls will be collectable as long as children are young.

The most cherished and timeless of antiques, and a truly vast area to look into, dolls date back thousands of years to the Ancient Greeks. They have been made of bisque (unglazed porcelain), wood, papier-mâché, wax, china, celluloid and other more contemporary plastics. The most desirable dolls tend to be those that date back to around 1700 – these are usually made from either bisque or wood and are mostly French.

Bizarrely, more modern items, from the 20th century, can sometimes make more money at auction than fine 18th or 19th-century examples. Dolls from 1900 to the late '50s are also highly desirable, particularly German makes (such as Kestner, Franz Schmit, and Kammer & Reinhardt) and American dolls like the popular Kewpies. Dolls made after 1890 are far easier to identify due to international marking laws (labels can be paper, moulded, an ink stamp or on cloth labels on clothing). Look out also for various doll-related items such as dolls' houses, costumes, and miniature furniture. This is a market in itself and prices for expertly crafted items, particularly single interior scenes (e.g. a kitchen), can make up to £20,000.

How much?

Barbie is still the business. Over one billion dolls have been sold since her birth in 1959. The first Barbie has a black-and-white striped swimsuit, pointy eyebrows, a blonde ponytail and holes in her feet. She can now fetch several thousand pounds. A number one 'ponytail' Barbie sold at auction in Ohio, USA, in June 2008 for $3,800. First examples of GI Joe (1964) and Action Man (1966) are worth over £350. (See pages 12 and 21 for more information about Action Man and Barbie.)

In the late '90s a Marque Bébé doll from 1913 fetched £56,500 at Christie's, South Kensington. Occasionally, very early wooden dolls (1600s and before) come on to the market. These can make £70–£80,000, or sometimes more.

Celluloid flapper doll with original outfit 3in (1920s): £35 (Jamie Breese. Item kindly provided by Neo Belle Bizaar)

Dolls' houses

Previously the plaything of the ultra rich, doll's houses began to be accessible to the children of the late 1800s. The best examples are works of art in their own right and sell for thousands of pounds, and tell historians exactly how we used to live. The more mass-produced ones remain accessible pricewise and, if kept well, may prove to increase in value. For collectors, there's a huge sense of nostalgia – but you'll need plenty of space if you're planning to start a collection.

Amazingly, dolls' houses were originally produced to teach young girls about managing the home! The earliest houses date back to the 1600s and originated in Austria, Holland, and Germany. The most splendid examples were not only a way for a merchant to show off, but were also used as display cases for the collectables of the time!

Original condition is one of the key factors. Of course, most houses have been played with, but substantial home improvement is not attractive to mini-home buyers of today.

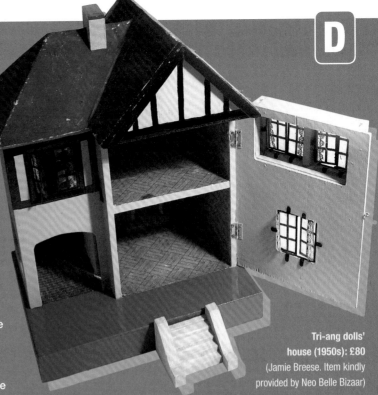

Tri-ang dolls' house (1950s): £80 (Jamie Breese. Item kindly provided by Neo Belle Bizaar)

How much?

In general, the furniture is worth more than the houses. Handmade examples by British makers of the past are the most sought after. Tin plate furniture by Rock and Graner can cost over £1,000 for a simple set. More affordable are the plastic examples created in the 1960s – these can be picked up for a few pounds at car boot fairs, if you are lucky.

One of the most stunning dolls' houses ever made was sold a few years back now in London at Christie's, the auctioneers. It had previously been on display at The Bethnal Green Museum of Childhood. Called Dingley Hall, it had been made for two boys in the 1870s and was a work of extraordinary quality, size, and awesome detail. The estimate was £30,000–£50,000, but it made a whooping £124,750. One of the greatest pieces ever constructed is a feature of Windsor Castle – Queen Mary's doll's house. It has running water.

If interested in starting a collection or viewing some remarkable pieces, readers can contact Maple Street (www.maplestreet.co.uk), the largest Dolls House and Miniature Shop in Europe. They also operate the National Museum of Dolls' Houses and Miniatures. Here you can see vast scale models of Wimpole Hall and even Chatsworth House.

The ten grand doll's house

Only 30 years ago, £10,000 could have bought you a house in East Kent. Recently, a resident of East Kent sold a superbly luxurious Georgian doll's house for close to that amount! Doll collecting is huge of course, and when a beautiful home comes up for grabs, the prices can go crazy.

The rare, palatial doll's house dated from 1760–1780 and was named 'Throstlenest House' after a real stately home upon which its design was based. The actual house was pulled down during the canal building of the 19th century, leaving the miniature model home as the only evidence of its existence today.

How much?

The property comprised three storeys, and the interior included a library with fully-fitted shelves, walls covered in silk, portraits, tapestries, and mirrors. How much for all that? Bonhams the auctioneers sold the pad in a London sale of Toys and Dolls for a mighty £9,600.

Other rare dolls' houses have attracted some serious money too. In January 1978, Christie's of South Kensington sold 'Titania's Palace', which was created in 1907 by Major Sir Nevile Rodwell Wilkinson. It went for a record-shattering £135,000.

Mettoy tin plate doll's house (1950s): £90–£100 (Jamie Breese. Item kindly provided by Neo Belle Bizaar)

Eames furniture

Charles Eames (1907–1978) is perhaps the most famous name in 20th-century furniture design. He is best known for his revolutionary chair designs, of which there were many, although you can still find various tables and other items, all of which would fit like a glove in today's funky designer homes.

Charles mostly worked, with his wife Ray, on projects for the huge American furniture company, Herman Miller Inc. They worked with new materials such as plywood and plastic, and were also one of the very first to offer self-assembly units. Today, original furniture is sought after and often copied. Sometimes the best pieces are sold at top auction houses for big bucks.

How much?

The most famous design is known as the 'Eames' LCW dining chair'. It was produced in 1946 and was a simple design using bent plywood on a metal rod frame. Originals can fetch quite a lot of money today, especially in sets and in mint condition. One original example from the mid-1940s sold at Christie's in London in November 2007 for £1,500.

Obviously you need to know what the originals look like. You can visit museums, such as the Design Museum, to see some examples, but because of their timeless appeal many modern versions are made and sold. Plenty of books and websites exist too. The bottom line is that, original or modern, Eames furniture is utterly timeless and is a good buy at whatever price, as you will keep it forever.

This original LCW dining chair sold at Christie's in London in 2007 for £1,500 (Image courtesy of Christie's Images Ltd 2008)

Eames ES 670 lounge chair

The Eames lounge chair and ottoman was a radical, affordable blend of the old club chair and the totally new.

The first was made in 1956, and was a birthday gift for their family friend and legendary film director Billy Wilder. It immediately caught people's attention when Charles appeared on the *Today* programme with the chair.

How much?

You can see the cherry plywood and black leather version most famously on the set of TV's *Frasier*. The actual early versions fetch between £1,000–£2,000, while the versions made today often cost more, which is quite odd in the antiques and collectables world.

It's probably the ultimate talking point in a living room. Check furniture auctions frequently to see if you can find earlier '50s or '60s chairs if you like the lived-in look. Around £4,500 would secure a brand new, modern, official design.

The famous Eames lounge chair is an iconic design that has stood the test of time. 1950s (Wikimedia Commons)

Elton John collectables

Elton remains as collectable as ever. He was one of the first artists to catch the early wave of rock and roll collecting back in 1988: his unwanted clothing, furniture, and other items were auctioned by Sotheby's and made an astonishing £4,838,022.

Elton's early singles are always worth snapping up if you find them cheap and in good nick. For example, his second ever single, 'Lady Samantha' from 1969, makes around £100 today. The high-end prices remain with memorabilia such as platinum or gold awards to recognise sales of records, or instruments, stage-worn costumes, and autographs. A signed colour photo makes between £60 and £125 at the moment. Many of Elton's personal items (not necessarily stage-worn) were sold by the Elton John Aids Foundation in a famous sale in Regent Street a few years ago.

How much?

Elton's records remain highly sought after. To spot the ultra-rare items, you need to know what you are looking for. For example, a special factory custom 12in pressing in blue of 'I don't wanna go on with you like that' is currently worth around £750+. Another rarity is his third Bluesology single

This 'matador' suit, worn on stage by Elton John, was sold at a Sotheby's auction in 1998 (TopFoto)

– 'Since I found you baby/Just a little bit' – this can make over £500. Elton's promotional disc 'Someone to watch over me' – a tie-in made with the French glassmaker Lalique – in 1994, makes up to £600.

The most cherished collectables are items that have a personal connection to the great man himself. For example, in April 2001, Christie's sold Elton's orange-tinted glasses for £2,585, and in 2008, autograph dealers Fraser's were offering a black felt top hat worn during one of his performances, signed on the top of the brim in silver ink, for £695.

For collectors on a budget, the Elton Tour Programmes make a realistic alternative. Most will set you back between £10 and £30, and there are many to collect due to the myriad of international performances and his length of time in the biz. Always seek out copies that are in the very best condition. There are a small number of Elton phonecards that have been issued in the past. A dealer will sell a group of three unused ones for, perhaps, £20.

Ephemera

Without knowing it, most of us are already collectors of ephemera! Ephemera are items, usually printed, the usefulness of which was intended to be short-lived. If you are the type of person who has kept your first school report or the ticket from the first Beatles concert that you went to – ephemera collecting could be for you.

You might have thought that you were making a wise decision keeping the Souvenir Edition of Charles and Diana's wedding. Alas, too many people did the same thing, as they did for the Coronation of the Queen in 1953. You need to save something that had a limited circulation but is still important to many others. Some people collect old cigar box labels, or even hotel luggage labels from the past – all these are traded at ephemera fairs around the country.

How much?

A souvenir newspaper from the Queen's Coronation is worth a couple of pounds, but a ticket to a Beatles' concert is possibly £100s. If you had got the Fab Four to sign it, however, you would be looking at £1,000s.

When it comes to ephemera, anything associated with the *Titanic* sells for a small fortune. Menus, tickets, postcards, letters from aboard, have all hit auction heights in recent years. These will soon run out, however, and new areas need to be spotted. Princess Diana related items are thought of as rare today, and prices for such items, especially if signed, are still increasing.

Your school report may be of interest to you and your family but, sadly, no one else is likely to think so. Old diaries and paperwork can stay at the back of the sock drawer, but there is interest in family and social photographs from the late 19th and early 20th centuries.

Fabergé

The famous Russian treasures of Fabergé are the very last word in crafted treasure. Works by Fabergé are almost outside the remit of this manual as they are broadly considered to be works of art.

Peter Carl Fabergé took over his father's jewellery workshop in St Petersburg, Russia, in 1870 and quickly took the firm in a new direction. The honour of 'Supplier to the Imperial Court' was quickly bestowed. Much of the work from the late 19th century was commissioned by the Russian Royal Family, and individuals from the Far East, the USA, and England. The Paris exhibition of 1900 was the high point, but the First World War, followed by the Russian Revolution in 1917, saw the company fail, and Carl was forced into exile, where he died soon after.

Tragically, there are fakes around – which means an expert's opinion is vital. Most examples are signed with either 'K.F.' or 'Fabergé', followed by a workmaster's name. These people were master craftsmen of the most exceptional standard, but they didn't just make eggs. Other wonderfully fashioned treasures included magnifying glasses, hand seals, cigarette cases, bell pushes, umbrella handles, and clocks.

How much?

Prices vary considerably. Unexpected finds are rare, although it has happened. Prices start at around £1,000 for silver and enamel desk bell pushes; mid-range items include jewelled gold flowers at £50,000 a stem; and lastly, £1 million and beyond for eggs.

Imperial Easter Eggs were made each year from 1884 to 1917. Commercially produced miniature eggs were also made and may be bought now for £1,000+.

About 500 people worked for a short period producing many items, so there is plenty to pick from, but because of the price, Fabergé is hard to collect.

Fabergé Eggs

Did you know that the greatest Easter egg hunt in the world is still on the go? Several of the most prized Easter eggs in the world are yet to be found!

The eggs in question were, or course, Fabergé's. To mark the 20th anniversary of his marriage, the Tsar commissioned the 'Hen Egg', and this became a tradition of yearly Easter commissions, which lasted until the murder of the Romanov dynasty by the revolutionary Bolsheviks.

How much?

It is known that only 50 Imperial Eggs were made, and the last may have been the supposed 'Twilight Egg', made just before the Russian Revolution. The fact is that eight of the Imperial Eggs are still lost. Nobody knows what happened to them. It is simply impossible to value these, but they are always millions per egg.

One of the finest eggs is the stunningly beautiful 'Coronation Egg' of 1897. It measures just 5in in length and was made from varicoloured gold, diamonds, rubies, and other precious metals. An estimate of over £10 million wouldn't be out of line, and it now belongs to a wealthy Russian businessman.

Other current owners of Imperial Eggs include Her Majesty The Queen, who possesses three in the Royal Collection. Five are located at the Virginia Museum of Fine Arts and a further three at the New Orleans Museum of Art. The Hillwood Museum in Washington has two, and others remain in Royal hands, foundations, or anonymous private collections around the world.

The Rothschild Fabergé Egg

An astonishing three auction world records came tumbling down in November 2007, all beaten by just one lot created by the world's most remarkable and illustrious craftsman in 1902.

This Fabergé Egg was not one of the Imperial Eggs (made for the Russian Royal Family) but it was made to Imperial standards. It is the only example of Imperial standards to have remained in the same family's ownership since its commission. The sale took place in London.

How much?

Over a ten-minute biding battle a Russian private buyer eventually purchased the egg for £8.98 million, a world-record price for a Russian art object at auction (not including paintings). A world record for a Fabergé work of art, and a world-record price for any timepiece (clock or watch) at auction.

The workmanship of the item is almost beyond belief. It is remarkably large, with exceptionally chased varicoloured gold work, and enamelled in translucent pink. Its face is a clock and it contains an automaton cockerel, which flaps its wings and nods its head each hour.

The Rothschild Fabergé egg which sold for £8.98 million at Christie's in November 2007 (Image courtesy of Christie's Images Ltd 2008)

A French advertising paper fan (Martin Breese)

Fans

Fans have been keeping us cool for many centuries. Originally they were a Chinese invention, and 16th-century Portuguese traders brought them back to Europe. Later the French court of Louis XIV and his descendants made fans fashionable. The fashion soon spread to England and Queen Anne became a big 'fan' of fans.

18th-century fans were small handmade works of art. London fan makers were some of the best in the world, and wealthy ladies commissioned exotic versions. Ivory was used to create the 'sticks' and the finest were intricately carved to form a pattern when the fan was spread out. The painted scenes were exquisite and often of a romantic nature, with a different scene on each side.

How much?

18th-century fans in good condition will sell for £1,000+. Move into the 19th century and prices start to fall, but good hand-painted Victorian fans will still make £500. As usual: the better the quality, the better the price. Heavy Victorian fans made from dyed ostrich feathers are a bit cumbersome and not so popular. They can be bought for under £100.

Exceptional hand-painted 18th-century fans with finely carved ivory sticks can sell for up to £10,000. They will have to be in perfect condition and preferably from a very good source to be worth this much!

Good 19th-century examples are certainly worth buying and could well rise in value as 18th-century ones become harder to acquire. If you buy a good fan, keep it in a cool place when not using it. Never display a fan opened out in a glass case – the temperature inside will rise and the fan's sticks will warp. Tears and splits will greatly affect the value. Avoid the temptation to flick the fan open with force for dramatic effect.

Fender Stratocaster

Considered one of the greatest guitar designs of all time, the Strat is also the most successful electric guitar, saleswise, in history. Invented back in 1953 by Leo Fender, it has remained largely unchanged and has been the choice of top musicians for decades now. Haynes have even published a Manual for this gem. Certain versions in certain colours can make substantial amounts at today's auction rooms.

The Strat was former British Prime Minister Tony Blair's choice of instrument when in a rock band! In 1998, he nominated it for inclusion in the Museum of Scotland when celebrities were invited to pick an object they thought best represented the 20th century. Prices vary for the more modern standard-coloured Strats. For example, many Strats from the 1980s are now worth more than they were when purchased – often fetching between £600 and £1,000. White models are probably the most sought after, followed by brown, and then black. The serial numbers on each instrument help in identification.

How much?

Commanding the highest prices are those guitars that have been used on hit records and by famous artists. The world record price for a guitar at auction was for one of Eric Clapton's legendary instruments. 'Blackie' realised $959,500 in 2004 at Christie's, New York.

The best Strats to go for, from an investment point of view, are probably those made prior to the buyout by CBS in the late 1960s. These earlier Strats, say from 1963, in custom colours, are usually the most valuable: look out for the fabulous, way-out colours like Mary-Kay Blonde, Burgundy Mist, Sea Foam Green, and Daphne Blue. These can make many hundreds, and sometimes thousands, of pounds at auction. The Lake Placid Blue variety is considered one of the most desirable. Other collectable vintage Fender guitar models include the Telecaster, the Esquire, the Jazzmaster and the Mustang.

Eric Clapton's 'Blackie' sold for $959,500 in June 2004 at Christie's New York
(Image courtesy of Christie's Images Ltd 2008)

First-edition books

Modern first-edition books have become extremely collectable over the last decade or so. Modern, here, means roughly from 1900 to the mid-1990s. Ultra-modern first editions are books from the present day. A first edition is not the first book off the press, as some of the prices might have us believe. It is a copy from the very first run of published books. This is a fun and highly accessible field of collecting that has, for some, made for a terrific investment.

Initial print runs for unknown authors tend to be low, so a popular author's first works are worth bucks. The presence of a dust jacket is very important and wildly affects values. To identify a true first edition, look for a single date on the title page. If it is followed by 'second impression' or 're-published in', then it's no gem. There is a more modern system used today with a numerical strike line of numbers 1 through to 10, in any order, to show which impression the particular copy represents. A system of grading is employed in collecting circles, and the Internet has become an easy way to trade copies.

How much?

As an example, Ian Fleming is highly sought after. A fine first-edition of *Casino Royale* in a fine dust jacket fetches up to £25,000 (see page 38). Agatha Christie remains desirable with *The Mysterious Affair at Styles* of 1921 being gold dust. The first US edition of Graham Greene's 1938 classic *Brighton Rock* is worth upwards of £11,000 in fine condition in a fine dust jacket.

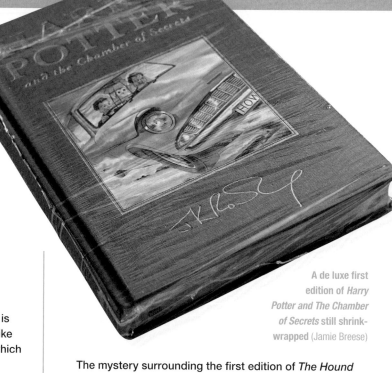

A de luxe first edition of *Harry Potter and The Chamber of Secrets* still shrink-wrapped (Jamie Breese)

The mystery surrounding the first edition of *The Hound of the Baskervilles*, published in 1902, is legendary – why are there only three copies known to exist with a dust jacket? If you ever did find a complete copy with dust jacket, it is easily worth tens of thousands. Ultra-modern first editions by authors like Philip Pullman and J. K. Rowling can be worth thousands too.

My advice is to go for either fine, excellent quality editions of valuable books like those mentioned as they have steadily increased in value each year, or to take a gamble on new unknowns. The onset of the credit crunch could affect values in the short- to mid-term, however.

The Amber Spyglass by Philip Pullman. First edition signed by the author, and pictured with promotional postcard and Alethiometer (both signed): £450 (Jamie Breese)

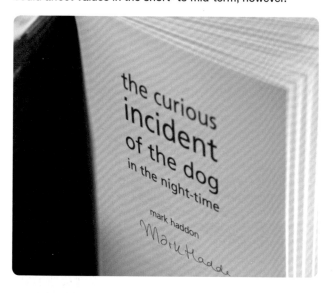

A first edition of *The Curious Incident of the Dog in the Night-time*, signed by the author: £100 (Jamie Breese)

'A Study in Scarlet'

A book handed in to a branch of Oxfam in Harrogate went under the hammer for a small fortune in May 2008, and what made it so desirable was that it was one of the rare copies of the title that contained the first ever appearance in print of master sleuth Sherlock Holmes. Sir Arthur Conan Doyle wrote this story while working as a doctor, aged just 27. He was paid £25 for the rights. No one then knew it would become one of the defining works of crime fiction.

How much?

A range of items gathered in by Oxfam shops across the country was auctioned by Bonhams in Oxford on behalf of the charity. The star lot, a copy of 'A Study in Scarlet', was estimated to sell for £7,000–£9,000 but eventually went for a mighty £18,600. This was an incomplete copy – a complete version in good condition would have been much more valuable.

The book (actually better described as a magazine) in which the story first appeared – *Beeton's Christmas Annual* 1887 – is thought to be one of the most desirable titles for collectors of fine fiction. There are rare editions that have commanded over £50,000 in the past, and there are just 31 known copies in the world. Tracking down any remaining 'lost' copies would surely be a challenge worthy of Baker Street's most famous fictional hero.

C. S. Lewis

It took a long time for Hollywood to take on the epic and hugely popular *Chronicles of Narnia*. The series has sold over 85 million copies worldwide since the books first appeared in the 1950s. The movies drew new attention to the rare first editions of these beloved stories by one of Britain's most popular authors, Clive Staples Lewis (1898–1963). He was also a close associate of *Lord of the Rings* author, J.R.R. Tolkien.

The jewel in the crown of any collector of children's literature must be a first edition of *The Lion, the Witch and the Wardrobe*. It was first published in the UK by Geoffrey Bles Ltd in 1950 in a green cloth-covered hardcover and came with a dust jacket designed by Pauline Baynes. Complete copies in good condition are extremely scarce and if you happen to own one, you are in for a nice surprise.

A first edition of *The Magician's Nephew*: £1,250 (Image courtesy of Adrian Harrington Rare Books)

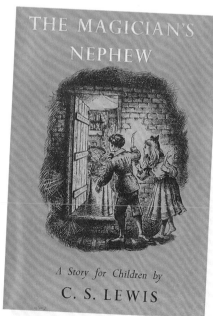

THE MAGICIAN'S NEPHEW

A Story for Children by
C. S. LEWIS

How much?

A nice, clean first edition of the *The Lion, the Witch and the Wardrobe* with dust jacket will currently sell for up to £5,000. The complete set is therefore hugely desirable.

Lewis was an Oxford scholar of Medieval and Renaissance Literature and his books aren't the only things collectors seek out. His autograph is prized, as are letters from him (around £1,000 to £2,000 for anything interesting, typed and signed). A complete set of American first editions are also prized and slightly more affordable.

A limited edition of *A Bad Beginning* by Lemony Snicket, signed by the author, still in its shrink-wrapping (Jamie Breese)

Lemony Snicket

Lemony Snicket is the pen name of Daniel Handler. This hyper-reclusive US author's extremely curious books have become some of the most affordable collectable books.

Since mid-2001 over two million copies of the UK version of the books in 'A Series of Unfortunate Events' have been sold. These cracking little hardbacks follow the comically unpleasant adventures of Violet, Klaus, and Sunny Baudelaire. In 2003, a beautiful leather-bound and signed 'limited edition' of book one appeared, and most of the 1,000 copies sold out straight away at £100 each. A few rare book dealers are already asking over £150. There's a 'Special Edition' version that might have proved to be a wise investment at £14.99.

How much?

These books were first published in America, and a set of US first editions of books 1 to 13 can sell for up to £1,200 if signed by the author. A full set of UK first editions are desirable, and a dealer would sell these for £400–£500 but it is the first three books which carry the most value.

What makes them collectable? Possibly their novel theme: Snicket has said, 'Not only is there no happy ending, there is no happy beginning and very few happy things in the middle.' Also, it is the fact that any movie release can bolster a book's collectability, and they're cheap to buy new at seven quid. The first movie hasn't to date been followed up with a further production.

These are good reads, but for investment it's the first editions showing numbers 10 to 1 on the reverse of the title page, which are worth snapping up if found cheaply. US first copies and UK limited editions are probably for the more serious Snicket collectors.

Agatha Christie

Over two billion copies of Christie's (Agatha Mary Clarissa Miller) books have been sold in 65 languages! She is the best-selling crime author and, along with J. K. Rowling, Ian Fleming, and one or two other big names, one of the most collectable writers of all time. Since the 1980s, the value of many of her early books – usually the first ten or so titles – have simply sky-rocketed.

The presence of the original dust jacket is particularly important with Christie and increases the value of a book many times. Collectors admire the early art nouveau-like designs, and all her first editions came with one. Finding one today on a title from the 1920s is very hard indeed. Most of her work was published either by John Lane, The Bodley Head (from 1921) or Collins (from 1926).

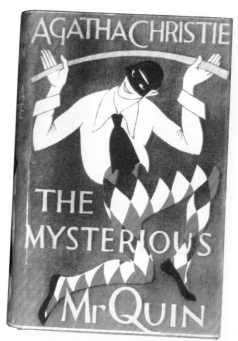

A first edition of The Mysterious Mr Quin (Martin Breese)

How much?

In late 2008, leading London book dealer, Peter Harrington, was selling a first edition (1937), with jacket, of her most popular title, *Death on the Nile*, for £4,000. In the mid- to late 1990s, a similar copy could cost around £600.

Her first book, *The Mysterious Affair at Styles* (1921), which introduced Hercule Poirot, is simply gold dust. There is almost no dealer with a jacketed copy for sale. Any very early, signed, first edition which appears for sale will shake the collectables world.

A first edition of Murder in Mesopotamia: £6,750 (Image courtesy of Adrian Harrington Rare Books)

Most book collectors will tell you not to buy 'Book Club' editions of any novelist for investment purposes. These are not first editions and are usually published much later on. Christie is different: many of her books were published as first editions by the 'Collins Crime Club'. Don't get the two descriptions mixed up! It is possible to find first editions at car boot sales and the like: I found a rare Christie book from the 1950s a few years ago while rummaging around a house when recording *The Life Laundry* for BBC2.

The Hobbit

This famous fantasy novel for children, first published by George Allen & Unwin on 21 September 1937, was written and illustrated by John Ronald Reuel Tolkien, the genius behind 'The Lord of the Rings', and has sold over 60 million copies since. 1,500 first-edition copies of *The Hobbit* were printed, and today they are astonishingly valuable. Perhaps you have one in the attic? Also, look out for Tolkien's three books in his 'The Lord of the Rings' series: *The Fellowship of the Ring* should state on the reverse of the title page 'First Published in 1954' and nothing else. *The Two Towers* should state exactly the same and *The Return of the King* should state just 'First Published in 1955'. All were hardbacks published by George Allen & Unwin and issued with dust jackets.

How much?

I took an unsigned first edition of *The Hobbit*, complete with its dust jacket, on to ITV1's *This Morning* a few years ago and it was priced at £30,000. A decade ago it cost under £6,000. A copy sold at Sotheby's in London in 2002 for £43,020. In 2008 you could find a first edition, first impression, in reasonably good condition but with an extensively restored dust jacket for £12,500. Some signed or inscribed copies appeared, too, and the prices asked ranged from £50,000 to £75,000. Even a third impression of *The Hobbit* can be worth £1500+.

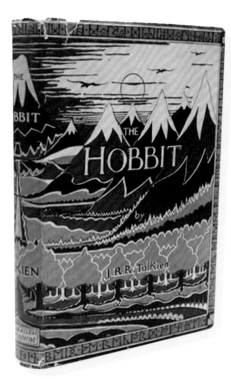

A first edition of The Hobbit: £37,500 (Image courtesy of Adrian Harrington Rare Books)

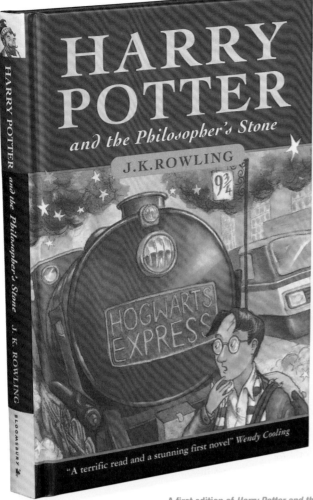

A first edition of *Harry Potter and the Philosopher's Stone* by J. K. Rowling: £30,000
(Image courtesy of Adrian Harrington Rare Books)

Harry Potter

The publishing world and collectors alike were amazed by the success of the Harry Potter stories by J. K. Rowling. In October 2007, fans and rare book collectors competed at auction to buy a pristine copy of the first ever Harry Potter book *Harry Potter and the Philosopher's Stone*, published by Bloomsbury in 1997. It made the headlines, as these sales of J. K. Rowling's books always do.

Out of the first print run of 500 copies, 200 were paperbacks sent to the reviewers, while many of the remaining 300 bound in hardback went straight to schools or libraries. The book was priced at £10.95 in 1997 and didn't come with a dust jacket.

How much?

A few years ago, I handled a signed, fine copy of *Harry Potter and the Philosopher's Stone* held by the well-known specialist book dealers Adrian Harrington Rare Books of London (www.harringtonbooks.co.uk). It was then priced at around £25,000. Currently, a copy in fine condition from the same dealers will cost £30,000.

In late 2008, Fraser's Autographs were offering three 12-page personal horoscopes by Rowling, each with a hand-drawn natal chart. These featured illustrations and writing dating from when she was writing the first Harry Potter book and were priced at £25,000 each.

Remarkable Rowling

One of just seven copies of a new book by J. K. Rowling – *The Tales of Beedle the Bard* – was sold at Sotheby's in December 2007 for a truly magical figure. It was handwritten and even illustrated by Joanne herself, and attracted interest from all corners of the world.

The book, containing five tales, was bound in brown morocco leather and embellished on the upper cover by Edinburgh silversmiths Hamilton & Inches. It features in the final Harry Potter book – *Harry Potter and the Deathly Hallows*. A spokesperson at the time said, 'This is one of the most exciting pieces of children's literature to have passed through Sotheby's. We have to reach back 80 years to find a comparison when we sold the manuscript of *Alice's Adventures in Wonderland* on behalf of the original Alice.'

How much?

The pre-sale estimate was £30,000–£50,000. On the day, six bidders battled to secure it, and the hammer finally fell to a representative from a London fine art dealer. The price it achieved stands as the highest ever at auction for a modern literary manuscript, an auction record for a book by J. K. Rowling, and also an auction record for a children's book. It sold for a simply spellbinding £1,950,000.

Proceeds from the sale went to The Children's Voice – a campaign run by the Children's High Level Group, the charity, co-founded in 2005 by J. K. Rowling and Emma Nicholson MEP, that seeks to make life better for vulnerable children across Europe. One of the campaign's central aims is to move children out of institutions and into loving families. A brilliant use of the magic of Harry Potter.

This handwritten and illustrated copy of *The Tales of Beedle the Bard*, one of only seven copies produced, sold for £1,950,000 in December 2007 (Getty Images)

Football memorabilia

One of the hottest sporting collectables of the late 20th century would have to be items relating to football. This is one of the few areas of memorabilia where modern items can fetch as much as the vintage stuff and, as the game is so ingrained in our national culture, it is difficult to see a time when values might tumble significantly.

How about the ultimate memento of England's finest year – 1966 and the World Cup? Items relating to this seminal tournament are hugely sought after.

As a general rule, mass-produced items, such as sticker-albums, don't have a market value, even if complete. For the future, why not collect the enamel club lapel badges (these can be picked up for under 50p at car boot fairs, etc.), or keep aside unusual programmes, e.g. a charity match from a Premier League team. Posters advertising matches often get chucked; these may be worth something down the line. Unused tickets and even the stubs from important matches are also worth something to novice collectors.

How much?

Signed footballs are not worth as much as you might imagine. A figure of around £200 is not uncommon, even for a top Premier League team such as Manchester United. The money lies in shirts that have been worn in a game: for example, a replica David Beckham shirt, signed, together with authentication, makes £400–£600+ at auction right now. If it was worn in a key game, then considerably more. An Arsenal jersey signed by 23 of the 2004/05 squad, including Thierry Henry and Patrick Vieira, on the reverse was up for grabs at Fraser's Autographs in late 2008 for £750. Signed photographs are a collector's must-have and, again, a good large print signed by Becks can currently make up to £175 at a good dealer.

A pair of (size 8) Adidas Predator football boots, with the heel numbered 7 and the tongue signed by David Beckham. The boots were worn by Beckham in the 1997–98 season and were sold by Christie's for £13,800 (Image courtesy of Sotheby's Picture Library)

Beckham Collectables

Beckham collectables can make their own headlines! Posh once accused an autograph dealer of selling a fake signed snap of her hubbie. As part of the settlement, signed Becks memorabilia was apparently provided as well as a hefty cash sum for compensation.

Becks is collectable because he was part of Manchester United, one of the most popular clubs in footballing history. He is also a star player with great skill and a high public profile. It is debatable, however, if signed items, particularly photos and autograph book pages, will hold their value in the long term. The best option would be to consider shirts – match-worn are the ultimate – or, better still, boots. These must have provenance (evidence to show they are what they are claimed to be).

How much?

So, how much will Mr Beckham's autograph set you back? Fortunately, he is a very generous signer. He rarely says no, especially if a charity is involved. The great news, therefore, is that it is relatively easy to come by good, clear signatures on photos, shirts, and footballs. The bad news is that the more examples in circulation, the less the value, particularly in the long run. Today, a signature on a photo, if nicely framed, can make around £150–£200 if sold by a specialist dealer. Once, Becks accidentally kicked a ball in the face of a young Leicester City fan and, being a nice chap, as a gift he gave his actual boots to him from that match. These were estimated at one point to be worth £2,000–£3,000: not a bad peace offering.

A souvenir World Cup book (Jamie Breese)

A 10inx8in signed photograph
of David Beckham playing for England: £175
(Image courtesy of Fraser's Autographs)

Just a few years ago, the auctioneers Sotheby's sold Beck's England shirt – unworn for an astonishing £2,280. Christie's once sold a pair of Beck's boots for £13,800 against an estimate of around £1,000! But the market can shift up and down – Christie's also sold a pair of boots, won in a competition by school kid Christopher Hawkins, for a lowish £1,500. Rumours abound that two famous personalities from music and TV bought two pairs each a few years ago for charity for nearly £30,000 a lot!

My advice is to buy items because you like the man and his skills. Don't necessarily buy for investment, for, as with all collectables, the market can rise and fall according to memories and fashions. Having said this, football has been one of the hottest areas of sporting collectables, and Beckham is a true international ambassador for the sport.

A pair of signed David Beckham football boots inscribed 7 and Beckham. These sold for £3,525 in September 2001
(Image courtesy of Christie's Images Ltd 2008)

1966 World Cup

Our biggest moment of World Cup glory – the 1966 World Cup Final. England played West Germany on Saturday 20 July at the Empire Stadium, Wembley. England's hero, Geoff Hurst (later Sir Geoff Hurst), scored two goals in extra time, leading to England's victory.

At the low end, you have used tickets, scorecards, magazines, toys, and replica shirts. Mid-range, you start to see framed signed team photos and signed balls, etc. The top end would be match-worn clothing, winners' medals and personal mementoes from the players.

In the mid-range, five rare, unused tickets for the '66 World Cup tournament, including the final, and the official souvenir, have been sold at auction for nearly £1,000. Here, the unused nature makes for a huge boost in value. Condition is important. If on a budget, look for the quirky items, and remember – most sticker albums, even complete, are not worth a lot.

How much?

Defender Ray Wilson's winners' medal from the '66 World Cup was sold at a Christie's sale in March 2002 for £80,750. Even more mind-bending was goalie Gordon Banks's medal, which sold in March 2001 for £124,750 – a then world record for any football medal. An extremely rare porcelain replica of the FIFA World Cup trophy, made only for FIFA officials, was once sold by Bonhams for over £4,300!

£91,750 was scored by Christie's for the very shirt worn by Geoff Hurst in the '66 final. Brazilian legend Pelé played in the 1970 World Cup final – to many, the best final ever – and his actual match-worn shirt sold at Christie's in March 2002 for an astonishing £157,750.

If you want a 1966 collectable, scan dealers, auctions, or your loft for the official souvenir book. A bunch were made but not so many will be around today in good shape. They're worth around £100–£250 at present.

A souvenir World Cup 1966 Jubilee SOS Celebration programme, signed inside by all 24 members of the squad: £1,750 (Image courtesy of Fraser's Autographs)

A Stewart Grand Prix cap signed by
Jackie Stewart and Rubens Barrichello,
and a Jaguar Racing cap signed by
Johnny Herbert (Steve Rendle)

Formula 1

With Lewis Hamilton now World Champion, it could bode
well for the exciting market in Formula 1 collectables. Driver
suits and helmets are particularly sought after and frequently
sell for high prices.

Motor racing started at the turn of the last century. After
the Second World War a fixed formula was established
for racing, which in 1948 became Formula 1. In terms of
merchandise, toy cars were the first to appear. These were
from Mercury. Corgi made a series of F1 cars in 1/36th scale
in the 1970s. More recently, companies such as Mattel pitch
them more as models.

How much?

A replica helmet signed by a current driver might make
£500–800+. A limited-edition helmet signed by Michael
Schumacher makes £800–£1,000. An actual race-used
example is of far greater interest: in March 2006, the Michael
Schumacher podium and race-worn Japanese and Australian
Grand Prix helmet from 1992 sold for £11,000 at Bonhams.

A good signed and framed photo of Jenson Button costs
around £100, as will a signed cap. A race-used visor signed
by Damon Hill can fetch £250. In December 2005, Bonhams
sold Nigel Mansell's 1992 World Championship
FW14B Grand Prix car. On average
a famous F1 car will cost you
over £100K, but a less
significant car
could be yours
for under £30K.

A Honda sticker
signed by the late
Ayrton Senna, whose
signature is highly
sought-after, and his
McLaren team-mate
Gerhard Berger (Steve Rendle)

Gentlemen's collectables

This is a relatively new field of collecting that was
created by the auction houses to group all the
charming items relating to the true gentleman! The
demand comes from those seeking original, classic
gifts, and international collectors who wish to acquire
a slice of the English gentry's lifestyle. The most
popular items date from the 1890s to the 1920s and
cover a wide variety of objects.

These items are always functional, and now
considered fun. Most households will have an item that
has perhaps been passed down from great-grandparents.
Popular items include hip flasks, and there are three types
to look for: silver-plated and leather (£60–£80), part silver
(£100–£150), and all silver (£300–£400). Other objects
include walking sticks, tankards, hunting flasks, letter
knives, match holders, silver-mounted shaving sets, and
silver card cases. The prices that most items fetch suggest
it is an affordable and accessible luxury for all.

How much?

Cufflinks are one of the most popular collectables in this
category, but value is affected by condition. Through use,
the chains wear thin, although these can be replaced for
around £40. Damage to enamel items (the most popular at
present) is less easy and more expensive to repair. A pair of
amethyst and enamel cufflinks might fetch up to £800.

American buyers sometimes pay through the roof to add
a good set to their collection. If you have a set that is old,
made from gold, or featuring jewels, and perhaps a motif
(such as a greyhound, polo mallets, or other novelty) why
not get it valued at a reputable auction house or dealer?
Some quirky sets have made several thousand pounds.
A rare pair by the artist Aleksandr Rodchenko (made for
Dobrolyot, the then Soviet Union state airline) sold for an
incredible £4,320 at Sotheby's in London in March 2005.

Very fine travelling sets are rare and command top prices
when they appear on the market. One such case, which
featured cut-throat razors for each day of the week, a letter-
writing kit, clothes brushes, silver soap dish, and manicure
set, once sold for around £8,000. This spectacular item
came in a canvas case to protect the leather one!

A rare pair of cufflinks by the artist Aleksander Rodchenko (made for
the Russian State Airline Dobrole) sold for £4,320. (Image courtesy of
Sotheby's Picture Library)

Goblin 'Teasmade'

The humble Goblin 'Teasmade' is part of our history and a true British design classic. Being awoken to the glow of the internal lights and a hot cuppa is something to behold. The automatic tea-maker was introduced in 1936 by the vacuum-cleaner firm, Goblin. Today it is getting a little harder to find mint condition examples.

The 'Teasmade' was a fine example of how the new electric wonder-gizmos started to replace the role of the domestic servant in the later inter-war years. The earlier art deco-influenced ones were often unwanted wedding gifts, so tended to be stored away, unused. Always look for the little orange plastic goblin on the front of the set.

The clock movement uses a synchronous mains motor. The water would start to heat up 10 to 20 minutes before the alarm; then it would, through steam pressure, pass into the stoneware teapot, and eventually the kettle would empty, tipping the switch and activating the alarm. Bizarrely, they were often noisy when boiling and usually awoke most users before the clock went off, which almost defeats the purpose!

How much?

The most familiar version is the Model D25 that appeared in 1955. It kept the art deco styling, with its curvy, streamlined, cream-coloured urea plastic frontage, and the dual opaque acrylic light covers. Machines with their original melamine trays are hard to find. A truly mint-condition set might cost £60, though not so clean examples can be found for £20 or less at auction.

The more opulent 'Teasmades' that were produced soon after the appearance of the first Goblins are worth more money if in good order. The later and smaller mid-1950s Goblin (Model D26) is harder to find – it uses a single kettle only, with no teapot. One of its contemporaries, the Hawkins Classic, is also art deco style, and has a stove-enamelled base and great lines. The 1970s Goblins, until recently just car boot fodder, are now appearing in funky apartments and loft conversions.

A Goblin Teasmade
(Image courtesy of Metro Retro)

A '2nd Period' (1881–1934) Goss Nautilus Shell. £275 (Image courtesy of Nicol Crests & Collectables)

Goss crested ware

Goss china is noted for its range of white glazed porcelain miniatures, each featuring a crest or coat of arms relating to popular towns in the UK. The pieces were mass-produced as souvenirs by the Falcon Pottery (Stoke-on-Trent) in many shapes – from old boots to simple pots with lids. They have been collected for years and remain affordable.

W. H. Goss began to produce these charming collectables back in 1858 after receiving permission from a variety of towns to use their crests. They were an instant hit with visitors all over the country as travel had become a brand new pastime, and returning with small affordable souvenirs of a resort was considered a must.

How much?

Interestingly, not all place names and their crests are equal. The better pieces to go for tend to be places that are not seaside resorts: these tended to sell less well at the time and are more rare as a result. Most pieces will cost between £5 and £50. Some fall into the early hundreds, and a select few have been known to make several thousands at auction.

The better money lies with the little ceramic models of famous British buildings that Goss created, again as souvenirs, and these are far more colourful. Some buildings and cottages can fetch several hundred pounds if found in fine condition. Goss also created a number of pieces detailing aspects of the First World War, such as cenotaphs or soldiers firing machine guns.

Goss started a trend in chinaware that was copied by other firms such as Shelly, Arcadian, and Carlton, but they are marked so are easy to spot. These are also worth looking out for – many pieces sell for over £50. If you want to find out more, visit www.gosscollectorsclub.org. The club organises fairs, holds postal auctions, and publishes a magazine for members.

Gramophones

The very first gramophone was made by Emile Berliner way back in 1887. Can you imagine a time when after each record you played you would have to change the needle? Technology has leapt forward, but the gramophone, and in particular the horn gramophone, still conjures up bucket loads of nostalgia, and can be worth a few quid too.

Gramophone collecting is quite a genteel pastime. However, there are many, many passionate folk out there – often members of societies, who care about the preservation and documentation of these charming machines. There are several types, most notably the tabletop horn variety and the portable player which came in a carry case. Some of the finest models of each type were made by HMV (His Master's Voice).

A 1930s Columbia portable gramophone: £50–£80
(Image courtesy of Metro Retro)

How much?

This is quite a specialist market – and yet, many may well have a gramophone at home, perhaps stowed away in the attic. Very few models make thousands – these tend to be original condition horn HMV players. As an idea, a nice portable HMV, with original soundbox and case, will make anywhere from £20 to £100+ at auction. A rare HMV School's model gramophone, Type GFO, with green 'Morning Glory' horn and gooseneck tone arm, sold at Christie's in London in May 2006 for £540. Don't forget the other manufacturers, such as Edison Bell, Decca, and Columbia. Condition and completeness is very important in this technology-based market.

A rare HMV School's model gramophone Type GFO, with green 'Morning Glory' horn and gooseneck tone arm, sold at Christie's in London in May 2006 for £540 (Image courtesy of Christie's Images Ltd 2008)

An very rare Berliner gramophone from 1888 – one of the first gramophones to use a disc, rather than a cylinder (TopFoto)

It is important to realise that many of the wind-up, horn gramophones on the market are in fact reproductions. Many of these comprise parts that don't match. Be very careful before parting with a lot of money if what you are seeking is a wholly original working antique that will increase in value. Ask questions and seek advice. The web is full of helpful enthusiasts who, if approached, may well offer words of wisdom. There are dozens of specialist books covering every possible aspect, and a good deal of swap meets and annual collecting fairs.

The HMV gramophone

HMV's very first store was opened on Oxford Street in 1921 by the composer Sir Edward Elgar. The HMV dog has a good story behind it. In short, there was a painting by an artist called Francis Barraud that was created for the 1889 summer exhibition at the Royal Academy. 'Nipper' the dog is shown listening to his master's voice on an Edison phonograph, all placed on a polished coffin lid! The Gramophone and Typewriter Company bought the work and asked for their latest model gramophone to be painted over the older phonograph and the coffin lid painted over to make it a coffee table! The company went on to use the image for HMV as a trademark from 1910, and the rest is history. The painting is now displayed at EMI Music's Gloucester Place headquarters.

How much?

Some particularly sought-after models have sold for substantial amounts at auction. For example, a rare phonograph by Edison went for £32,200 at Christie's. An unusually fine HMV Model 202 gramophone from 1929 sold in 1995 for £14,625. In general, it is the original condition HMV tabletop gramophones that attract the most interest. HMV made some of the finest portables from 1928 onwards.

An HMV Model 102 portable gramophone, c1930s – a highly collectable model (TopFoto)

Harley-Davidson

2003 was Harley-Davidson's 100th birthday year. One of the world's most familiar brands started life way back in 1903, in a tiny wooden shed. The first year of production saw just three bikes made. Owners, including myself, talk about the magic of this most marvellous mode of transport. With such a long production history, there are plenty of collectors of classic machines out there and the bikes don't have to cost the earth.

More and more people are getting the habit, especially among women and younger riders. New Harleys depreciate in value quite slowly, and on the strength of that they are reasonable investments as general transport. Many of the early bikes can be classed as antiques, but these machines require expert knowledge to properly maintain them.

How much?

The great thing is, there are so many choices. For example, if you love the old 1940s and '50s look you could opt for a gorgeous modern Road King Classic (complete with white-wall tyres and 1550cc engine) at around the £15,000 mark; or you could track down an original vintage Harley, say the 1940s WLC models – some are around half that price on the second-hand market and need more attention, but both ooze style and romance.

The Harley Owners Group (HOG) has become the world's biggest motorcycle owners' club, with around 750,000 members! Each bike is a Holy Grail to their owners, but few of them are likely to have ridden a Model No. 1 – a good condition example would be off the scale, price wise.

A vintage Harley-Davidson at the Goodwood Revival (Jamie Breese)

Harry Potter

With the hype in the late 1990s at fever pitch, *Harry Potter and the Philosopher's Stone* (published in the US as *Harry Potter and the Sorcerer's Stone*), and the following movies, created a huge market for toys and collectables. As well as this, the collecting world was spellbound by the often astonishing value attached to related items.

The precedent for merchandise was already set before the first movie came out when items connected to the first four books appeared on shelves a year before. Some of this was changing hands on the Internet here and in the US for substantial profits. The film tie-in toys, calendars, figures, etc. were all collected once the films appeared. Many people may have bought film items for investment. Remember, though, some speculators were stung by the over-production of merchandise for the last *Star Wars* film, so with any movie, choose carefully. Limited editions are often a wise choice.

How much?

The Pobjoy Mint's Harry Potter limited-edition coins came in sets of six, and in silver, gold, or plain metal (unlimited), were legal tender, and may well increase in value. Prices ranged from £9.95–£239.70. The 'Mirror of Erised' wristwatch was a limited edition of 3,500. It now makes £200. Look out for the well-made 'Hogwart's Express' train set: one pristine example sold for £60 in June 2006.

The absolute treasure for any collector is one of the first editions (the first print run) of the first book by J. K. Rowling, *Harry Potter and the Philosopher's Stone* (Bloomsbury, 1997). Out of the 500 printed, 200 were paperback review copies. A mint-condition (unread) hardback could be as much as £30,000 from top rare book dealers. Any original artwork used in these books is utterly priceless. See 'First-edition books' in this manual for more information about these rare books.

Harry Potter film props

One of the big explosions in the collectables market in recent years has been the focus of props, and for the budget-conscious, prop replicas. The former offers a chance to get close to the magic of the movies, and the latter make great gift or display pieces. According to the police, the demand for authentic items from Harry Potter is likely to have even inspired the theft of Ron Weasley's flying Ford Anglia from South West Film Studios in Cornwall several years ago.

The items themselves come from several sources. Some are acquired and passed on by studio folks, some are donated to charities to auction, and some are presented to the film executives who later sell them on. The dark arts are not just up there on the big screen: fakes do exist and, due to the potential cost, you need to be vigilant. Having a DVD of the movie in question is useful to check exact details, and buying from more respectable dealers offers some extra protection. Top auction houses occasionally sell the best pieces and these are clearly genuine, but they often attract a greater number of buyers and, therefore, the bigger hammer prices.

How much?

At the top end of the current market you would need to keep the original film-used props safe in Gringotts vaults! £100 plus is the going rate for one of the actual envelopes that flew through the air in the *Philosopher's Stone*. You would pay a lot more for the actual letter that Harry opened – the acceptance letter from Hogwarts School of Witchcraft and Wizardry. That went up for sale in 2002. Way over £10,000 was paid for Hagrid's crossbow, and the 19th-century globe, which again featured in the first movie, was sold for £17,750 at auction. Items relating to the books themselves remain in high demand: the original painting from the cover of the very first book, created by Cliff Wright, made £85,000 once upon a time.

If the real thing is just too costly, there is an alternative: there is (as mentioned above) a growing market in prop replicas. Nicely presented items, such as the Noble Hermione Wand (around £30), the Quidditch Broom, or even a replica Triwizard Cup.

Harry Potter coins produced by the Pobjoy Mint to tie in with Harry Potter and the Goblet of Fire (Image courtesy of Pobjoy Mint)

Alfred Hitchcock

Hitchcock remains one of the greatest film directors of all time, with worldwide interest built up over 50 feature films. He was also one of the first filmmakers to become a 'celebrity' director through his publicity stunts on and off-screen.

Hitch is collected around the world, and his popularity seems likely to continue for many years to come. Top of the collecting tree are the finest movie posters from his classic films: *Rear Window*, *The Birds*, *Marnie*, *Vertigo*, *Rebecca* and *Psycho*.

How much?

Today, there are actually specific sections at some of the top poster auctions that are dedicated to Hitchcock poster art. In fact there is even a book on the subject! One of the Holy Grails would be the original US poster for his masterwork *Vertigo*. You need to know the subject well – especially the different sizes. American posters are called 'One Sheets' (41inx27in) and British examples are called 'Quads' (30inx40in). Either way, any original *Rear Window* poster in good shape will start at about £500 at auction.

Hitch's autograph is a must-have: it has risen in value by over 250% since the end of the last decade. A signed photo often starts at around £1,000, and if it has something extra like a great pose or a personal trademark doodle of his profile, then possibly twice that amount. Autograph dealers Fraser's suggest a current value of £2,950 in 2008, compared to £775 in 1997.

In the mid-1990s, Royal Doulton asked modeller David Briggs to produce a Hitchcock commemorative character jug. Showing Hitchcock behind a shower curtain (from *Psycho*) on top of which is a bird (from *The Birds*), it came in two colour schemes. The large pink curtain version (number D6987) is incredibly rare and worth over £800.

Homemaker

Homemaker was a style of earthenware produced by the huge Ridgway Pottery in Stoke-on-Trent. The bold and instantly recognisable transfer-printed patterns in black-and-white were an iconic design of the 1950s, and the Homemaker range is collectable today for its kitsch value.

Designer Enid Seeney created the range in 1956, and the pieces were sold exclusively in Woolworths from 1958 right up until 1970. The stylish designs featured 1950s 'boomerang' tables, chairs, plant stands, and other classic home items from that decade.

How much?

It was fairly cheap to buy back then: a standard plate would cost just 6d (2½p). Today, many pieces can be picked up for quite reasonable prices if you know what to look for! I love the expresso coffee cups and saucers – very stylish. However, one of the hardest to find pieces – the fabulously rare 'Cadenza' teapot – and some of the rare coloured pieces could call for hundreds of pounds. There are now books on the subject, and a red-coloured 10in dinner plate which features on the cover of one of these would be a top find. A breakfast service with 43 pieces, including an oval serving plate, sold at auction in March 2008 for a very respectable £150.

One of the best places to start building a collection is your local auction house. Here you will often find a part dinner or tea service, and it will be reduced as a result of its incompleteness. You can go out to other auctions, good dealers, or car boot sales to find the missing pieces and build complete sets, which will only increase in value as time goes on.

Hornby

The legendary British inventor Frank Hornby founded the world-famous Meccano toy company way back in 1901. In the early 1920s, he manufactured a tin clockwork train set to rival the famous German makers like Marklin, and in 1925 he produced his first electric model. Many trains and sets are collectable today.

The famous Dinky toy cars were an offshoot of Hornby as demand grew for cars to accompany the model railway worlds that owners had created in their attics. Perhaps surprisingly, there is a demand for the better homemade sets. Also, look for the more valuable pre-Second World War model trains that were marked 'Hornby Series' as opposed to 'Hornby Trains'. Die-cast metal models are more desirable than the later plastic ones.

How much?

Serious collectors go where the serious money is: Hornby's '0' gauge trains. These were very accurate sets, the track being 1.25in wide. Prices for basic sets or locomotives begin at around £200 for good condition, boxed models. The 'Dublo' gauge sets appeared in 1938 in date-marked blue boxes: these were smaller but retained the excellent detail and are more affordable today. A 'Hornby Series' electric Southern E120 Special Tank locomotive B 28 painted in

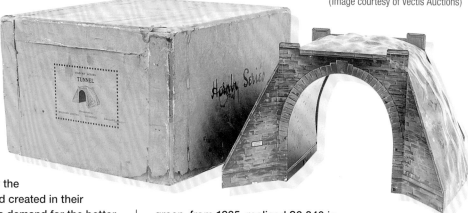

Rare Horby accessories are also very desirable. This boxed Hornby '0' Gauge tin tunnel sold in January 2009 for £80
(Image courtesy of Vectis Auctions)

green, from 1935, realised £3,840 in December 2006 at Christie's, South Kensington.

The most sought-after Hornby train could be the famous 'Princess Elizabeth' locomotive of the late 1930s. Though thousands were made, collectors look for the rare '0' gauge three-rail version with the London, Midland & Scottish Railway paint job. Boxed and mint versions sell for big money today: one such fine example with tender realised £2,640 at Bonhams in Knightsbridge in November 2007. At their Train & Toy Sale in September 2008, Vectis sold a superb boxed red set for £1,800.

A rare 'Princess Elizabeth' locomotive in excellent condition with box. This made £1,800 at Vectis Auctions in September 2008 (Image courtesy of Vectis Auctions)

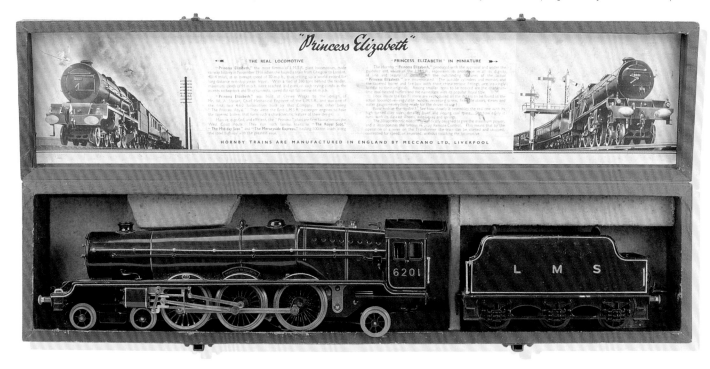

J

The Magic Roundabout jigsaw puzzle (1960s): £10 (Jamie Breese. Item kindly provided by Cream and Chrome Collectables)

Jigsaws

The first jigsaw puzzle was made in the 1760s by the British inventor and cartographer, John Spilsbury. For the first hundred years, such items were known as 'dissected puzzles' and usually featured geographical images. The name jigsaw came about in the 1860s, with the development of the actual tool – this allowed for intricate designs and mass production. Some fine early examples can make fortunes today.

Jigsaw puzzles are often referred to as 'Juvenilia' and are an early example of what we now call interactive 'edutainment'. Children were not well catered for in terms of toys and games at that time. An acceptable pastime, however, would have been to while away the time by learning your geography with a map puzzle. Almost all early puzzles are made of wood, and these examples were made from a very fine hardwood, usually mahogany. The image would have been hand-coloured and the cuts were made around the different countries or counties.

How much?

A jigsaw really must be complete for it to be valuable. Popular manufacturers include Victory Puzzles (these are 20th-century items and can fetch upwards of £10) and Chad Valley (who are also famous for Teddies). Look out for cheaper examples from firms such as Ives (which became Parker) and Milton Bradley (which became MB Games). Railways and steam trains prove a popular subject to collect – some rare items made with the Great Western Railway can be worth hundreds of pounds. The rare 18th-century jigsaws are particularly sought after – a set of several John Spilsbury jigsaws fetched £26,000 at auction a few years ago.

The value of jigsaws drops with the introduction of mass-produced cardboard examples in the 1940s (though card was being used as early as the 1820s in Germany). Car boot fairs have proved to be fertile hunting grounds for these cheaper sets, but who knows what might turn up at your next sale?

Jukeboxes

Multi-selector phonographs, or jukeboxes as they became known, first appeared in amplified form in 1928. They were often more expensive to buy than a car in their heyday, but have held their value well over the decades. The most successful model ever made was the Wurlitzer 1015 of 1946, which held 24 78rpm discs. 60,000 were made and these days they fetch several thousand at auction.

The Golden Age of jukeboxes, contrary to popular belief, was in fact the 1940s, not the '50s. The key makers of the 20th century were AMI, Wurlitzer, Seeburg, and Rock-Ola. These were all-American companies and they shipped machines all over the world. The value of a jukebox is almost entirely dependent on its looks and condition. Popularity dwindled in the '60s with TV and home record players.

How much?

Landmark machines always fetch thousands of pounds: the Seeburg V200 of 1955, the AMI Model I of 1958, and the Wurlitzer Model 2000 of 1956.

The Wurlitzer 850 of 1943 is one of the most sought-after jukeboxes on the market, along with the 1015. Being mechanical, they were very reliable. The Model 950 from 1942 was one of the Paul Fuller designs. It is, as of 2000, considered the most valuable jukebox in the Wurlitzer family. A stunning example in unparalleled condition came up for sale at Christie's, Los Angeles, in June 2001 where it made a remarkable $22,325. Collectors can pick up a good Rock-Ola Ultra jukebox (Model N437) at auction for under £1,000 currently.

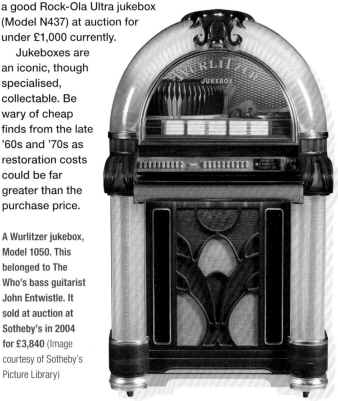

Jukeboxes are an iconic, though specialised, collectable. Be wary of cheap finds from the late '60s and '70s as restoration costs could be far greater than the purchase price.

A Wurlitzer jukebox, Model 1050. This belonged to The Who's bass guitarist John Entwistle. It sold at auction at Sotheby's in 2004 for £3,840 (Image courtesy of Sotheby's Picture Library)

Kitchenalia

There's money in ol' pots and pans, believe it or not. Not only are many of these cherished objects true antiques, they are also quite functional in today's world. Every provincial auction house in the UK features such items, and many can be picked up for under £20.

One approach for investment would be to look for kitchen items created by the world's best designers. For example, Dr Christopher Dresser made objects like soup ladles (in 1879), the biggest American design hero, Loewy, made the Super Six fridge in 1934. These can cost big bucks today. Smaller collections feature vintage breadboards and chopping blocks (can be worth over £400!), antique coffee mills (average £50) and spice racks. A good oak butter churn from the late 1800s makes around £80 on average. Homepride and Horlicks are even collected in their own right!

'Homepride Fred' spice container (1970s): £8 (Jamie Breese. Item kindly provided by Cream and Chrome Collectables)

How much?

Very popular at auction are whole sets of 19th-century copper saucepans (or batteries de cuisine). These were essential for the lucky few in Victorian times and can make hundreds if complete. Victorian copper jelly and chocolate moulds sell for £50 upwards if original and of an intriguing shape. Sets of six often make £200+.

The most cherished item must still be an old Aga. It was a Swedish Nobel Prize winner who created the first one back in 1922. Like original cast-iron fireplaces, these are fiercely sought-after working treasures and change hands for small fortunes, regardless of age.

Vintage '40s and '50s refrigerators from the UK and US are wildly sought out by trendy city dwellers. These huge metallic beasts made by Prestcold and others sell, reconditioned, in smart shops for £600 upward. Enamel ware items, such as bread bins, teapots, and flour bins can all be found in fairs, sometimes for under a fiver. More modern items are set to become design classics. The Italian and British designers of more recent years are creating instant mini-treasures with items like the famous Alessi 'bird' kettle and beautifully crafted cutlery sets.

Rare 'Homepride Fred' kitchen wall thermometer (1970s): £25 (Jamie Breese. Item kindly provided by Cream and Chrome Collectables)

Collection of 1950s/60s kitchenalia (Jamie Breese. Item kindly provided by Neo Belle Bizaar)

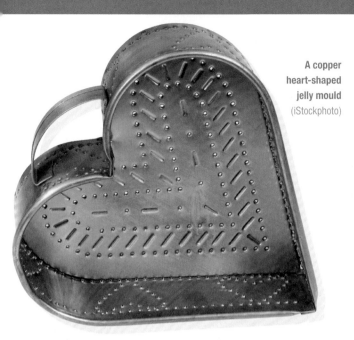

A copper
heart-shaped
jelly mould
(iStockphoto)

Jelly moulds

Believe it or not, jelly has been around since medieval times, but was a savoury luxury and made with horrendous ingredients such as sheep's heads. The arrival of sugar heralded an explosion in many sweeter puddings, and all sorts of mould designs made from stoneware and creamware appeared. Today antique moulds make for an affordable and easily found collectable.

The most imaginative designs came during the late Victorian and Edwardian era. Copper examples tend to be the most popular and come in all shapes and sizes, often in graduated sets that look great today in a period-style kitchen or country cottage. These were lined with tin for safety and were used for cakes too. Glass moulds made by top firm Sowerby are prize finds today, and top potteries such as Minton and Wedgwood all made fine and collectable moulds in earthenware.

How much?

The larger castellated copper shapes command the best prices. These, as the name suggests, tend to show eight 'turrets' and range in price from between £100 and £200. Most ceramic moulds from the late Victorian period, by firms such as Copeland, tend to fall into the £25 to £75 price band, though lucky and eagle-eyed 'kitchenalia' car booters may pick them up for a few pence. A three-tier copper mould sold in November 2008 on eBay.co.uk for £217. It carried the St Pauls Sceptre mark for Benham & Froud and was in great shape.

If copper moulds are too pricey, the later ceramic designs from the 1910s and '20s, by firms such as Shelly and Malin, make an affordable alternative. These don't look as authentic as copper ones, but like most glass moulds they are easy to pick up, even from dealers, for between £20 and £40. Ceramic moulds bearing a transfer-printed recipe look great on display. Aluminium and plastic moulds have yet to prove their desirability on the collectables market.

Honeypots

Honeypots are collected internationally, though there is a limit to how much they will make. Surprisingly, there is great diversity in colour and decoration, and their relative affordability makes them a good area to start collecting.

Many key potteries have made honeypots, including Royal Doulton, Carlton Ware, Spode, Radford, Wemyss, Charlotte Rhead, Shelly, and Hancock. There are several different types to keep a look-out for: the most familiar are the rounded beehive shaped 'Skaps' which are the most popular and have been in production since the 1930s. A single bee on the lid often surmounts them. The other design is the rectangular, butterdish-shaped style upon which a honeycomb would be placed (many of these were created by Poole potteries).

A good tip for cleaning your collection is to use a brush for the corners and in delicate areas. An overnight soak in bicarbonate of soda or mild detergent can work wonders. There are several organisations about to bring collectors together and share information: the European Honeypot Collectors' Society has been around since 1998. (www.geocities.com/tehcsuk)

How much?

Condition is important, as with any ceramic, and also make sure you have the correct lid for your pot. Most are affordable in the £20 to £100 bracket. Back in 1999 Christie's the auctioneers had a Clarice Cliff sale and sold several important honeypots – all in a beehive shape and with variations of tree designs and patterns, from 1929 to 1935. A piece with a 'Gardenia' pattern made £1,000, while a 'Blue Firs' pattern item achieved a record auction price for a honeypot at the time of £1,260. A 'May Avenue' pot went at their South Kensington rooms in 2000 for an incredible £3,680.

A 'Gayday' Clarice Cliff honey pot and cover (1930s). This sold at auction for £352 in November 2007 (Image courtesy of Sotheby's Picture Library)

Lamps

From the humble and ever-popular Lava lamp of the early 1960s, to the rare designer pieces from craftsmen like Jean Perzel and Sergio Mazza, the electric lamp has been around for over 100 years. But did you know that some of the better designs, especially those from the '60s, '70s and, now, even the '80s, can be worth more than a few bob?

Most of us can only dream of owning a tabletop creation from the early 1900s by Louis Comfort Tiffany. Highly influential, when they do come up for auction, they can make hundreds of thousands of pounds. Some are priceless: a particularly fine 'Lotus' example went under the hammer back in 1997 for a gob-smacking £1.8 million. Clara Driscoll's gilt bronze 'Dragonfly' Tiffany lamp is more affordable at the £200 grand mark!

How much?

The first 'Anglepoise' lamp was designed by George Carwardine in the early 1930s, and his inspiration came from the movement of the human arm. The rare version one has a three-stepped base to it and carries the manufacturer's name, Herbert Terry & Sons. This costs up to £400 today.

Other superb and rare electric lamps include Poul Henningsen's famous PH table lamp (Model No. 3/2) from 1933: one example fetched £6,250 at Sotheby's in London in September 2007. A rare PH 5/3 standard lamp of his went for £14,900 in April 2008 at the same auctioneers.

'Shatterline lamp'. Originally sold through BHS stores with orange base and spun-fibreglass shade (1960s/70s): £60 (Jamie Breese. Item kindly provided by Cream and Chrome Collectables)

Below: A vintage photo from the Mathmos Archives (Image courtesy of Mathmos Ltd)

Cult designer Joe Colombo made the Topo 'Anglepoise' table lamp in 1970, and that easily makes £150+. Verner Panton's 'Moon' lamp of 1960 is ultra-funky and now sells for £200–£400 at auction. If a Tiffany original is beyond your reach, or you don't have a piece by contemporaries such as Daum or Emile Gallé, then remember that the original Tiffany style has been oft imitated and has inspired quite reasonable reproductions which can sometimes be found for under £500 or so at high-end high street lighting stores.

Lava lamp

The incredibly successful Lava lamp was first designed in 1963 by the Dorset-based inventor, Edward Craven Walker. Amazingly, it started out as a wacky adapted egg timer: when the blob rose to the top, the egg was ready! Lava lamps have become an icon of the 1960s and '70s – it was recently declared a design classic by the Design Council – and the unpredictable, psychedelic effect is now fascinating a whole new generation once again.

The lamp worked by heat convection: when the lamp was switched on, a light bulb would heat up the fluid. Then the wax would melt and float to the top and eventually cool and drop down again. The contents are made from a mixture of coloured wax, water, and a secret formula. The first production runs of this classic light were actually made from the bottles of a popular orange juice drink. Its cult status was achieved after appearances on TV programmes like *The Prisoner*, *Doctor Who*, and *The Avengers*.

How much?

Lava lamps vary little from the very first examples which were mass-produced in the early 1960s. The original designs are still used today by Mathmos. Their range of lamps starts at around £30 for a small lamp.

Other lamp-related collectables include the 'Space Projectors', which showed slides of moving colours, and the 'Galaxy' fibre-optic dome, which now changes hands for around £200. The Glitter lamp was an early '70s pop art – influenced offshoot of the Lava lamp – small pieces of sparkly silver foil would float around, giving a magical, disco light effect.

The design of Lava lamps has changed little since they were first invented. Here are two popular lamps in an advertising still (Image courtesy of Mathmos Ltd)

Letters written by Claude Monet (above), and Charles Dickens (right) (Images courtesy of Fraser's Autographs)

Letters

A sale of important rare letters at Sotheby's in London highlighted the buoyant market for this unique type of collectable. Many people across the land are probably sitting on such paperwork, blissfully unaware of the potential treasures they have tucked away.

Important historical figures always fetch a premium, as do the best-known literary figures. For example, a few years ago a four-page illustrated letter to a young girl from Beatrix Potter made £8,000. Letters from Royalty are also keenly sought, even if conveying fairly standard messages. T. Vennet-Smith Auctions sold a five-page personal letter from Princess Diana for £3,600 some years back. That will most likely have increased in value by now.

How much?

Notable historic figures are probably the most desirable. A signed letter and other documents from the legendary Captain James Cook sold for a superb £33,600 a couple of years ago. Topping the bill at the same auction was a series of over 320 letters and postcards from Samuel Beckett. This one lot raked in an astonishing £243,200. A letter signed by a survivor of the *Titanic* disaster made twice its estimate when the hammer went down at a mighty £20,400. A letter from Charles Dickens to a colleague, and signed 'C. D.', was up for grabs for £2,950 at Fraser's Autographs in late 2008.

The type of letters I, as an expert, come across most frequently are those from a notable royal at a time of war, or a letter from a well-known politician or film star. Collectors should be careful not to count their chickens here, as quite a few are sent out. Sometimes an Autopen is used to replicate their signature, or they are just standard thank you messages in print. Experts do know how to spot them, and it is always worth first checking with a specialist at an auction or a dealer before getting too excited.

Liberty

Liberty & Co. was founded by Arthur Lasenby Liberty (1843–1917) and the first shop was opened on London's prestigious Regent Street in 1875. He sold a fantastic array of branded goods, as well as commissioned items. Famous all over the world, today much of the furniture, textiles, and metalwork is highly sought after.

The company developed in the era of the Arts and Crafts movement and later, through art nouveau. Many items were made with an organic, Celtic or classical theme. Most famous, perhaps, are the swirling Liberty prints. Arthur forbade the designers to sign their work, so the mystery of who made what remains.

How much?

The company was revolutionary in its heyday of the early 1900s because it mass-produced items which were traditionally craft-made (hence expensive). This made such gems affordable to the new middle classes. Some of the cheaper items are from the pewter ranges. A fabulous Liberty & Co. three-handled vase from the early 20th century will set you back a few hundred pounds. A designer chair might cost several grand, while a fine Liberty Voysey 'Donnemara' carpet made £17,400 in April 2007 at Sotheby's.

The most celebrated treasures are the items from the 'Tudric' (pewter) and 'Cymric' (silver) ranges. These include the famous 'Cymric' mantel clocks (£0000s) and the 'Cymric' silver jewellery made by W. H. Haseler. An elegant silver pendant, enamelled in turquoise and blue, would make £300–£500 at auction currently. A 'Cymric' silver tankard by Archibald Knox sold for £10,000 a few years ago at Philips.

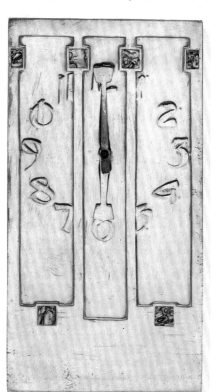

A Tudric pewter and abalone clock designed by Knox in around 1903. This made £28,200 at an auction held at Christie's, London (Image courtesy of Christie's Images Ltd 2008)

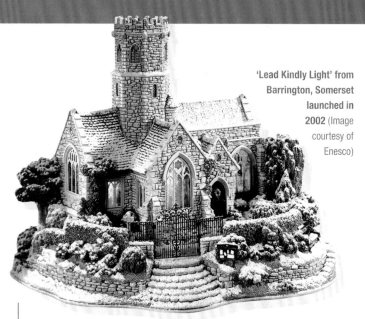

'Lead Kindly Light' from Barrington, Somerset launched in 2002 (Image courtesy of Enesco)

Lilliput Lane

These highly collectable miniature cottages (made of resin) have become increasingly collectable in recent years. Now part of Enesco Ltd, Lilliput Lane was founded in 1982 and quickly built up a worldwide reputation for producing handcrafted and handpainted recreations of popular landmarks and buildings. Each creation undergoes a very long and painstaking production process with each model mastered in wax. There are a number of collectable series, from 'Britain's Heritage' and 'Britain in Miniature' to 'Snow Place Like Home' and 'The Dutch Heritage Collection'.

How much?

Many of the charming models have gone up in value on the worldwide collectors' market. A retired piece called 'Chatterbox Corner' – a sweet English village scene with a red telephone box – was made between 2000 and 2004. This cost £29.95 at the time, but now sets a collector back by up to £40. Look out for the amazing 'Millennium Bridge' model (L2170), which was created for the year 2000 and came in a limited edition of only 2,000 worldwide. It is a jaw dropper. 'Cliburn School' was a model donated free of charge to pupils and staff at the school when it closed in July 1983. There was no retail price. A current secondary market price stands at £1,750. 'Cotman Cottage' from Hoxne, Suffolk, launched in 1993 with a retail price of £59.96. Around £125 is now mentioned for this on the secondary market.

Collecting cottages like these (and the David Winter designs too) is an international trend now, and there's a collectors' club boasting over 40,000 members. Readers can join the Lilliput Lane Collectors' Club based in Carlisle, Cumbria (www.lilliputlane.co.uk). Members receive a quarterly newsletter and exclusive members' pieces.

'Little Moreton Hall' from just outside Congleton in Cheshire is a 2009 annual piece and retails at £69.95. One to watch, perhaps?

Lord of the Rings

On the collectables front, *LOTR* has long been established as an exciting and dynamic field – from the ultra-valuable, brutally scarce 'first editions' of the original 1950s books, to the huge swathes of film merchandise, much of it of a fine and limited nature.

The best items in my opinion are those that are sold as limited editions or high-end collectables. A visit is advised to your local 'Forbidden Planet' store (or online at www.forbiddenplanet.com) to take a peek at the glass display cases. There are incredibly detailed collectable replica swords – the limited-edition broken Narsil sword cost £439.99 a few years ago, and might go up in value. Handmade wooden pipes: Gandalf's is great and cost £175 new a few years ago. The most detailed busts and statues of the key characters are superb. One of the best places to locate a related item to suit any pocket is www.ebay.co.uk There are currently several thousand items up for auction.

How much?

There were, of course, many collectables produced in the decades prior to the films. Royal Doulton scored a hit with a sensational set of affordable figurines. There were 12 in total and they sold for up to £20. These were designed by D. Lyttleton and issued in the late '70s and early '80s. It was called the Middle Earth series, based on the animated film

A photograph of Gollum signed by the actor who voiced the character – Andy Serkis (Image courtesy of Fraser's Autographs)

version, and they are superb to look at. The prices (as of 2008) if you were to buy them from a good dealer can be high: Barliman Butterbur can command £600, Samwise £600, and Tom Bombadil £600. A complete, exceptional set could cost £3,000–£4,000 today.

Perhaps authenticated signed photographs by the film cast could prove to be a worthwhile investment. *LOTR* is the *Star Wars* of the new millennium, and the very best autographs have not dropped in value. Keep all collectables in boxes, together with any paperwork to stack the odds in your favour in years to come.

One of the classiest collectables is a 24-carat gold proof set of five coins which depict five key characters. Made by the Pobjoy Mint, they were a limited edition of 1,000 worldwide, and cost £1,395. They came in a presentation box and featured a 9-carat gold replica of the actual ring.

The Pobjoy Lord of the Rings series. The centrepiece is a 24-carat gold proof set which features five coins, each portraying a different character from the film (Image courtesy of Pobjoy Mint)

Large vintage leather trunk: £820; Gladstone bag (c.1910): £380; hat box (c.1880): £395; small case: £190. All from Henry Gregory (Paul Raeside. Image courtesy of *BBC Homes and Antiques Magazine*)

At the turn of the last century, Louis Vuitton travel goods were the last word in luxury. Nothing has changed, and it remains the choice of the well-heeled and movie stars of today. See right for more information about Vuitton. Other fine names to look for include John Pound & Co., Asprey & Co., Harrods, Finnigans, and Hermes.

If you are on a budget, it is quite easy to find reasonably good condition leather cases, Gladstone bags, and trunks for under a tenner at some car boot sales. Check the handle is secure before purchase, then clean up with a damp cloth and use a dark shoe polish to buff. Bar Keeper's Friend is a good brass cleaner. It is amazing how nice these old cases can look after some attention. Beware of imitation leather cases (brown vinyl or board) – these are numerous but low quality and were made for young evacuees.

A variation on the regular case, and more desirable, is the travelling case, complete with brushes, bottles, and the like.

How much?

Prices vary from dealers: £50 to £500+, depending on the maker and condition. Finding one with an intact cloth interior and brass fittings is a bonus, and on the open market a basic, clean, tidy leather suitcase will set you back £100 upwards.

Hatboxes are more a showpiece these days, but still, fine leather 'buckets' start at £80 from a good dealer. A decent picnic hamper, complete with '50s crockery and keys will start at £100.

Writing case (1940s): £120; silver-plated and leather hip flask (1920s): £200. From Henry Gregory (Paul Raeside. Image courtesy of *BBC Homes and Antiques Magazine*)

Luggage

With the travel boom in the early part of the last century, leather and canvas cases were mass-produced and often monogrammed for the customer. Together with the exquisite hotel labels often stuck on the item, old luggage makes for a nostalgic, classy trip.

Most of these cases and bags date back to the '20s and '30s and can be seen in many of the Merchant Ivory films.

Vellum case (1930s) from Henry Gregory: £280 (Paul Raeside. Image courtesy of *BBC Homes and Antiques Magazine*)

Picnic sets conjure up images of years gone by.

Louis Vuitton

Louis Vuitton trained as a master packer for rich clients in the Paris of the early 19th century. By 1851 he had risen to the heights of packer for the Empress Eugenie. Old trunks were of the dome top variety which enabled rainwater to run off them when travelling on the tops of carriages but with the arrival of speedier transport Vuitton had a bright idea…

For the visit to the opening of the Suez Canal by the Empress, Vuitton designed a suite of flat-topped cases and trunks, which everyone admired and wanted. Suddenly every rich and titled person in the world wanted a Vuitton trunk. The famous LV design did not make an appearance until 1896 but has changed little since and has become a design classic.

How much?

Louis Vuitton trunks and cases cost thousands when bought new today, and old ones will cost thousands as well, but a smaller case could be found for £500 or £600. As long as the condition is good, a big trunk will sell for between £1,500 and £3,000+ at auction. Special fitted ones will make much more – these floor-standing versions often have pull-out clothes rails, shirt drawers, and hatboxes!

Many famous clients, such as the Duke and Duchess of Windsor, have owned special Vuitton cases, bags, and trunks. Anything with a direct connection to someone of note, whether pop star or princess, will be worth a premium. One hard-backed case belonging to Katharine Hepburn sold for $10,800 at Sotheby's New York in June 2004.

A selection of contemporary Louis Vuitton bags (Getty Images)

Picnic sets

Picnic sets conjure up images of years gone by. A vintage set brings a touch of class to any outing today. Though they are still made today, there are very few manufacturers that design sets that match the standards of those made between 1900 and the late 1940s. The decline in popularity is linked to the cost of manufacture and the enormous expansion of other leisure activities in the last half century in this country.

There are broadly two options if you want to buy a vintage picnic set: the cheaper sets (which usually come in a square, lockable box) are the most common. These look more like an early portable record player from the outside, and are mostly found with the maker's nameplates: usually either Brexton or Sirram. Those sets from the 1950s are perhaps the most colourful and feature classic motifs on the glasses, plates, and flasks.

How much?

With the cheaper Brexton type sets, all the pieces must be present and the keys should also be included. Usually, £50 to £80 will secure a good example. The earlier leather and leather/cloth examples with good names often start at £3,000!

The second type of set to look out for are those made for automobiles in the 'golden age' of set design – 1900–1945. Sets which are covered in leather, or leather cloth, featuring high-quality accessories and made by names like Vickery, Finnigan's, Coracle, and Asprey, can fetch fortunes. These were usually 'step board' or 'foot rest' sets made to fit into or on to the luxury cars of the time. Amazingly, a fine set for four people by Coracle from around 1910 was once valued at £20,000. A six-person picnic set by G. W. Scott & Sons Ltd in a green leathercloth suitcase, with two brass carrying handles each end, made a mighty £5,520 at an automobilia sale at Bonhams, London in December 2007.

One general rule is that picnic sets didn't really develop until the turn of the last century with the arrival of the car. These very early sets mostly came in wicker baskets and often had fold-down fronts. The later leather cloth examples came in several colours and arrived in the 1930s.

Unused picnic set in wicker hamper (1962): £45 (Jamie Breese. Item kindly provided by Cream and Chrome Collectables)

The Magic Roundabout

Created by a Frenchman, Serge Danot, in the mid-1960s, and originally called *Le Manège Enchanté*, this classic children's TV series has enchanted and puzzled generations of children – and adults. The British version (*The Magic Roundabout*) was narrated by Eric Thompson, father of actress Emma Thompson. Its surreal storylines and setting has made it the stuff of legend.

In general, TV toys are known to have a better chance of steadily increasing in value. Dozens of toys were made available, though British firm Corgi produced perhaps the finest models in the early 1970s. There are a number of books, jigsaws, and even bath products to seek out. These could all be worth keeping (stockpiling) for the future.

How much?

The true Holy Grail would be any of the original figures used in the animation, but little is known about these. Other than that, *the Magic Roundabout* playground set made by Corgi is rare today. This nostalgic gem (Model No. H853) featured a musical carousel, a complete plastic garden, and a train track. At good auctions, boxed and 'Good Plus' examples were making £600+ in the early 2000s. Today, a similar set could fetch between £200 and £300. The musical carousel (Model H852) from the playset featuring Dylan, Florence, Paul, and others was also available individually and now makes around £200 at auction if in generally great condition with a tidy box.

The Citroën car, driven by Brian the Snail, fetches several hundred pounds, and the Train with Mr Rusty makes £400 in top nick.

The best money, as ever, tends to lie in items that are boxed and in mint condition. This is true of most collectable toys, but particularly with Magic Roundabout collectables. Internet auction sites such as eBay (www.ebay.co.uk) often feature these great, colourful collectables. There are also some great specialist toy auction houses. Alternatively try your local toy or retro dealer.

A *Magic Roundabout* lampshade: £29 (Jamie Breese. Item kindly provided by Cream and Chrome Collectables)

Matchbox cars

Who would have thought that these little micro toys would one day turn out to be one of the good toy investments? The market for die-cast cars is always quite good, and some models of Matchbox cars (originally sold for pennies) are continuing to fetch fine prices.

The Lesney Company was started in 1947 by two former Royal Navy friends. The name Matchbox came from one of the founders who made a diesel road roller and fitted it into a matchbox so his daughter could take it to school. The 'Models of Yesteryear' followed in 1956, and the Superfast car range was added in 1969. Rarity of colour is everything when collecting Matchbox toys. The great news is that the rare colours, which bump the value up so much, were available to the average customer. The presence of the correct box adds a great deal to the value. The early German and French models made from 1977 are perhaps the most difficult to find.

How much?

A No. 46 Morris Minor in pale brown has sold for £4,000. A Thames Trader cattle truck in metallic copper sold for £3,750. The red version of No. 45a, the Vauxhall Victor, is one of the most sought-after toys: it could make thousands at auction.

In September 2008, a Superfast No. 24 Team Matchbox pre-production car sold for £1,600 against an estimated £360–£500. The Matchbox painting books are good sellers – these can command £150–£200 at auction.

Matchbox toys are now made by Mattel, who were celebrating 50 years of Matchbox production a few years ago. Look out for a number of the newer vehicles to keep aside, if you are feeling lucky and have the patience.

Matchbox 'Regular Wheels' No. 33C Lamborghini Miura (c.1968). This realised £100 in October 2008 (Image courtesy of Vectis Auctions)

Matchbox 'Models of Yesteryear' No. Y23 AEC Bus 'Miniature Car N.M.C.C. Japan' (late 1980s or early 1990s): £130 (Image courtesy of Vectis Auctions)

Matchbox 'Regular Wheels' No. 9A fire engine; No.10A Scammell articulated truck and trailer; No. 12A Land Rover; No. 13 wreck truck; and No. 14A ambulance.

This collection of vehicles (manufactured between 1953 and 1969) realised £150 in October 2008 (Image courtesy of Vectis Auctions)

Medals

Medals are an inspirational collectable and you'd be surprised how many families have one or two tucked away. There are several types: the campaign medals from a certain battle; the more commemorative types marking a key event, and lastly the medals for valour and bravery.

The most sought-after medals are those given for bravery, as there is often an inscription with the recipient's initials and a ribbon, or even bars. The George Medal was the second highest award for civilian bravery, second only to the George Cross (which the island of Malta was famously awarded in the 1940s). An expert should have records of all those people who received one, which helps in identification and valuation.

How much?

The most common medals in this country are probably the campaign type. For example, the War Medal was awarded to all those people serving in uniform in the Second World War. These make around the £10 mark if resold. If you had served three years, then you might have received the Defence Medal, which can make about £16 on the open market.

There are a few very special awards for gallantry. The VC, or Victoria Cross, is the best known. One from the Second World War was sold a few years ago by the London experts Spink for nearly £140,000, while an earlier Indian Mutiny Victoria Cross sold for £27,500 at Sotheby's in 2000. In 2004 Spink created an auction record for a Victoria Cross when one sold for £230,000. A gold medal awarded to

This Second World War Victoria Cross was sold by Spink for nearly £140,000 (Image courtesy of Spink)

Captain Hardy – Nelson's right-hand man after the Battle of Trafalgar – once sold for £248,800 at Christie's.

Of course, people are reluctant to sell a part of their family history, but there is a healthy flow of buying and selling on the medals market. The true value must be the bravery which underlines most of these precious pieces of metal. With special awards, consult a reputable dealer or auction house for specialist advice.

This collection of Orders and medals, awarded to Air Chief Marshal Baron Dowding of Bentley, architect of the RAF's victory in the Batttle of Britain, was auctioned by Spink in 1997 (TopFoto)

Memphis Group

In 1980 a ground-breaking, radical group of designers, consisting of many leading names from many countries, set out to create a look for the decade. They called themselves the Memphis Group, and the inspiration for the name came from a Bob Dylan record that just happened to be playing at the time! With all things '80s undergoing a revival at the moment, and the group's short life (they closed down in 1988), Memphis pieces are becoming increasingly rare and sought after.

The group produced everything from glassware and ceramics to furniture and clocks. Despite being based in Milan, the collective had an international flavour – key names were Michael Graves and Ettore Sottsass. Their work is extremely distinctive, with the very bright pastel colours, the reliance on plastic and laminates, and playful designs, which often have a 'Legoland' appearance. Almost all the work is marked 'Memphis' and some pieces can be found with the designer's name, and date too.

How much?

Sottsass's 'Tervas' vase can cost as much as £2,000, while his 'Euphrates' vase can fetch £800 a time. The 'Super' lamp by Martine Bedin is hot. The famous 'Carlton' room divider from 1981 is an auction piece and makes thousands, as does the 'Carlton' bookcase. A sterling silver 'Murmansk' centrepiece from 1982 sold for over £15,000 at Christie's New York in December 2006.

Though cheap materials were often used, some pieces were made in very small numbers and were expensive to buy. Perhaps the most famous rare Memphis piece would be the eccentric dressing table produced by Graves in 1981. Called the 'Plaza', it looks like an art deco New York office block and fetches sky-scraping figures today: £15,000+ on a good day at a top auction.

Some of the plates can be picked up cheaply today. The 'Lettuce' plate designed by Sottsass costs around £100, while the smaller 'Indivia' plate costs around £60. The 'Superior' porcelain toothpick holder, or 'Ontario' pepper shaker, both designed by Matteo Thun in 1982, can cost as little as £50. If you are a lucky owner, it's worth having a look at your piece again and considering getting an appraisal from an auctioneer.

Midwinter

Midwinter Pottery was founded in 1910 and became one of the key potteries in the 1950s. The colourful and modern patterns were a breath of fresh air in post-war Britain.

The big change in direction for the firm came in 1953 when Midwinter produced the Stylecraft range. This was a significant step away from the more traditional wares and the previous art deco inspired designs. They were one of the first to bring the funky, noticeably '50s, look to British tableware, and were inspired by the fashions of the day. Two of the key names to look out for are Jessie Tait and Terence Conran who worked on various patterns for the popular Fashion shape. Midwinter was bought by Meakin, and then again by Wedgwood in the late '60s. Sadly, the company closed in 1987 and left a long legacy for collectors to seek out and enjoy.

How much?

Some pieces have realised large figures in the past. The Colin Melbourne Brontosaurus and Polar Bear are two such rarities among the animal figurines, but they have probably halved in value since 2002 to £200–£300 on eBay. A 6in tall teapot alone sold on eBay in November 2008 for £200. In the same month, a stunning 1950s Salad Ware teapot decorated with vegetable motifs by Terence Conran attracted a remarkable £1,120 and 15 bids on eBay. A single jug from the same range made £185.

A favourite for many collectors is the 'Zambesi' patterned tableware produced in the Fashion shape/range. These items are classic 1950s designs by Jessie Tait. They have a zebra-like pattern with red details and can fetch a lot of money. A 15-piece coffee service will be in the region of £300 currently. The vases are incredibly varied in design and this is matched by the values. A tube lined vase might make £40–£50 online. The 'Red Domino' pattern is simple and stylish: a complete dinner service would be a great find, and prices for a fine condition set will be in the region of £150–£250 at a good auction.

Midwinter 'Nature Study' large plate designed by Terence Conran (1950s): £35
(Jamie Breese. Item kindly provided by Cream and Chrome Collectables)

Moneyboxes

Moneyboxes make for a great collectable. They come in all shapes and sizes, though the best tend to be the early cast-iron or tin examples, which can be worth hundreds, sometimes thousands of pounds.

The first boxes appeared in the 1850s, were mostly made of cast iron, and usually featured some type of clever movement. In the 1920s, with mass production of tin boxes, their popularity was sealed. These often featured elegant lithographed decoration. There are earlier ceramic moneyboxes, and these are even harder to find in good condition.

How much?

J. & E. Stevens of the USA is perhaps the most famous name in moneybox manufacturing. The Paddy and the Pig mechanical bank is worth around £500 if near mint, while the famous greedy mayor by Tammany (1873) makes about £250+ now. Among the ceramic Wemyss Ware pigs, you can find a moneybox: the cabbage rose pattern is popular. If one sold at auction it would make £350–£450 at present. The Crawford's biscuit tin bank, featuring a fairy house, makes about £200.

The Holy Grail find could possibly be the legendary 'Skipping Girl' box made in America in 1870 by J. & E. Stevens. If you are lucky enough to have one of these on your mantelpiece, you might be able to pull in between £12,000–£17,500 at auction.

Collecting moneyboxes isn't just for the adults. It makes for a great kids' hobby as so many banks can be picked up for £5–£10, or even less at car boot sales. The NatWest Piggies are perhaps the most famous (see page 96). Look for the more recent iconic cartoon characters like Pooh Bear, Snoopy, Mickey, and Noddy. These could all increase in value.

A 'Rupert Bear' moneybox: £20–£30
(Martin Breese)

A hair (approximately 10mm long), which was part of a lock cut from the head of Marilyn Monroe by her hairdresser Robert Champion. Mounted, framed, and glazed, together with a photograph and a signed statement from Champion, this sold for £495
(Image courtesy of Fraser's Autographs)

Marilyn Monroe

Along with James Dean, The Beatles, and Elvis, Marilyn occupies a very special position in contemporary culture. Her continued status as an icon has kept buoyant the interest in her life, and the collectables and memorabilia market is as strong as ever.

Anything with a personal connection carries a premium price tag. With a single hair from her head being sold, you'll start to get the picture. The hair (approximately 10mm long) was part of a lock cut from Marilyn's head by her hairdresser Robert Champion, and was offered in 2008 by Fraser's Autographs, selling for £495. Like Dean, Monroe died well before her time, was both an exhibitionist and a vulnerable and insecure screen goddess, and this has just added to her desirability. In the '60s Marilyn's image was boosted again by pop artist Andy Warhol's screen prints of her. A few years ago a set of ten were sold for £241,000.

How much?

The top items go for mega bucks. In October 2005, a US-based auction saw the sale of her birthday gift to President Kennedy (a gold Rolex which was inscribed with the words 'Jack with love as always Marilyn May 29th 1962'). Together with a poem she wrote for him, the lot went under the hammer for £66,650. A signed, single photograph taken in 1949 and given to her agent went for £14,000 in 2002. In 2003, an outfit she wore in the classic flick *The Seven Year Itch* went for £34,150.

You don't have to have a movie star's pay packet to buy into Marilyn, but it helps. A single signature on a small piece of paper was valued by Fraser's at between £6,000 and £7,000 in 2008. This extraordinary figure is testament to Monroe's timeless popularity. Whether prices will increase from this level is hard to predict.

Moorcroft Pottery

Moorcroft is one of the few factories to be doing well during the current difficulties experienced in British pottery. In the last ten years, Moorcroft has been selling more of its wares than it ever has done – more even than during its golden age in the 1920s.

The pottery was founded in 1912 in Colbridge by the youthful William Moorcroft, who decided to break away from the Macintyre ceramics company and set up on his own. The company went from strength to strength and was given the Royal Appointment in 1928. Moorcroft was known for glossy, largely floral, glazed pieces. Dominant colours included purple, olive green, and deep blue. Queen Mary had admired examples of Florian Ware as far back as 1913 during a visit to the potteries and later bought several pieces from Harrods. Until the outbreak of the Second World War she was a regular visitor to the Moorcroft stand at the annual British Industries Fair.

How much?

Moorcroft has a habit of increasing in value. Christie's the auctioneers hold a specialist yearly sale, and there are key pieces on permanent display at such prestigious venues as London's Victoria and Albert Museum. On the low side you can pay just under £100 for a small cabinet vase. Earlier, larger pieces, such as Moorcroft Macintyre 'Yellow Iris' patterned vases can fetch a grand or more each. A lot of modern, cheaper pottery uses similar designs: so look for the impressed 'Moorcroft' and the signature William or W. Moorcroft on decorative wares.

The modern output is equally charming and collectable. Often, today's wares will be strictly limited editions of as few as 50! Becoming a member of the Moorcroft Collectors' Club provides access to factory tours, special club pieces, and special member-only events. Details can be found at www.moorcroft.com.

A late 20th-century design called 'Spiraxia' by Emma Bossons FRSA
(Image courtesy of W. Moorcroft plc)

Moorcroft sale

The biggest single-owner collection of Moorcroft pottery to appear on the market was in a sale of Ceramic Design by Bonhams the auctioneers in London in late September 2008.

The collection was started in the 1920s by Mr and Mrs Bracewell at their home in the Lake District. They loved the designs of William Moorcroft, and their passion was shared by their son Peter who inherited the collection upon their passing. The collection comprised 200 lots from 1900 to around 1955 in many desirable patterns. Among the lots up for grabs were inkwells, jugs, vases, fruit bowls, desk sets, bowls and covers, teapots, and teaware.

How much?

The Bracewell collection was estimated at approximately £150,000, and one of the star lots was a William Moorcroft Hazeldene large-footed bowl, circa 1920, which sold for £3,120.

'Tigris' by Rachel Bishop. This was produced during the 'Phoenix Years' period of the company, when it was under new ownership
(Image courtesy of W. Moorcroft plc)

An incomplete 'Imperial Stormtrooper' helmet from *Star Wars* sold for £16,450 at Christie's in December 2002 (Image courtesy of Christie's Images Ltd 2008)

Movie memorabilia

Surely, this is *the* collectable of the last century, and a true indicator of the special importance of the movie star. You'll have to have a movie star's pay packet to acquire the real gems, but more accessible items like props, photos or posters are widely available.

The big bucks are in the screen idols of Hollywood's first 50 years. These obviously include Hepburn, Laurel & Hardy and Monroe. Equally large amounts lie in the exceptionally rare models, props, and costumes from the major movies, e.g. the Bond series. Oscars and actors' scripts are often considered to be Holy Grail items. Unique *Star Wars* items are perhaps the most exciting at present. Naturally, good condition and impeccable provenance are essential.

How much?

Sometimes, a lot of money, as you will see. Charlie Chaplin's bowler hat and cane made £82,500 at auction. Clark Gable's *Gone with the Wind* script sold for over £160,000, while his Oscar went for over £400,000. Oddjob's steel-rimmed hat from the Bond film *Goldfinger* is worth over £60,000, and you would have had to shell out a cool £20,000 if you wanted to get close to Monroe with her shimmy dress from *Some Like it Hot*.

In December 2008, Bonhams sold the 1976 Lotus Esprit, driven by Roger Moore in *The Spy Who Loved Me*, for £111,500. This was one of two cars used in the film and attracted international attention. In the end it was bought by a private US collector.

Twenty-two grand for a hand

A strange lot from a galaxy far, far away attracted international attention in late 2007 at a London auction house. Up for grabs was a metallic-looking hand that once belonged to one half of cinema's most likeable double act – C-3PO from *Star Wars*. The 'hand' was in the form of a glove modelled in plastic and vinyl with metal details. It had red and yellow painted wire details running from the palm base to fingers and, of course, was made for Anthony Daniels as the iconic but worrisome android, C-3PO. Originally it had been donated by the writer, director, and producer George Lucas to the Friends of the Joffrey Ballet. It was sold with a plastic display case and signed photo of Anthony Daniels.

How much?

The sale of Film and Entertainment Memorabilia at Christie's, South Kensington, realised a whopping £228,550 in total in 2007. The top-selling lot was Lot 135, the hand, which fetched an incredible £22,100 against an estimate of just £4,000–£6,000. It was sold to an anonymous buyer. What makes this figure even more remarkable is that, according to Lucasfilm Archives, it is suggested that this 'hand' was made for *Return of the Jedi*, but was probably not screen-used, as evidenced by its excellent condition.

A rare C-3PO hand, and signed cast photograph, which realised £22,100 at Christie's in 2007 (Image courtesy of Christie's Images Ltd 2008)

Movie posters

Well-designed cinema posters relating to great pictures are hugely enjoyable and can be worth fantastic amounts if the size, country, movie, and condition are right. American examples are called 'one sheets' (41inx27in) and British examples are called 'quads' (30inx40in). A knowledge of who the early printers were and the variety of paper used makes identification of desirable originals possible.

US posters are generally worth many times more than the European equivalents. Condition is crucial, and a poster is best rolled as opposed to being folded. Posters are sometimes found in lofts, where they have been used as insulation, or under carpets, and the prices paid reflect the true rarity. Not many posters for cinemas were produced and few survived.

How much?
Prices were certainly high in the 1990s. *The Invisible Man*, from 1933 (if a US example), once would have achieved £36,700, while *King Kong*, from 1933, is always popular and has reached up to £28,750 at auction. *The Invisible Ray*, *Alice's Day at Sea*, and Mickey Mouse in *Lonesome Ghosts*, are gold dust, and James Bond, Hitchcock, and Monroe's films are all worth big bucks.

Christie's made the headlines with a French poster of *Casablanca* (1942), which at the time cost £54,300, while Sotheby's, New York, once flogged a poster for the original movie *The Mummy* for £283,000.

A quad poster for the movie *Goldfinger*
(Image courtesy of Christie's Images Ltd 2008)

The new money is in the cult films of the '50s and '60s. Michael Caine, Steve McQueen and Clint Eastwood are on the up. Horror-related posters are increasingly popular, as are the great films of the '90s.

Attack of the 50ft Woman
Five world records were shattered at a sale of classic movie posters in March 2008. Posters are collected all over the world and movies, together with vintage travel, are two of the best performers.

The highlight of the auction was a one-sheet version of the 1958 Allied Artists classic *Attack of the 50ft Woman*. Alison Hayes was the star, and the film was directed by Nathan Hertz.

How much?
This superb, iconic poster sold at the Vintage Film Posters auction at Christie's, London. It made a whopping £11,875 (a world record price for this poster at auction) against a pre-sale estimate of £3,500–£4,500.

Four other records were also shattered at the same sale. Posters for James Bond movies are always well liked. One up for grabs was a British poster promoting the film *Dr No* from 1962. The estimate had been £1,500–£2,500, but it made £11,250 on the day. Another record was created for a poster for the film *La Dolce Vita* from 1960. It was an Italian version. The estimate for this one was £4,000–£6,000, but a US private buyer came up with a mighty £10,000.

A poster for *Raiders of the Lost Ark*
(Image courtesy of Garry Johnson)

This superb 'Hero' pulse rifle is from the hit movie *Aliens*. It is valued at £30,000 (Image courtesy of Propstore)

Movie props

Collecting movie props can be a fun and rewarding pastime to match any pocket. Prices have steadily increased for several years now. The high end is dominated by important costumes or on-screen props relating to major blockbusters or the classic films of Hollywood's Golden Age, and these usually come with some clear authentication. For example, Superman's costume worn by Christopher Reeve in 1978 sold for £38,000 and the Cowardly Lion's paw-shaped shoe, worn in *The Wizard of Oz* of 1939, sold a few years ago for £17,500.

Perhaps the most desirable and rare movie props are those relating to the *Indiana Jones* and first *Star Wars* trilogies. Sci-Fi films tend to be a safer bet, probably because of the elaborate and interesting props which are created for on-screen use. Smaller items rarely have authentication, so it helps to purchase from reputable dealers.

How much?

A popular watchword for collectors is 'owning a piece which you can identify with on screen'. Around £40 can buy you a production-used prop, but it will cost more if it can be recognised clearly on screen. For example, you would need to pay £150 for a prop computer seen in the film *Judge Dredd*. A prop flag from the film *Indiana Jones and the Last Crusade* was priced at £200 a few years ago. This compares with its current valuation of £800, which serves to indicate how prices have escalated.

Christie's New York once sold the actual Maltese Falcon from the famous Bogart movie of 1941. It went for nearly £285,000.

Anyone interested in starting a collection can visit the truly huge memorabilia fairs held in the UK and abroad, and one of the largest prop dealers in the UK can be accessed online at www.propstore.com.

Terminator memorabilia

Arnie still remains a sought-after celebrity, and here we focus on items from the hugely successful *Terminator* trilogy. If he gets remembered for doing a fine job as a politician as well, it might seal his fame and, therefore, collectability for another decade or more.

There are four areas to consider if you wish to invest in these types of collectable. First, there are the original movie props and costumes (the larger pieces are mostly found at movie sales at big international auction houses or top dealers). Second, you have the licensed replicas of items (e.g. I spotted a replica chrome head from T2 (1991), complete with red light-up eyes for £500 at www.propstore.co.uk). Third, you have the promotional items made for the general public or limited availability (e.g. a promotional cap and umbrella from T3 *The Rise of the Machines* (2003) currently costs around £75, or there was the entire Kenner toy line. Best is the Bally Midway T2 pinball game). Fourth, there are some unlicensed items made for profit or by fans for fun.

How much?

An original theatrical quad-style *Terminator* (1984) poster from the UK will set you back around £250 currently, while a T2: *Judgment Day*, Special Preview Screening ticket for London will cost around £5. You can buy a specially mounted piece of latex face make-up used by Arnie in the first film for around £600, or pay £80 for replica chrome 'bullet hit' from the second film.

Some of the very finest props and costumes can be seen at some of the Hard Rock Cafés around the globe. If you keep your eyes open, online auctions, often for charity, take place on the Internet.

Arnie once helped raise $400,000 for charity with a sale of limited-edition T3 merchandise.

Authenticity is one of the first concerns of potential buyers. Most key prop collectable companies will offer a guarantee of provenance or have the reputation to back it up. If you are spending a lot, then ask: a good dealer or auction house will provide whatever info they can offer.

An instantly recognisable 'Hook Arms' T1000 shirt from the movie *Terminator 2*. £10,000 (Image courtesy of Propstore)

Musical instruments

There are one or two entries in this book that, it could be argued, fall outside the area of 'collectables'. While not strictly collected as such, musical instruments are important and cross over quite a bit into the 20th and 21st centuries, so they are included here.

Prior to 1800, most instruments were handmade by craftsmen, but with the coming of mass production to meet the growing public interest in owning and playing musical instruments, this changed. Like furniture, handmade instruments are 'living' antiques, and professional players appreciate the timeless quality of sound that an original design can produce.

All other early instruments tend to play second fiddle to violins in terms of value, although prices do fluctuate according to fashion. However, the products of certain master craftsmen, such as Antonio Stradivari and Joseph Guarneri, maintain their high values. One of the greatest instruments ever to appear at auction was Stradivari's 'Mendelssohn' violin, which fetched over £900,000 at Christie's in 1990. Another Stradivari violin, known as 'The Hammer' sold at Christie's New York more recently for an astonishing $3,544,000.

If an item belonged to a famous musician, then this also plays a part in ramping up the price. Condition is, not surprisingly, of great importance, and more so with stringed instruments. Some repair is acceptable as long as the key parts are complete.

A violin by Antonio Stradivari (Cremona, 1716). This sold for £767,200 at Sotheby's in November 2003 (Image courtesy of Sotheby's Picture Library)

How much?

Price is ultimately determined by the identification of the craftsman who created the instrument. Saxophones made by Adolphe Sax are sought after, as are very early pianos by Cristofori. More modern fine pianos tend to be worth under a grand, with the exception of those made by Bluthner, Bechstein and Steinway. Harps vary in value, with the market dominated by Sebastian Erard who was making innovative designs in the late 1700s (late examples of his can still be found for around £1,500). Flutes can cost tens of thousands if made from ivory and boxwood and are from the 1600s, whereas percussion instruments, regardless of age, tend to be undervalued at a few hundred pounds, tops.

As you might imagine, identifying and dating instruments is best left to the experts. There are endless reproductions, particularly of violins, and to the untrained eye these are impossible to distinguish, leading to many heartbreaks when the truth is unveiled. Reputable dealers and auction houses will often examine and give you an estimated value without obligation.

Bob Dylan

The recent film documentary made by Martin Scorsese has created renewed interest in the unique talents of one of the last century's greatest musical geniuses. For many, he was a spokesperson for a generation – the king of protest songs.

It's not just the documentary and recent BBC TV Dylan season that caught the public's imagination; Dylan's memoirs were published in 2004 too. If you were a fan or still are, who knows, you might have a piece of paper signed by him. Better still is a signed photo. In 2008, autograph experts Fraser's valued a top-end example at £1,950.

How much?

In November 2005, an auction held by Christie's in New York saw a 16-page document featuring poems by this great artist sell for an astonishing £45,000. They were penned while he spent time at the University of Minnesota between 1959 and 1960. What made them even more special was the fact that they are the first known documents to be signed with his performing name – 'Bob Dylan'. One of the true Holy Grails of rock and pop is a copy of Dylan's *Freewheelin'* album; some have estimated a value of many thousands if it is the rare earlier stereo version with four extra songs absent from the later release. A rare handbill for Bob Dylan at Town Hall in 1963 made $2,750 at Christie's New York in June 2008.

Possessing a piece of rock history may not cost you an arm and a leg. A few years ago, a Bob Dylan acoustic guitar fetched £1,410 at auction; a small price to pay to own a used instrument.

A harmonica used and autographed by Bob Dylan, circa 1982. It sold at Sotheby's in June 2002 for £1,116 (Image courtesy of Sotheby's Picture Library)

The NatWest pig family
and 'Cousin Wesley'
(Image courtesy of Wade)

one. A complete set of five will make about £250–£280 online at present, while a good dealer might sell a sparkling set for up to £350.

In 1999, a limited edition called 'Cousin Wesley' was produced for those parents who invested in a children's savings bond. He is dressed in a green shirt and a blue cap, and changes hands now for £250–£350 online. 'Wicket' was one of the latest additions to the NatWest family. He was a strictly limited edition, and was offered exclusively to cricket fans attending the NatWest international matches. Younger cricket fans in attendance were able to get a 'paint your own' 'Wicket' when applying for a Young Savers account or a Child Trust Fund.

The pigs are worth more if you can find them with their original stoppers. Pigs which don't have the 'Wade, England' marking on the base were made by other companies and are worth less.

NatWest piggies

In December 1983, the NatWest Bank started giving away these charming piggy banks. The object of the exercise, supported by a colourful advertising campaign, was to encourage children to save. Almost everyone knows somebody who still owns one, but how many have seen the complete set of six?

Three quid was the initial payment. Then, in exchange for every £25 deposited, the child would receive one of a family of five pigs made by the British pottery, Wade. Alternatively, if £100 was deposited straight off, they would be sent a pig every three months. The first was 'Woody' the piglet, and the last was 'Sir Nathaniel', the father. Sunshine Ceramics actually produced the first batches and these were unmarked on the underside.

How much?

'Woody' and his sister 'Annabel' were the two figures that were easiest to acquire. The parents are, understandably, harder to acquire, as it took longer to become eligible for

'Wicket' – a very limited-edition pig
(Image courtesy of The NatWest Bank/RBS)

Newspapers

Britain has a glorious history of producing the greatest newspapers that goes right back to 1622. Not surprisingly, the most popular editions are usually worth the least, as people tend to keep them for posterity.

Age is not a guarantee of value. Vintage examples on rag paper (pre-1850) are often found in better condition, as less stable pulp paper was favoured in the 20th century. Papers which feature the important battles of Nelson's naval career, from 1805 and beyond, can command prices upwards of £500. Many top collectors go for a certain subject and, curiously, murders are popular. Beware of facsimile editions of papers, produced to celebrate a certain anniversary.

How much?

The Sunday Pictorial was the first incarnation of *The Sunday Mirror* and cost a penny. It first appeared on 14 March 1915 and featured the headline 'The Task of The Red Cross', accompanied by a touching picture of a soldier giving another a piggyback. It started as a mainly image-based paper, but became the more familiar newspaper (and was renamed) in 1963. It's worth around £220. The first edition of *The Daily Mirror* appeared on 2 November 1903 and is worth around £200.

There are some extremely rare papers that can fetch thousands, but these tend to be *very* hard to find. Some of the disasters of the 20th century also prove desirable, from the sinking of the *Titanic* to the Kennedy assassination.

Newspapers covering important historical events can be well worth preserving for the future (Getty Images)

Not all important historical events covered in papers are sought-after. Many people have carefully kept aside issues relating to Coronation and Royal events for nostalgic reasons (Getty Images)

A real find would be a contents bill taken from a *Mirror* paper stand on 20 April 1912. The headline on it was 'Hymn Played While The *Titanic* Sunk', and in good nick it can be worth well over £400. An online dealer in 2008 was asking over £500 for one rare copy of *The Glasgow Herald* of 16 April 1912 relating to the *Titanic*.

Other more famous occasions are easier to find, as many people kept them as souvenirs at the time. Some of the more bizarre headlines have also proved to be collectable – 'Freddie Starr ate my hamster' being one such gem. Other issues are collected because they are the last issues of a particular title or format, e.g. *Today*'s last issue in 1995 would be priced at £90 with a specialist dealer.

For the future, always keep aside a first edition of any new paper or journal. When moving or decorating, look under your carpets – some people used papers for crude insulation. Keep your collection away from light and leave preservation to the experts.

Noddy collectables

Enid Blyton's most famous creation has captivated millions of people around the world. Noddy first appeared in 1949 in *Mr Tumpy and his Caravan* and then his own book, *Noddy goes to Toyland* (also that year). He's recently been revived into a naughty but innocent little boy in an animated series, which has sold around the globe. Over 200 million copies of the books have been sold.

There were 24 books in all, spawning a huge industry, and Noddy books are believed to be in the top ten of children's books in faraway Japan – the Japanese are often the leaders of the collectables world. Top buys are the Noddy items from the 1950s and '60s that were much loved by their owners. The fact that few have survived unscathed pushes up the prices.

How much?

Noddy can go for mega-money because of his huge international appeal. 'Big Ears' and 'Policeman Plod' are also popular, but Noddy's other friends don't fare so well. A Wade first series 'Noddy' from 1958–1960 will cost you £180–£200 (without a box) on eBay, and prices have remained steady for this piece for the last six years. 'Miss Fluffy' cat is a disappointing £40–£50. Other toys fare well, with an original tin car with Noddy driving going for around £200 in its box. Also popular are tea sets, especially in their original boxes, and they fetch around £200–£250. Most sought after are the Wade versions, with porringers (porridge bowls) selling for £80+.

Committed collectors want the original artwork drawn by Van der Beek, who died in 1953. He admitted that he'd drawn so many Noddies, he used to see little ones clambering all over his desk! Sotheby's held two sales of original artwork in 1997 and 1998. The first fetched twice its estimate at £350,000, while the second netted £137,425 for 363 original pictures.

A 'Big Ears' eggcup: £5. A 'Noddy' eggcup: £5 (Jamie Breese. Item kindly provided by Cream and Chrome Collectables)

Three medals won by athlete Heather Armstrong, including Olympic medals from Helsinki 1952 and Melbourne 1956, were auctioned by Christie's in 1999, and were expected to make £8,000–£12,000 (TopFoto)

Olympics

There are few events in history that see such a varied and colourful range of collectable merchandise than the Olympics, but they are not so hot on the collectables front. Since the modern games began in 1896, much of the produce has been either free or cheap to acquire and, of course, it makes for a worldwide market. In short, anything that has a connection with any of the games is desirable to somebody, somewhere. The Internet has expanded the market a great deal.

The lower end is dominated by toys, pins, buttons, posters, proof coins, watches, stamps, and souvenirs; while the high end attracts bidders for winners' medals and torches. One of my favourite mid-range examples is the rare Carlton Ware 'Walking Ware' mug made for the Moscow Olympics. This has the familiar legs holding the mug upright, and makes up to £750 from a good dealer depending on condition. Only 100 were made.

How much?

The torches vary in price: the idea of the flame was brought forward from the ancient event, and the torch relay has operated continually since the early '50s. There are quite a few in circulation and prices seem to fall between £1,000 and £3,000.

One collectable which is still strong worldwide, albeit quieter in Europe, is phonecards. If you have plenty of money to spend, then there are always a few Holy Grails. Chris Boardman, the Brit cyclist and Olympic winner, rode a Lotus bike. The model used by him on his double record-breaking win in 1992 was once sold by Philips the auctioneers for £25,000.

One of the most accessible of Olympic collectables is pins: there are bid pins, countdown pins, media pins, sponsor pins, mascot pins, and sport pins. The newest hot Olympic item has proved to be the London 2012 Olympic Games bid pin badges! They were limited items made for staff members and guests at the launch of the bid. Now they are appearing on eBay.

Paddington Bear at 50

It was Paddington's 50th anniversary in 2008. The much-loved bear has never lost his appeal since he first appeared on our shores with a name tag saying 'Please look after this bear'. Naturally, such a star attracts collectors, and among the most popular collectables are the figurines and plush toys made in his honour.

Many of the collectable figures were made by the British pottery Coalport. The first ones started to be sold in the mid-1970s. Later pieces were made in the '80s and even more recently. There are plenty of nice pieces to choose from, and there have been recastings and limited edition pieces sold aplenty. Most examples stand around 9cm tall and make a pleasant display.

How much?

You can pick up a signed luggage label by author Michael Bond for around £50. However, the most desirable figurines, such as 'Magician with Wand', will command around £145 at the moment. 'Waits for a Train' (the first version from the '70s) makes around £100 on eBay. Some of the more common pieces sell for £10 to £20.

If these are too small, you might want to consider the larger plush bears made by Gabrielle Designs that was Shirley Clarkson's company (mother of presenter Jeremy). They were good quality and made from the early '70s onwards. Early and collectable bears make £100–£150 and need the Dunlop wellies, not the later PB marked ones. Aunt Lucy is harder to find today, and in good shape will cost £200–£250. The Danbury Mint have made various limited-edition collectors' plates, and these sell for £20–£40.

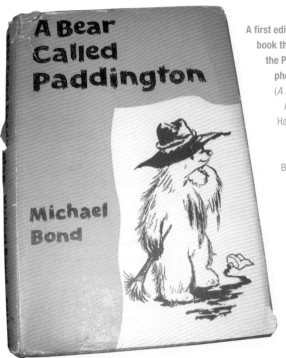

A first edition of the book that started the Paddington phenomenon (*A Bear Called Paddington*, HarperCollins Publishers, © Michael Bond, 1958)

A 20th-century glass paperweight: £10 (Martin Breese)

Paperweights

The golden era of paperweight design was between 1845 and 1860. It was the three legendary French manufacturers Saint Louis, Baccarat, and Clichy who were the first to produce this elegant yet functional object. George Bacchus & Sons of Birmingham also made some fine examples. Unlike other antique glass, paperweights have steadily increased in value, and consequently are a good area to invest in. They are attractive to collect, and they require little space to store or display. With knowledge gained from some good reference books, you can hunt around at antique markets, car boot fairs, and provincial auctions looking out for hidden treasure. Collections can be formed from themes (such as particular sorts of flowers; a certain maker; antique or 20th-century objects) or the vast number of glass-enclosed motifs (from animals to historical characters, from flowers to silhouettes). The only constant is really the size, which is usually 10cm or less in diameter.

How much?

Key factors affecting value are when it was made, its rarity, whether produced by a well-known artist, and its condition. Over £100,000 was paid in the early 2000s for a rare 19th-century lampworked Pantin salamander magnum paperweight, while over £7,000 was once paid for a paperweight that was presented to Elvis by the Beverly Hills Police Department.

The Holy Grail was found and sold in 1990 by Sotheby's New York, though there will be others – somewhere! Sotheby's sold the fabulously rare and beautiful 'Basket of Flowers' paperweight made by the Clichy works for a record prive of over £170,000.

The chances of finding an item from the golden era are slight, but it could happen. If you can't face trawling the flea markets of France, then why not consider the annual modern paperweights from makers such as Perthshire or Baccarat.

Pelham puppets

Pelham remains one of the great names of British toy manufacturing. The company was founded by an ex-serviceman after the Second World War and went on to become one of the best-loved toy brands. Sadly, the company closed in 1993, and their fabulous puppets have become increasingly collectable in recent years.

Over 500 different characters were created. Age does not always guarantee bigger bucks, though the rare blue-labelled Pelhams (called Wonky Toys) were the very first made and are more sought after. Boxes give the clearest indication of age, with the unusual brown box being the earliest version of the Pelhams proper.

How much?

Because of the changing market and huge variety of toys, it's best to get some guidance on prices. Look on the web for Internet auctions as a source of information. Details such as whether the puppets had moving or fixed mouths affect the value. Most puppets fall into the £30 to £80 bracket, which really makes Pelham a great, affordable collectable.

As with any collectable, there are some treasures out there. One of the most unusual is the Pelham Electronic Theatre that was an expensive accessory for the lucky kids of the day. These have made around £1,000 in the past. Look out for the *Blue Peter* characters, 'Bleep' and 'Booster'. Together with their strange and rare alien friend, all three could be worth £300–£500+.

Condition is very important. Just as with any toy, Pelhams were played with a lot and were quite fragile in the first place. Always go for the best condition puppet, in the best box. Check that the strings aren't tangled and that the cellophane window is clean and undamaged.

Pelham Puppets large scale Pinocchio (1970s/80s):
£190 (Image courtesy of Vectis Auctions)

Two PenDelfins
(Fred Woodward)

PenDelfins

From a garden shed in Pendle, Lancashire, founders Jean Walmsley Heap and Jeannie Todd planned to make Christmas presents for their friends: today some of the rarest rabbit characters sell for hundreds of pounds and are eagerly traded at auction and on Internet sites.

Formed in 1953 as a true homegrown cottage industry, the PenDelfin Studio has successfully been producing their highly collectable rabbit figurines since 1956. There have been several hundred rabbits and buildings created to date. More recently limited-edition collector plates have been produced, and even Carlton Ware produced licensed editions of earlier pieces.

How much?

If you bought the earlier items, you are possibly sitting on a small fortune. There are variations with some characters, which makes them even more sought after. There are specialist dealers and even auction rooms – all selling PenDelfins. Look for 'Aunt Agatha' (1963 and retired in 1965) or the mega-rare 'Cha Cha' who was produced from 1959 to 1961 and can cost over £750 today. The same goes for the earliest 'Father' figures. If you own a few, don't wrap them in newspaper: the print tends to transfer to the piece! Get one of the few guidebooks out there and check your pieces for a valuation. Most figures produced from the mid-1960s onwards are more affordable.

The PenDelfin range has expanded to incorporate a brand new series called 'Shillingsbury Tales', depicting mice instead of rabbits. Prices of the new characters range from around £15. The PenDelfin website is a good source of information: www.pendelfin.co.uk or you can join the PenDelfin Family Circle for around £25.

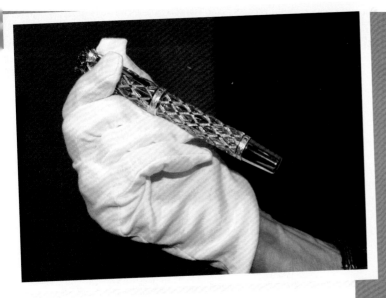

A Montblanc Prince Rainier III Limited Edition 81 Pen, produced in 2007. An artistically skeletonised fountain-pen edition limited to only 81 pieces worldwide
(Francois Durand/Getty Images)

Pens

Pens have been around since the first feather was dipped into some ink, but it wasn't until 1889 that George Parker patented his first fountain pen. By 1894 he had patented a pen that didn't drip, and very soon the pen became something of a status symbol. The golden era was the pre-Biro days of the 1920s and 1930s when makers such as Parker, Waterman, Montblanc, and Sheaffer produced pioneering models in celluloid and plastic, as well as precious metals.

The outer case of the pen soon became a designer's dream and, although the size was standard, the case could be fashioned from any material and in any style. Most popular were the marble-effect cases, but for the very rich silver, gold, and diamond-encrusted pens were available.

How much?

These de-luxe pens are highly sought after today and still turn up at auction. Parker was famous for designing the snake pen in 1906 that had a snake entwined around the body of the pen. This model cost $10 when it was first produced, but today would sell for many thousands.

A high price was achieved for a fountain pen at Bonhams the auctioneers a few years ago: a Namiki Dunhill model fetched £23,000. More recently, in October 2008, Christie's New York sold a rare White House fountain pen by Montblanc. The 18-carat white gold pen, which was designed to reflect the architectural style of the White House, made $26,250.

Most pens are worth less than £100, but it is worth checking out any that look unusual. Never scrape dried ink from the nib, as nibs are usually made from 14-carat gold and are easily damaged. Beware of dents in silver and gold pens, and look out for hairline cracks in lids made of celluloid or plastic where discoloration may also appear. For investment purposes, look for models by the major manufacturers.

Rare fountain pens

The craftsmanship of the best fountain pens has made them very attractive to collectors around the world. They were something to talk about in the early days and, like a fine timepiece, they remain a status symbol today.

The quality pens of the late Victorian to the late Edwardian period were often handcrafted and could take several weeks to decorate. Particularly in the early days, plastic was the choice of many, but the casing lent itself to fine designs, and gold, silver, and even diamonds were used by the top quality manufacturers. Condition is of vital importance to collectors – the most enthusiastic of which tend to be British, American, and Japanese.

How much?

Fountain pens in top-notch shape can be worth five times as much as worn examples. Most desirable pens fall into the £300-£600 bracket, with others of greater rarity making £600-£1,200. The super sought-after pens would include the Parker No. 60 'Awanyu Aztec'. Fashioned using 18-carat gold, one such pen once sold for £48,000.

As a rough guide, most fountain pens made before the Second World War by top makers such as Montblanc, Wahl-Eversharp, Parker (before 1930), Dunhill-Namiki, Waterman, Mabie Todd and Sheaffer are all worth buying if they are undamaged and cheaply priced.

A Caran d'Ache fountain pen made with 18-carat gold and studded with a diamond and a ruby. Caran d'Ache produced 10 limited edition models, this one selling for $174,000 (Getty Images)

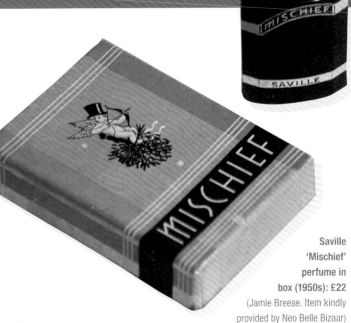

Perfume bottles

Around 700 perfume houses are known to have been in existence. There is an incredible variety of elegant bottles to be sought by collectors, and though the use of them can date back to the Romans, it was the 20th century which produced the greatest variety, with the huge influence of popular art and fashion.

Perfume bottle collecting is serious business. In the 19th-century, the greatest glass masters, such as Baccarat and Lalique, made astonishing examples which can cost as much as £20,000+ today. Fabergé also made bottles. Many books have been published – some just about certain shapes: you'll find barrel-shaped bottles (French), double-ended bottles (one end for smelling salts, the other for scent), handpainted porcelain bottles, and many novelty shapes. Their development in the last hundred years has been a marketing triumph, with extensive advertising, clever packaging, and increasingly more complex and sophisticated designs.

When it comes to collecting, the perfume inside is of little value. However, if it was originally sold with a fragrance (usually from 1907 onwards) a sealed example in mint condition and in original packaging will demand a premium. Because so many are thrown away once the scent is used up, perfume bottles are actually quite scarce and can hold their value well.

Saville 'Mischief' perfume in box (1950s): £22
(Jamie Breese. Item kindly provided by Neo Belle Bizaar)

How much?

One of the most modern bottles is also one of the most desirable. Jean-Paul Gaultier regularly produces limited editions of his outrageously designed own-brand perfume. It appeared in the early 1990s and the female, headless body shape has many guises, always in a tin. Unopened examples of certain fragrances have been changing hands for over £300. Older names like Lalique still dominate the higher end of the market, however.

Art deco glass perfume bottle (1930s): £28.
(Jamie Breese. Item kindly provided by Neo Belle Bizaar)

Bourjois 'Evening In Paris' perfume in box (1950s): £22
(Jamie Breese. Item kindly provided by Neo Belle Bizaar)

There are plenty of Holy Grails for collectors: 'Le Roi Soleil', of 1945, was designed by Salvador Dali and had a fabulous stopper – it's worth thousands. Look out for the name Julien Viard from the 1920s, with the human-shaped stoppers. Many of the most exotic and truly valuable bottles are those from the 1800s, but they are hard to find today.

For the future, keep an eye on more recent designs. To have a better chance of appreciating in value, modern perfume bottles need to be kept unopened and in the original packaging as well as the neck tags. The most famous perfume of the 1980s, Calvin Klein's 'Obsession', was designed by legendary French sculptor Pierre Dinand and was a revolutionary shape as well as scent. It might well increase in value over time. A more modest collection may be formed this way with Dior, Chanel, and others.

Superb scent bottle

Perfume bottle collecting has become an international activity, and occasionally a magnificent example will hit the headlines as it steals the show at auction. In January 2007 a superb gold-mounted nephrite scent bottle came up for sale at Christie's in London. It was just 6cm in length and shaped like a gherkin. It dated back to 1890 and was set with a band of rose-cut diamonds. Novelty or figural shaped bottles are hugely popular. Better still if they are from the St Petersburg workshop of one of history's most important craftsmen – Carl Fabergé.

How much?

This nephrite bottle was sold as part of the former collection of King George I of the Hellenes. The pre-sale estimate was perhaps a touch on the conservative side, being 'just' £10,000–£15,000, because on the day, as is often the case with fabulous Fabergé, it made a mighty £66,000.

A Fabergé scent bottle made £66,000 at auction in 2007 (Image courtesy of Christie's Images Ltd 2008)

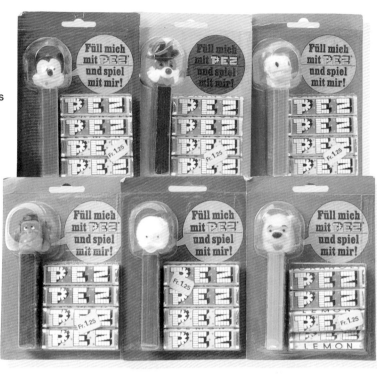

A group of PEZ dispensers in near mint or excellent blister packs – including 'Winnie-the-Pooh' and 'Mickey Mouse' – made £60 at Vectis in April 2008 (Image courtesy of Vectis Auctions)

PEZ dispensers

PEZ, despite being huge in the US, started out in Austria in the 1920s. The name is derived from the German word for peppermint. It wasn't until the 1950s that the familiar character heads appeared, and this is what transformed it into a true hot collectable.

PEZ dispensers are quite hard to date. One of the quickest ways is to look at the base of the body. If the base is square, then it is 'non-footed' and is older. Mis-packaged dispensers are worth a lot more money.

How much?

A rare PEZ is the red plastic 'Space Trooper' robot from the mid-1950s. He can pull in around £200. The 1970s Popeye PEZ makes about half that. A few of the vintage examples were shipped in a box, and can make over £100. Even Swarovski Crystal made a 'Daisy Duck' version handcrafted by Katherine Baumann of Beverly Hills. These were produced in limited numbers and sold for over £100. Quite a few reasonably recent designs are worth big money, e.g. the 'Little Orphan Annie' dispenser from the early 1980s makes over £100.

There are PEZ newsletters, conventions, special cruises, and several books out there on the subject. If you want to find out more you could look at the newsletter – www.pezcollectorsnews.com

Phonecards

As the march of the mobile phone overshadows the usage of phonecards in Europe, their popularity has dipped and values have tailed off considerably since the mid-1990s. The first phonecards were produced in Italy in the late 1970s, and the endless variety of designs, colours, and currencies made this one of the most collectable collectables.

Phonecards were often produced to mark special occasions, to promote films and sporting events, for charities, and were even commissioned privately in very small runs. Some BT cards were made for HM Prisons. Germany, Japan, and the UK seem to be the hotspots for international collecting. Those made for BT and Mercury are the easiest to collect. Remember, like most plastic collectables, these cards will fade if displayed in direct sunlight.

How much?

The 'Star Trek Voyager' card, made in 1999 and worth £1, at one point could be found for sale at nearly 55 times the face value. The IMRA conference card from 1992 was once valued at several hundred pounds, while the most famous British example is the 100 unit Muirfield Golf Festival card which was once worth thousands.

There are still lots of highly-prized cards. Many of these are the earliest Japanese examples and have made hundreds of pounds in the past. The first Italian cards were kept by the payphone machines when they expired, making them especially hard to find. A standard 1983 card from Taiwan was rumoured to have sold for thousands of pounds once. The eBay site in late 2008 showed whole collections of 150+ cards being sold for £30 or so. The rest of the listings remained unsold.

With so many cards produced there are quite a number of error cards. Much like banknotes or stamps, cards produced with incorrect spelling, the wrong picture, or other quirks are usually more valuable. Look for the rare trial cards too. Remember that the value drops if the card has been used. These might be worth looking at during the credit crunch as a possible investment for the future?

A BT Phonecard: £3–£4 (Martin Breese)

'Magic box pig' from King Bladud's Pigs in Bath – a public art event staged in Bath in 2008, featuring over 100 decorated pig sculptures, all later sold at auction to raise money for the 'Two Tunnels Greenway' cycle route (Paul Buckland)

Pig collectables

Pig collectables are huge. What makes pigs so endearing? Not only are they intelligent (apparently) but, according to the Chinese horoscope, those born in the Year of the Pig (1935, '47, '59, '71, '83 and 1995), are generous-natured, honest, and loyal – traits that are definitely desirable.

What makes a good pig? Look at Miss Piggy – she's attractive, cute, and fun. Translate that into china, glass, silver, jewellery, and even paintings, for top buys. Even George Clooney has been tempted by a pretty porcine – but his is real. There are so many types to choose from that you might decide to stick to one genre (e.g. moneyboxes, or cruets) or even type of pig – Vietnamese are the most fashionable. Prices start from a few pence and go on to several thousand pounds.

How much?

You can pick up a cute pig collectable for as little as 50p at your local car boot sale, or even antiques fair, but the weightier the pig, the higher the value – a good one can cost you around £5,000 – more for a good painting. Three guinea pigs in a basket (a design for a Christmas card by Beatrix Potter), made £12,600 at Bonhams, London, in November 2008.

A limited-edition Cousin Wesley Natwest ceramic piggy bank made by Wade. £170 (Image courtesy of Vectis Auctions)

There are plenty of collectable pigs for under £30 but, with so many pig collectors about, if you like something, buy it quickly – before someone else snaps it up. Look for the novelty wares by Royal Copenhagen, Goebel, Wade, and Carlton Ware. The latter produced a great pig-shaped water-jug (looks like a teapot) which is worth around £75–£100. Studio potters (small potteries such as Basil Matthews and David Sharp) have produced some great piggies, which start from around £30. Royal Doulton flambé pigs are extremely rare and can fetch hundreds of pounds at auction.

One of the top names in the pig collecting business is Wemyss. These were collected by the late Queen Mother. If you can't afford that, why not splash out £30–£50 on their cheaper cousins made by Wemyss' counterpart, Plichta? The most common pig is about 5cm–8cm long and has a thistle or rose painted along its back, with the maker's name on the base.

My advice is not to be a pig and buy up every pig in sight, but to concentrate on better quality ones, or ones by specific makes – moneyboxes are a particularly good buy as they also appeal to moneybox collectors (useful if you change your mind and decide to sell them on – they'll certainly bring in the bacon!) Check out the pigs by Royal Doulton and their sister company Beswick, if you want to buy specific types of pig. Other popular animals include dogs, cats, owls, and elephants, but pigs are the pick of the litter.

These highly collectable toy pigs made by Schuco of Germany were auctioned by Vectis in April 2005 (Rex Features)

A small Wemyss Pig Moneybox (early 20th century). This sold at a Sotheby's auction in August 2005 for £1,104 (Image courtesy of Sotheby's Picture Library)

Wemyss pigs

Scotland's most famous pottery was created at Robert Heron and Sons in Gallatown, Kirkcaldy, Fife, between 1882 and 1928. It is their unusual Wemyss Ware pigs that caught the imagination of the Victorian public. Today, some individual pigs sell for thousands of pounds.

The pigs were initially designed as doorstops and were quite expensive to buy at the time. Their decoration was overseen by a Czech artist called Karel Nekola, who was credited with the attractive, handpainted floral designs which most pigs sport. Other motifs used included cabbage leaves, shamrocks, and thistles. The rustic country style has been imitated by many other firms but hardly surpassed. Beware of quite accurate fakes that are lurking around. If in doubt, consult an expert.

How much?

It's not just the pigs – a sleeping piglet from the early 20th century painted with the thistle motifs, once made £12,575 at a dedicated sale. However, it is quite possible to find fine original pigs for around the £200–£400 mark.

In September 2001, world records tumbled as the auctioneers Sotheby's held a specific sale of Wemyss Ware in Scotland with an astonishing array of pigs up for grabs. The highest amount paid was £16,600 for a single, large pig, from around 1900. This pig was seated on its haunches and had unusual sponged markings.

There are no hard rules when chasing Wemyss pigs. Certainly, the larger ones seem to make far more money – these usually have very 'human' eyes, when compared to the smaller pigs with simple 'dots'. Look out for the pottery's other wares, like washbasins, cats, and even the extremely rare garden seats (an oriental-themed example made £12,650 once).

Pin-ups

Pin-ups became popular during, and immediately after, the Second World War, with the US bomber's 'nose art' – painted-on, scantily-clad, ladies who became mascots. They also appeared on writing kits, issued to GIs abroad with the legend 'Thinking of you – what every Serviceman needs!', written across the pack. These days they have stayed very collectable and are relatively cheap to buy.

Pin-up artwork is most collectable when it is on playing cards. Mostly appearing from the 1950s, these risqué items are now more valuable if they feature paintings instead of photographs. Other items include glass tumblers, calendars, postcards, magazine covers, posters, and photographs. One rule of thumb is that pin-up art should never be gratuitous and, at most, only semi-nude.

How much?

A complete set of pin-up playing cards from the '50s will usually cost you somewhere between £30 and £140. Look for top models, like Bettie Page, as these fetch more on the open market. Also look for products with the '50s starlets from the fashion world, or movies. A set of six tumblers featuring a forces' sweetheart can be picked up for under £45.

When looking for playing cards, try to spot those painted by the top artists of the day – Varga, Petty, Dickens, or Gil Evgren: they're worth more. Marilyn Monroe is the ultimate icon for most collectors. Her image appeared on merchandise, though much of it is modern (see page 90 for information about Marilyn memorabilia).

The innocent golden age of the swimsuit sweetie has passed, though contemporary icons from today will surely be of value in the future: from Jordan to girl-next-door Louise. American icons like Kim Basinger or Cameron Diaz are worth watching. The famous Pirelli calendars continue the tradition, and even fairly modern editions can be worth considerable amounts. Most modern starlets feature on merchandise – collect now, though it may take 40+ years to become desirable.

It isn't just the forces' sweethearts who are in demand – movie stars and glamour girls from decades gone by are also sought-after (TopFoto)

Pirelli calendars

These world-famous calendars are a yuletide gift from tyre-manufacturer Pirelli to promote their company at Christmas time. The first one arrived in 1964 and was the idea of Derek Forsyth of the UK Marketing Department. It has remained a desirable gift ever since, and today good condition, early calendars are quite collectable.

You would be surprised how many people own a copy. The calendar has steadily grown in status, with the world's greatest photographers – like Terrence Donovan, Mario Testino, and Herb Ritts – taking the helm. It has even attracted supermodels such as Naomi Campbell and Kate Moss. It costs over £1 million to put together each year.

How much?

You can't buy a new Pirelli calendar! They provide it each year as an exclusive corporate gift, and it is limited to a worldwide distribution of around 40–45,000 copies to selected customers. They also send it to VIPs and royalty. Prices range from between £20 and £200+ on the secondary market, and a first issue has been sold for £400.

Many consider calendar art to be a follow-on from, and natural successor to, the pin-up 'nose art' of American Second World War bombers and 1950s culture. It is possible to find them cheaply at charity shops, but the word is out on the earlier 1960s editions, and you may have trouble tracking one down. If you have a more recent copy, keep it unopened, safely away from direct sunlight and in a dry place. It will no doubt increase in value, as it probably cost you nothing in the first place!

A collection of vintage glamour items (Image courtesy of Metro Retro)

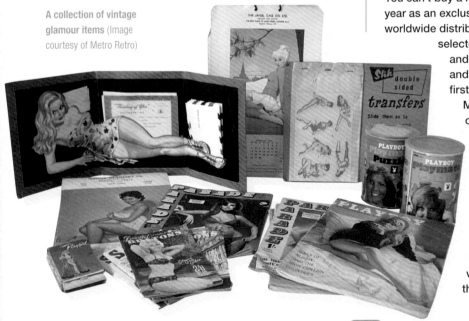

Plastic furniture

It might seem incredible today, but mass-produced plastic furniture was only a development of the 1950s. The problem was that the former wonderstuff, Bakelite, required vast machines to make the smallest items. Today, even smaller moulded plastic furniture, such as chairs, tables, and trolleys from the '70s are now desirable.

The real boom for this stuff was in the 1960s and '70s, with some extremely funky designs appearing in funky people's houses. The clean, space age, or futuristic, feel of so much of it is what makes it so collectable today. The most famous item might be the hanging ball chair, made from transparent plastic and hung from the ceiling. Original versions of these make thousands at international auction.

How much?

The famous white 'Ball (or Globe) Chair' designed by Eero Aarnio in 1963 was used in the cult TV series *The Prisoner*. There's a good chance such items will increase in value as the years pass.

When rummaging through car boots, shops or fairs, always keep your eyes peeled for the top names in fashionable, valuable plastic furniture: Verner Panton, Eero Aarnio, and Steen Ostergaard. All these designers produced some startling and very influential chairs and tables for companies like Olivetti, Knoll, Hille & Co, and Heals of London: all big buck items today. Snap up or dig out any wacky looking plastic chairs and tables; check the maker, and then check with your local auction house if something hot turns up.

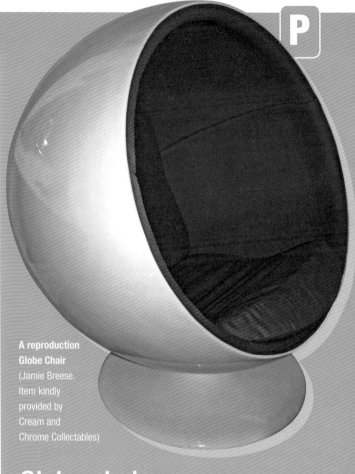

A reproduction Globe Chair (Jamie Breese. Item kindly provided by Cream and Chrome Collectables)

Storage unit (reproduction): £40 (Jamie Breese. Item kindly provided by Cream and Chrome Collectables)

Globe chair

Also known as the 'Ball chair', the 'Globe' was designed in 1962 by modern master craftsman Eero Aarnio. When this chair arrived on the scene it shook the design world, and it has been noted as one of the most influential and radical pieces of furniture of the 20th century.

The first prototype took nearly one year to make in fibreglass. When finished, it was put into production by Asko and quickly became a symbol of the swinging sixties. It gained cult status through featuring in the TV series *The Prisoner*, and in films like *Tommy* and *Dazed and Confused*. The Globe chair is full of surprises. One treat is the way the ball shape swallows the sounds and makes you feel as if you are in a room within a room!

How much?

The original Asko '60s versions cost around £1,500–£3,000 at auction for a standard model. Look for the ultra desirable original chairs with built-in telephones – these are legendary, and will cost you too! Adelta reissued this classic design in the early '90s. Today, you can buy the modern versions, which are all around the £2,000 mark. These are official Eero Aarnio versions.

If you like them, some of Eero's original designs are still in manufacture. You could go for an amazing brand new 'Bubble' chair created in transparent acrylic plastic and designed soon after the Globe in 1968. It literally hangs from the ceiling! They can often be picked up for around £1,000 to £1,500.

Poole Pottery coffee set (1950s/60s): £45 (Jamie Breese.
Item kindly provided by Cream and Chrome Collectables)

Poole Pottery

Pottery has been made in Poole in Dorset since the 19th
century, but it was the early years of the 20th that saw the
factory become one of the best producers of art pottery
in the country, changing its name from Carters to Carter
Stabler Adams, and later becoming Poole Pottery.

Two husband and wife teams, Harold and Phoebe Stabler
and John and Truda Adams, ran the business early on.
All were talented artists and designers in their own right,
and were joined at the factory by many local paintresses
who handpainted all the pots. Pre-war items have a mainly
distinctive floral pattern, but jazzy abstracts were popular
too, and in the 1960s the Delphis range introduced bright,
psychedelic designs.

How much?

Items from all stages of the firm's history are collectable,
and some pieces from the 1960s are worth more than some
from the 1930s, and vice versa. A small floral pot from the
'30s will cost up to £50, as will a small Delphis bowl, but
larger pieces might cost £500+, especially those with rare
designs. For example, a single-edition charger called 'Owl'
from 2000 realised £600 at auction in March 2008.

Collectors will pay large amounts for rare patterns and
designs. Exhibition-size pots are extremely sought after,
and one sold at auction in Wareham, Dorset, in 2001 for a
mighty £19,100.

There are plenty of vases, bowls, and plates by Poole
around, with prices to suit all pockets. Look out for art
pieces signed by Guy Sydenham (GS). They are already
selling well, and in years to come could reach the high
prices people pay for Bernard Leach pottery.

Portmeirion Pottery

Intrinsically linked to the weird and wonderful Portmeirion
development on the edge of Snowdonia, North Wales, this
pottery has become famous and makes for an affordable and
useble collectable of the now.

The pottery was founded in 1960 by Susan Williams-Ellis,
daughter of the architect Sir Clough William-Ellis. It sprung
from Sir Clough's idiosyncratic complex that achieved cult
status as the location for the infamous 'Village' in the 1960s
TV series *The Prisoner*. Later, the pottery was produced
in Stoke-on-Trent, but can still be bought back in 'the
Portmeirion Village' and in fine stores around the world.

How much?

Quite a few pieces are now turning up at auction rooms
around the UK and often sell for more than the cost when
new. The majority of Portmeirion seems to fall conveniently
into the £15 to £40 bracket. There are more desirable gems:
for example, a 'Totem' patterned coffee pot in the later white
colourway makes around £50 at present.

A classic Botanic
Garden water jug from
Portmeirion (Image
courtesy of Portmeirion)

'Little Miss Muffet' plate:
£15 (Jamie Breese. Item
kindly provided by
Cream and Chrome
Collectables)

The most popular design, and one of the best-selling ranges of pottery in the world is the series known as 'Botanic Garden'. During the early 1970s, while looking for inspiration for a new range to succeed 'Totem', Susan chanced upon a rare antiquarian book entitled *The Universal Herbal* by Thomas Green that featured a number of floral images. It is to these that this enormously popular range owes its origins. The plant and insect motifs still grace the plates, cups, and other tableware pieces to this day. Most early pieces cost £10 to £30 each on the secondary market. A Malachite coffee pot sold in November 2008 on eBay.co.uk for a mighty £325. It is regarded as an extremely rare piece and was designed by Susan Williams-Ellis in 1959 and launched in 1960. Because of high manufacturing costs its retail price was high, and it was produced only for a few years.

Keep a look out for the earliest sets from 1963 onwards – they were cylindrical tableware items with the famous 'Totem' pattern and were available in olive green, blue, and an amber colour, although many colourways were trialled. There alreadymis a Portmeirion Collectors' Forum and this popular pottery celebrates its 50th anniversary in 2010 – for collectors this means collectors' exclusive limited-edition items, as well as competitions. For further info, why not visit www.portmeirion.co.uk?

An extremely rare Portmeirion Malachite coffee pot (1960s). This sold on eBay for £325 in November 2008 (Image courtesy of Beryl Wrigley)

Totem Design

The Totem embossed range helped to put Portmeirion Potteries on the map in the early sixties, and today the Totem range of wares has become quite collectable.

Totem was released in 1963 along with Cypher. This was one of Susan Williams-Ellis's earliest creations, and her tableware collection went on to become a design icon of the swinging sixties. The design was produced by cutting abstract shapes into the actual cylinder moulds – stars, spirals and other forms inspired by ancient ceramics. Totem was highly unusual for its time, and was affordable. Examples can now be found in museums, as the Totem design is a classic of its time.

A superb Portmeirion Totem Coffee Pot (Image courtesy of Portmeirion)

How Much?

Prices vary and, as with many collectables, the 'crunch' may see falling prices. In March 2009, a pair of deep green. tall cups and saucers sold for a very affordable £10 on eBay. A large oval plate in blue made £22, while a green Totem coffee pot in good condition attracted 11 bids and sold for £11.50. Hard-to-find colours fetch bigger figures, as is the case with so many good ceramics.

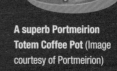

A Portmeirion Totem Milk Jug (above right) and Portmeirion Totem Cup and Saucer (right) (Images courtesy of Portmeirion)

Postcards

Cartology is an increasingly popular pastime, and in recent years the low prices have started to creep up on some items. The Post Office sold the first types, pre-printed with a stamp in the 1870s. It was 1894 when rules were changed to allow companies to make picture cards which could be posted without envelopes. E-mail (with attached digital photos), may well be the death of the postcard, but I sense there will always be nostalgia for the real thing.

Because of the vast diversity of postcards available, collectors tend to home in on particular subjects: travel is the most popular – these are topographical pictures which show a view of a place; transport (aircraft, cars, trains, and ships); politics and satirical cards are also sought after. Unmistakably British are the plethora of seaside postcards (£2–£10 on average), which were produced as the railways made the resorts a popular break for the Victorian and Edwardian family. Look for key name artists such as Donald McGill and Dudley Hardy – these are usually accompanied by a lighthearted poem or joke.

Cat themed
vintage postcards:
£3–£5 the set
(Martin Breese)

How much?

Photographers often set up at resorts and attractions: they would take a photo and sell it to you afterwards so it could be posted. The most valuable examples are those with a historical connection: cards posted from the *Titanic* can be worth £2,000 or more, while those relating to the Suffragette movement are collected in their own right.

Not surprisingly, condition is important to a collector. The message and stamp on the card is less crucial, though they do provide an intriguing snapshot of our social history, particularly those sent from the front during the First World War (often made with embroidered silk).

Postcard collecting is a more accessible area of collectables, as most cards can be picked up cheaply at junk shops, car boot fairs, or one of the many large, dedicated postcard sales. There are also a number of specialist auctions which take place throughout the year. The ideal find would be a collection in a photo album. 1900–1920 was the postcard's golden era, and small collections were treasured.

Postcards have been produced to commemorate all manner of events and places (Getty Images)

Prams

Aside from the more obvious items made for very young people, there is a wealth of other types of wares that were aimed squarely at babies. The pram was just as much a style statement for the parents as it was a comfort ride for their babies.

The word 'pram' is actually short for 'perambulator' which itself was taken from the Latin word, 'ambulare' meaning to walk. Perhaps surprisingly, it wasn't until Victorian times that they actually became popular. These early devices were very much the preserve of the wealthy, and a nanny was almost certainly part of the parcel. Though the poor made makeshift versions from grocers' boxes, the ones worth looking out for today are the best names and largest or most ornate models.

How much?

Though there are quite a few popular manufacturers, in general a fine looking, good condition late-Victorian pram will start at about £100 and occasionally go up to and beyond £500. Some feature the original leather hoods, and sometimes, if you're lucky, you can find a Leveson or Silver Cross. Film and TV props buyers are regular customers of these antiques, as sometimes they have to recreate an Edwardian park scene and need a few dozen at a time.

Prams can be collectable and some smaller models are particularly sought-after by doll collectors for display purposes (iStockphoto)

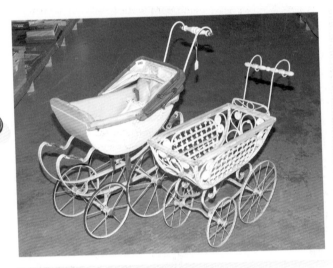

This pair of doll's prams sold for £50 at a Vectis auction in 2007 (Image courtesy of Vectis Auctions)

A Lines Bros Tri-ang Pedigree wooden doll's pram, British, c.1930. This sold for £15 at an auction held at Vectis (Image courtesy of Vectis Auctions)

The ultimate in baby carriages is Sliver Cross. They are known the world over as the Rolls-Royce of the perambulator world. The company started out near Leeds in the 1870s, and today they remain the choice of top celebs and royalty – Posh and Becks, Catherine Zeta Jones and Michael Douglas, Celine Dion, and Princess Caroline of Monaco are all customers. Though modern flagship models cost over a grand today, antique versions for a collector can be picked up at auctions for much, much less.

In general, vintage prams should not be used for their original purpose for safety reasons.

Dolls' prams often cost more today than the larger ones made for real little people. These are often wickerwork and are wheeled away usually by either doll or teddy collectors, and dealers who wish to display their wares. These Victorian or Edwardian dolls' prams usually cost £25–£100 at auction, depending upon condition.

Radios

Britain has a rich history in broadcasting, and consequently in radio design. From the 1920s to the 1950s we were a world leader in valve radio manufacture, with names like Ekco and HMV dominating the market. The BBC made the first broadcasts in the early 1920s, and owning a wireless set soon became the norm. It was crucial during the war years.

Appearing first were the less collectable wooden sets, usually featuring the 'sunburst' motif, and these were followed in the early 1930s by Bakelite plastic designs. The market for most British vintage radios probably peaked in the early 1990s when many classic Bakelite models were fetching well over £1,000. The best US-made 'Air-King' models are, however, still making very serious amounts at auction today.

With any set the shape is important, and the money lies in the larger art deco-inspired models such as the Ekco RS3 or the Defiant M900 which was manufactured by the Co-Op. Models like these are now considered design masterpieces and are particularly sought after. Old radios can be repaired and the valves are still available.

How much?

Straightforward British models can usually be found for £75 to £200 today. Look out for the smaller Second World War era Pye sets, with a plastic 'sunburst' grille. At the time, most were destroyed because of the similarity to the famous Japanese motif – so they're very rare indeed.

The famous 'Round Ekco' radios, such as the AD65 of 1934, are still very collectable. A handful of coloured circular Ekcos were made for exhibition or to order, and these are sought after. Prices would start at £2,500. The American 'Air King' radios, which look like 1930s skyscrapers, come in a variety of colours. Visit the Victoria and Albert and the Design Museums in London to see some classic models.

The early transistor radios are starting to become popular.

A Philco 'People's Set' radio in brown Bakelite cabinet: £350 (Jamie Breese)

The Philco 'People's Set'

This strange object is a Philco radio set. It was given the nickname 'The People's Set' and was designed, according to the manufacturer, to be affordable to the masses. The name sounds ominously like a product of Blairism, but this set has proved to be, along with the fabulous 'round Ekco' radio, one of the greatest radio designs of all time.

It dates from the days of art deco, and appears to have a bit of Flash Gordon, with a liberal sprinkling of neo-Egyptian. The design features lightning bolts straight out of the famous futuristic film *Metropolis*. 'The People's Set' was made of the then new super material, Bakelite, known popularly as 'the material of a thousand uses'. The distinctive streamlined edges were also way ahead of their time.

How much?

Made way back in 1936, a golden era of radio, the sets came in a variety of forms, including battery-operated for those without electrical supplies, and in different wavelengths. They started at around six guineas (£6.6s). This was quite cheap by the day's standards. Today a nice and tidy Bakelite example will sell for £250–£350 at a specialist dealer. These need to be in original condition without any reproduction parts. Check the website of 'On The Air' to find out more – www.vintageradio.co.uk.

'The People's Set' came in either a mottled brown Bakelite cabinet or a slightly more desirable black. Oddly, back then, there was a de-luxe version made from wood, which was far more expensive. Because Bakelite models are more popular today, the pricing has reversed, with a de-luxe having sold fairly recently for a mere £65. A harder to find radiogram version also exists (this featured a gramophone too, and was also wooden).

An Ekco AD36 radio in black Bakelite cabinet will cost at present £600–£750 from a good dealer (Image courtesy of On The Air)

The Bush DAC 90

Here we look at one of the most popular British radios ever made. The Bush DAC 90 has stood the test of time, and remains a design classic which many people will still own, whether it is in the attic or on the sideboard.

This legendary wireless first appeared at the 'Britain Can Make It' exhibition in 1946, towards the end of the golden age of radio design. It originally cost £11.11s and came in three colours: brown (or walnut), black, and ivory (or cream). It was a smash hit and sold by the truckload. At the time its four valves put it at the high end of home user stuff, and the Bakelite plastic (used for the cabinet) was still the wonder material of the age. Through various modifications, it stayed in production for nearly ten years, a feat most home entertainment systems would struggle to achieve these days.

How much?

Sets in a brown cabinet tend to be the most common and as such will cost between £60 and £90 on the high street today. The stylish cream cabinets will cost a bit more, perhaps £90 to £120, and the black cabinets, a bit more still, say £100 to £140.

These sets were very popular and quite hard wearing. Always try to pick a set in the best condition, as you can afford to be a bit fussy. The DAC 90 may be found in second-hand shops, and its distinctive streamlined toaster-like shape is easy to spot. You may pay as little as £20 for a non-working example.

An SH25 radio in brown Bakelite
cabinet (Image courtesy of On The Air)

Landmark Ekco radio

The all-electric Ekco RS3 Consolette was a true landmark design. Back in the days when the wireless was a necessity for every household, along came this groundbreaking machine – one of the first cabinets to be made from the legendary Bakelite. Today it is an affordable museum piece.

Manufactured in 1931 by E. K. Cole Ltd, and standing at around 18in tall, this radio set was not only a technical masterpiece, but also an astonishing design, mixing flavours of the prevalent art deco fashion with motifs of the outgoing art nouveau movement. It was groundbreaking in that it was the first set to actually print the station names on the dial.

How much?

Many of the Ekco radios of the 1930s are popular among collectors and those fancying a touch of class for the front room. An uncracked example of the 1932 version can be picked up from dealers for £500–£650. It cost 24 guineas (£25.4s) back then – a lot of money. A truly mint one was sold for £795 by specialist dealers On The Air. Don't expect to be able to tune in to your favourite FM station – FM wasn't even invented back then!

The RS3 and the SH25 are almost identical and are both truly desirable machines, and are priced as such. However, other great Ekco radios from the same era can be picked up for less. A black AC74 costs between £250 and £350, while a brown AC97 commands £350–450 from a dealer.

Records

Despite the relative demise of vinyl there is still a healthy interest and value in the realm of fantastic plastic. There are two broad categories: 12in (78rpm) classical discs, and 7in (45rpm) rock and pop singles. Emile Berliner patented the flat recording disc in 1887, and later he used a shellac compound for the commercial release of the very first 78rpm record in May 1898. These early 7in discs were of pub singers and other musicians, and were on his own label (which later became HMV, then EMI).

Sadly, around 95% of all 78rpm records are relatively worthless, in monetary terms at least. It is only the single-sided operatic recordings, preferably in a foreign language, which are of most interest to collectors these days. These must also be unscratched, and some knowledge is required to find the treasures. 45rpm singles were created in 1949 and appeared on our shores in the early 1950s. Rock 'n' Roll and Blues singles, often by more obscure artists, are perhaps the most sought after of all. The majority of commercially available smash hits from the era are usually worth £5–£30.

How much?

One of the truly rare, almost mythical classical recordings is the boxed set of seven LPs of Mozart. Entitled *Mozart à Paris* (191/197) and conducted by Fernand Oubradous, this set was released in mono by Pathé Marconi in France in 1956. In April 2008, a US collector paid $11,300 for a near mint condition set.

Possibly the most desirable 7in 45rpm single is 'God Save the Queen' by the Sex Pistols. This was initially released on the A&M label with a black paper sleeve. The band were sacked by the label after just seven days. Copies of the famous 'A&M Redundancy Sweeteners' issue (only 9 or 12 known to be out there) were handed to long-serving A&M executives in a brown mailer as a golden handshake when Polygram closed their London A&M office in 1998. The later, popular Virgin version of the single is worth just a few pounds currently, but one of the former sold on eBay in March 2006 for £12,675!

Again, it is The Beatles who are responsible for the Holy Grail records. A copy of their *The Beatles Yesterday And Today* album with the infamous 'butcher' cover and still sealed in its original packaging once sold for $38,500 in a US auction. Capitol Records' original cover depicted the band in white coats with lumps of meat and bits of dolls. The album was quickly recalled from stores, but quite a few got out there.

Look out, too, for the early Elvis 7in 45s on the yellow Sun Record label: mint examples make many hundreds of pounds. This is a truly vast field in collecting, and a degree of expert knowledge is required to navigate the fairs, shops, auctions, and sites.

Rock 'n' Roll records

In its heyday, there were two types of rock 'n' roll single: the older 78rpm and the 45rpm discs. 78s from the late 1950s are rare and now more valuable. In general, with the most sought-after rock 'n' roll singles, the demo (or promotional copy) is actually worth less than the sold-in-the-shops version.

When purchasing for love or money, remember the presence of a 'tri-centre' (the centre piece, often removed when using a jukebox) is very important with these discs, as is the general condition of the surface and label. A few scratches on a mint disc can drop the value by a half. Original sleeves are nice but less crucial.

How much?

The most famous rock 'n' roll record remains 'Rock Around the Clock' (1955) by Bill Haley and the Comets. First released on the Brunswick label, it makes around £5 on a 78rpm disc and £30 on a 45. At the other end of the scale, early Elvis 45s, such as 'Heartbreak Hotel' (on a label known as HMV Golds) can make £300–£400. A copy of Presley's 'That's All Right' on the Sun label, described as 'better than near mint' condition, sold for $11,000 not so long ago.

The most sought-after record Is quite possibly 'Walking the Blue' by Willie Dixon. Issued on the famous London American label (gold letters on black), it can make as much as £2,500 in mint order. The Penguins' version of the doo-wop classic 'Earth Angel' is hot to this day. Nearly 15,000 doo wop bands recorded in that era. The Penguins were a Californian outfit that formed in 1954 and disbanded in 1959. Recorded in their garage, 'Earth Angel' was their greatest legacy, and on a 45 in mint condition, it can make a mighty £1,000–£1,500.

Led Zeppelin are considered one of the great rock acts of the 20th century, and anything signed by them is desirable. This is a rare, signed, French-edition Led Zeppelin III album sleeve (Getty Images)

A group of 78rpm records
(Image courtesy of Metro Retro)

78rpm records

It's time to set the record straight! One of the questions I get asked, as an expert, relates to classical 78rpm records. At any given time, and at any auction or car boot sale, you will find boxes of them.

Their original mass production, size, and weight, coupled with enthusiasts preferring a classical recording on CD, means that about 90% are usually worth nothing financially, certainly in the UK market. There are approximately 600 serious collectors around the world who will pay, but only for the most rare 78s. Sought-after examples tend to be classical opera recorded in a foreign language and single-sided only (i.e. from 1898 to 1923).

How much?

Early recordings by Angelica Pandolfini (she only made four records) are generally worth between £1,500 and £1,800+. The most desirable 78 of hers, however, would be the 1903 recording of *Chanson de Florian*, and this makes up to £5,000. A collector recently found a copy in an Italian car boot sale for 50p. The most famous rock 'n' roll record, 'Rock Around the Clock', makes around £5 on a 78rpm disc.

The Beatles, as the Quarrymen, recorded a version of 'That'll be the Day' on a 78rpm acetate pressing in 1958. This is the world's rarest and most valuable record, and was bought by Paul McCartney in 1981. He reportedly made 50 special copies for friends for Christmas – these have been valued at over £10,000 a piece.

As with 45rpm records, condition is very important. Mint, or even unplayed, is infinitely preferable. Almost all violin and piano recordings are worth nothing. Enrico Caruso is worth a lot of money on the Zonophone label, but on HMV is worth very little.

Elvis memorabilia

Since The King's death, items relating to him have become ever more sought after. There have been dedicated sales at which fans have clamoured for one-off items, and prices have rarely been higher for original items.

There are too many types of collectables to list, but categories include: rare singles – early Elvis 45rpm records such as 'Heartbreak Hotel' (on a label called HMV Golds) can make £400 or more; merchandise (e.g. a plastic guitar with a facsimile signature makes £600); handwritten lyrics (his lyrics for 'Mississippi River' sold for £19,550 in 1996); and over £7,000 was once paid for a paperweight that was presented to Elvis by the Beverly Hills Police.

How much?

In 1999, a three-day Elvis auction was held at the MGM Grand Hotel in Las Vegas. Organised by Lisa Marie Presley, it featured over 2,000 original items and made several million pounds. Items included a signed credit card (over £7K), his 1956 Lincoln Continental (around £167K), a guitar plectrum (over £6K), and his first piano (around £60K).

Certainly, handwritten lyrics to his songs, important stage costumes, personal vehicles, and guitars top the wish list of any fan or museum. Two examples: in 1993, an American collector paid £99,000 at Christie's for an acoustic guitar used by The King, and in 1999, somebody paid nearly £20,000 for a 1970 stage shirt made for him.

You are unlikely to uncover Elvis's guitar at a car boot sale, but his timeless appeal means genuine, personally-used memorabilia is less likely to drop in value than other acts.

A superb signed photograph of Elvis on a motorbike
(Image courtesy of Fraser's Autographs)

Robots

There is still quite a vibrant market in toy robots. Collectors look to recapture their youth, and the prices at one point almost went into outer space. The term 'robot' was supposedly coined by the Czech, Karel Capek, in the early 1920s. The launch of Sputnik in 1957 started a worldwide Sci-Fi craze, and robots became hot toys.

Almost all of the vintage robots were produced in Japan by companies like Yoshiya and Nomura. One of the first robots was the 'Lilliput', which was made in Japan in the early 1940s. The earliest robots are fairly crude and very difficult to find in A1 condition. With widespread manufacture at the start of the '50s, more mechanical parts were included and wonderful colours were used. Their demise came in the late 1960s with changes in toy laws relating to the metal and paint which were used in their manufacture. If you discover an old tin example, do not overwind it or keep batteries inside (they rot), and seek specialist advice. The presence of a box increases the value tremendously.

Part of a collection of vintage toy robots and space toys sold by Christie's in September 2005. The complete collection was sold for over £200,000 (Peter Macdiarmid/Getty Images)

How much?

'Robbie', based on the character from the classic 1957 movie *The Forbidden Planet*, is the most popular robot, and is produced in two colours – black and silver. Known as 'The Mechanical Robot', it was made by Nomura, and in 2000 a rare silver version, complete, sold for $11,400 in the USA.

More affordable toys like a 'Dalek' (friction-controlled *Doctor Who* toy) from 1963, or the radio-controlled 'R2 D2' from the movie *Star Wars*, can be found for around £100, or £150 in a box.

There are a number of examples which will still be hidden away in lofts – somewhere. The 'Gang of Five' by Masudaya included 'Machine Man', who sold at the end of the '90s for over £25,000. In June 2007, Christie's sold a Yonezawa battery-operated 'Mr Robot' for a more affordable £840.

The traditional vintage robots are now available as reproductions. A possible investment for the future could be the more recent Japanese-produced robotic toy dogs and cats. 'Nikko the Cyber Dog' is a good example. There are specialist dealers, fairs, and specialist toy auctions held at larger salerooms.

'Machine Man' sold for £25,000 in July 1999 at Christie's (Image courtesy of Christie's Images Ltd 2008)

'Mr Zerox Robot' by Horikawa. He made £220 in December 2005 (Image courtesy of Vectis Auctions)

Robbie the Robot

This fabulous toy was from the groundbreaking Science Fiction adventure movie *The Forbidden Planet* of 1956. It is an exceptionally iconic collectable – not only was 'Robbie the Robot' the star of the hit film, but he was made at the dawn of space travel, with the launch of Sputnik a year after the film's release.

This legendary toy was made mainly by Nomura Toys of Japan from 1956 onwards. Probably for copyright reasons, they were always given different, often bizarre-sounding names, such as 'The Mechanical Robot' or 'Action Planet Robot'. The Japanese dominated the market until robot popularity waned in the 1970s. 'Robbie' helped to start a worldwide craze for all things Sci-Fi, and he is still an enduring image for the children of the post space-race world.

How much?

If you have the larger 12.5in model and he's complete and clean, with the clear plastic domed helmet, you could be talking £2,000+ today. The pistons in his head move and light up, and his antennae swivel as he walks. Look for examples with the delicate rubber hands intact; and the box, as with all toys like this, is worth nearly as much as the robot!

Robbie is still the undisputed King of the Robots, and his price has more than doubled in the last ten years or so. More affordable robots to look out for include C-3PO from the very first *Star Wars* toy range in 1978: the small figure in clear packaging can make hundreds, the larger toy, over £300 in a box.

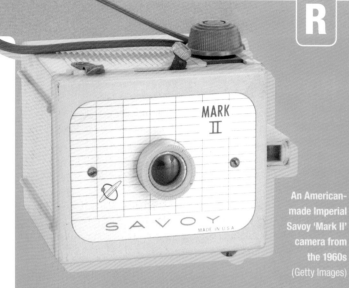

An American-made Imperial Savoy 'Mark II' camera from the 1960s
(Getty Images)

This 'Mechanized Robot' made £1,200 at Vectis
(Image courtesy of Vectis Auctions)

Retro

Over the last few years there has been a boom in all things 'retro', and a host of fascinating books have been published to shine light on this colourful part of the collectables and design world.

Retro is a broad term which covers all manner of objects from the recent past. There is no fixed time period, but it is fair to say that objects made from the '50s to the late '80s would comfortably fall into this bracket. Retro items also need to have something a little colourful or iconic about them, whether it be a kitsch lampshade or a lava lamp. Ceramic items such as the Homemaker tableware by Ridgeway is included, as are the tabletop electronic video games of the late '70s and early '80s. Telephones are a good example too: the comparatively recent 700 series phones and the culty Ericofons are top of the wish list for many retro addicts. See page 136 for more information on these colourful collectables.

How much?

Fortunately, most retro collectables fall comfortably into the sub £100 price bracket, though there are many exceptions. A classic framed print of the Chinese Girl (commonly known as 'The Green Lady') by Tretchikoff was a best seller in the '70s, and today a good example costs £50–£75. A nice Homemaker dinner plate costs £20–£25 from a specialist dealer, while a wholly retro Atari 2600 video games console will set you back around £90, together with some games. A good dealer should have a wide offering of wares, from chrome soda siphons to retro lampshades and plastic furniture.

If you research the subject you can build up a great collection quite cheaply. The three biggest groups of buyers are those in their 30s and 40s affected by a big dose of nostalgia, those who appreciate classic design, and those who want to finish their funky homes with an array of iconic wares: they make great talking points. For more information, contact Cream and Chrome Collectables at www.creamandchrome.co.uk

Rock and Pop memorabilia

The values attached to items of pop memorabilia took the world of antiques and collectables by storm. Unlike other collecting crazes, the desirability of this most eclectic of subject matters seems set to last, as it is so much part of Western culture, and there are huge doses of nostalgia mixed in with it all too. The rock star is certainly a modern phenomenon, yet prices for some exceptional items, particularly those closely associated with an idol, can far surpass those attached to, say, a rare piece of furniture. Since the early 2000s, key items belonging to Kurt Cobain, for example, have become extremely valuable. The surge in collectability began in the 1980s and has steadily increased, as have many of the prices.

The most collectable bands are The Beatles and The Rolling Stones, and solo artists such as Madonna, Elvis, Jimi Hendrix, Eric Clapton, and even Michael Jackson still, can all fetch gob-smacking amounts. Whether the credit crunch is going to stamp down on the greatest gems in this category, only time will tell. Certainly, some items are still grabbing the headlines with high prices – Jimi Hendrix's Fender Stratocaster, the first he burnt on stage – sold for £280,000 at The Fame Bureau and Idea Generation auction in September 2008.

Look for (in order of importance): musical instruments played by the star; handwritten lyric sheets; items of personal clothing (especially if worn on a landmark video or tour); Gold and Platinum discs; original album artwork; personal letters; signed records and photos, and lastly promotional items and ephemera (concert programmes, tickets, etc.).

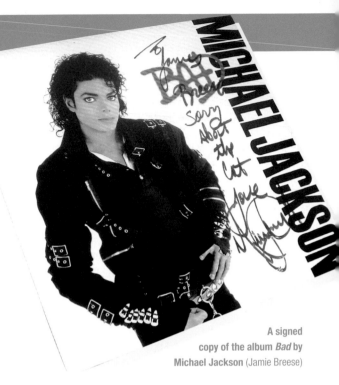

A signed
copy of the album *Bad* by
Michael Jackson (Jamie Breese)

The original handwritten lyrics to
Michael Jackson's 'Beat It' (Image
courtesy of Sotheby's Picture Library)

A one-off Stagg guitar, in sunburst finish, signed in silver ink by John Paul Jones, the body signed in black felt pen by Roger Waters, Nick Mason, David Gilmour, Jimmy Page, Charlie Watts, and Ronnie Wood, as well as by Robert Plant in gold ink. Accompanied by a letter concerning the provenance: £8,950 (Image courtesy of Fraser's Autographs)

Gone for a song!

One of the great memorabilia bargains of the last ten years was bagged at auction in 2007 by an anonymous private bidder for his six-year-old daughter. That lucky girl was given the chance to practise her piano skills on the very same piano that a certain pop classic was composed upon.

The old Chappell upright Joanna was the former property of a certain James Blunt and was used by him to compose his number one hit 'You're Beautiful' and, from the same *Back to Bedlam* album, 'Goodbye my Lover'.

How much?

I don't know how this little gem slipped through the net, but I can guarantee that in a few years a theme café or museum will be trying to track down this little girl with a big bag of wonga. Surely it has to be worth three or four times the £1,200 that the bidder paid at Bonhams in London in July 2007. The piano was sold with the two-bedroom London flat that the singer/songwriter – whose real name is Blount – lived in with his sister, and was mentioned in the deeds.

The big hit love ballad 'You're Beautiful' reached No. 1 on the American Billboard Hot 100 in 2006, making Blunt the first British artist to top the US singles chart for nearly a decade. The song has now become a wedding favourite, and 'Goodbye my Lover' one of the most popular funeral songs. Life and death encapsulated for so many in two songs created on one piano.

Marc Bolan's guitar

Marc Bolan, the immensely influential T-Rex lead singer, died in a car crash at just 29 years of age. He was one of the major glam rock stars of the early 1970s. A Gibson Flying V electric guitar, used by Bolan in the 1970s, was sold in 2007 and made a big noise.

A few years ago I was lucky enough to be able to take on to ITV1's *This Morning*, Jimi Hendrix's very own 'Flying V' guitar called 'Flying Angel'. This was used extensively in the studio, and live at the Rainbow Bridge, Atlanta Pop, Isle of Wight, and Paris Olympia concerts, among others. It was insured for one million pounds!

How much?

The Gibson was one of the flamboyant Flying V electric guitars used by stars of the era and, occasionally, of today. It was a model made in 1970 and used by Bolan on many occasions, including on *Top Of The Pops* in 1972, while performing his hit single 'Get It On'. The pre-sale estimate had been £30,000–£50,000. It sold at a special Pop Memorabilia auction held at Christie's, South Kensington, in April 2007 for £36,000.

On the same day, an elaborate stage costume worn by David Bowie for his last performance as Ziggy Stardust, at The Marquee Club in London, sold for £10,800. The estimate had been £4,000–£6,000. Another lot included was a long cloak costume worn on stage by Freddie Mercury during Queen's 1986 European tour.

A 10inx8in colour, photograph of Kylie from her famous music video, sporting the defining gold short shorts: **£175** (Image courtesy of Fraser's Autographs)

Pop star dolls

Pop star dolls are older than you might think, and some vintage mini icons have become sought after. With any new band, the big question for many fans and toy collectors is 'do we buy two sets, one for fun and one for the treasure chest?'

Dolls of The Beatles dominate the high end of the market, not surprisingly. There are dozens to pick from and prices vary enormously. For example, you can pay £35 for a single Beatle doll by Rosebud, or £120 for a set of four 13in blow-up dolls which were available by coupon from packets of Lux soap. For a '70s revival, look out for the Abba dolls made by Matchbox toys in 1978 – these are worth up to £80. Condition is vital for achieving top prices. The packaging's cellophane window remaining intact is useful and the box condition is often given a grade by dealers.

How much?

A Cher in a box from the '70s by Mego will set you back £70, or why not look out for Boy George, made by LJN in 1984 (circa £150). Another version was made by Sharpendale and now makes £70. Donny and Marie Osmond were available in one gift box from Mattel in 1976. They now make £50.

The 8in Beatles 'Bobb'n Head' dolls made by Car Mascot Inc. are perhaps the ultimate pop star figures. A complete and boxed set was sold by Bonhams in December 2007 for £480. The 14in versions are even harder to come by.

In July 1984, LJN Toys Ltd created the first of five Michael Jackson dolls. Standing 12in tall, these can make £100, proving that even popular dolls in mint condition can sometimes increase in value. The Spice Girl dolls, available in different guises made by Galoob, could be hot some day; so could the various boy/girl band dolls by Vivid Imaginations. After 13 bids on eBay £40 was paid for a single 'Girl Power' doll. This was the hardest to acquire Sporty Spice. The 'Viva Forever' Spice Girls dolls made by Hasbro in 1999 are quite rare and relate to one of the band's most enduring recordings. A set sold on ebay.co.uk for £119 in 2007.

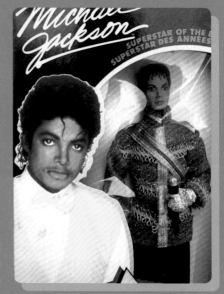

A Michael Jackson doll (Jamie Breese)

Rocking horses

Wooden rocking horses have long been admired by both children and adults. In the 1700s they were provided to teach riding positions to the children of the very wealthy. They came of age, however, in the Victorian and Edwardian period of around 1880 to 1930 which is considered the golden era for design. Like musical boxes, these magical items were often seen as a sign of prosperity among the emerging middle classes in Victorian Britain.

One of the very oldest horses was said to have belonged to Charles I in the early 17th century. The most popular is the English 'Dappled Grey' type. Famous makers to look out for include F. H. Ayres and G. & J. Lines Ltd, both of London, and the top German makers like W. Graeffer. There are generally two sizes (medium and large) though miniature horses can be found. Early horses were made with 'bow rockers' and the 'safety stand' (also known as trestle base) followed in the late 19th century. Pedal cars marked the demise of the mass popularity of the horse, but they are still used today.

How much?
The rocking horses that will set you back the most are those that are in the very best, original condition. These are prized antiques, and top manufacturers like those mentioned above start at a grand in good nick. Antique but home-made horses, made with wood off-cuts, can be picked up for a few hundred quid, while around £600 will secure a classic Dapple Grey from the '20s made by a good maker like Collinson & Sons.

Original condition rocking horses by F. H. Ayres tend to be the most desirable. £5,000 or upwards is not unheard of for fine examples. A professional restoration adds dramatically to the auction value in many cases. It's a very specialised job, where hair, paint, joints, and leather are carefully restored.

Modern replicas, or original designs, are available today, and the finest examples by firms like Stevenson Brothers can easily make several grand. A cheaper alternative is to invest in a smaller tinplate horse from the '50s or '60s (these can be picked up for under £100), or consider Hobby Horses which cost even less for more modern examples.

Royal Doulton figurines

Possibly the most famous British collectable of the 20th century, the Doulton figurines, have inspired collectors for generations. The firm was founded by John Doulton in 1815 when he set up in Lambeth, London. Doulton began to produce the figurines from St George's Day in 1913: this was the day King George V and Queen Mary visited. After several thousand creations, the figurines were still made until recently. Dating and identification are quite easy with the clear HN registration number on the base of most pieces.

How much?
Prices vary enormously according to the character. At one point the 'Myths and Maidens' set (HN2825-9) from 1982–86 was worth over £8,000. Very few figurines can be found for under £30. Another rare piece is HN33, called 'An Arab' – it was designed by Charles Noke and painted by Eric A. Webster in around 1920. It's currently worth a mighty £2,000. The 'Sunshine Girl' (HN1348), holding a parasol, was valued in 2008 at £1,800–£2,400.

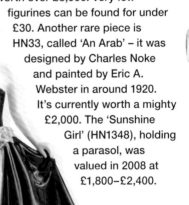

A Lady Jester figurine (HN1221) sold for £2,820 at Sotheby's (Image courtesy of Sotheby's Picture Library)

A bone china 'Pretty Ladies' time-limited edition, 'Olivia' (HN 5114) 'Figure of the Year 2008', modelled by John Bromley: £147 (Image courtesy of Royal Doulton/Wedgwood)

The Old Balloon Seller

Arguably the most famous ceramic figure ever produced, this legendary piece was produced by Royal Doulton and has stood the test of time. Almost everybody knows somebody who has one, and the colour and charm of the piece has entertained generation after generation.

The Old Balloon Seller was designed by Lesley Harradine and was first released in 1929. It has the special registration number of HN1315. Only recently, in 1998, was she discontinued. She was one of a series of street seller figurines, but her popularity ensured that she outlived all her contemporaries.

How much?

In 1999, Royal Doulton brought back our seller in a different colourway for a special set of events hosted by Michael Doulton, the great-great-great-grandson of the founder, John Doulton. This special figure sells for over £150 today. The original figures tend to make around £100 on average from a collectables dealer, if in good condition, and a bit more if mint.

Interestingly, one of the rarest of all the Doulton figurines is also holding balloons: she is called 'Folly' and has an art deco appearance, a cone-shaped hat and a short skirt. She was Model No. HN1750 and is worth £1,000–£1,500 if early and unrestored.

Buyers don't tend to mind so much whether they have the older Balloon Sellers or not. The older models were earthenware, but in the mid-1960s they were made with English translucent china – porcelain. All in all, a timeless, charming collectable.

'The Old Balloon Seller': £100 (Image courtesy of Royal Doulton/ Wedgwood)

Rubik's Cube: £10 (Jamie Breese. Item kindly provided by Cream and Chrome Collectables)

Rubik's Cube

This will be a blast from the past for most readers. The tiny coloured cube, created by accident, took the world by storm and proved to be the ultimate fad, outliving most toys and spawning a whole industry, and even championships. Today, the '80s retro trend makes an original cube a desirable collectable. Have you still got yours?

The cube was actually created in Hungary in 1974 by Erno Rubik, but didn't take off until it appeared at the main international toy fairs in 1980. It benefited from massive press interest and the demand was vast worldwide. It won the 1980 Toy of the Year Award and managed to last several years as a number one must-have. The number of possible combinations of Rubik's Cube is a mind-bending 43,252,003,274,489,856,000. Over 100 million Cubes were sold between 1980 and 1982 alone. Not many are unopened.

How much?

If you want to get collecting, why not opt for a truly retro Rubik's Cube Atari 2600 console game cartridge? This didn't sell well at the time and commands £50 today. There is a rare Charles and Diana cube to track down. The cube bears a picture of Diana on one side and a picture of Charles on the other, together with images of the Union Jack. This makes £25–£40 in good shape and boxed. A standard 1980 mint cube unopened and sealed can make £40–£50.

For the real fan, you can pick up a Rubik's Cube lighter and ashtray combo. These are typical kitsch, and affordable at about £4 or £5. Cheapest of all, but essential for any true collector, would be the series of Teach Yourself books and spin-off puzzles which followed, such as the Rubik's Barrel and the Magic Rings of 1986.

Rugby collectables

English rugby has come a long way since William Webb Ellis first picked up a football and ran with it at Rugby School many years ago. There is no doubt that from Downing Street to the man in the street, English rugby has been undergoing a new era of popularity. It is quite possible that the collectables market may be subject to the price increases that English football memorabilia saw in the 1990s.

Touch judge's flag, England v. France, 1911 (Image courtesy of World Rugby Museum, Twickenham)

How much?

Anything could happen, given the excitement around our triumphant World Cup victory a few years ago. Rugby has been a collectable field, but always subordinate, pricewise, to football, golf, and equestrian memorabilia. You can now imagine autographed items, especially clothing, balls and World Cup match-worn attire to appreciate. Keep any World Cup mementoes safe for the future. The autograph value to watch out for is that of fly-half hero Jonny Wilkinson. An autographed print of Jonny playing Australia in 2002 sold for £7,000 in 2003, though charity auction prices aren't always reflective of true market values. His autograph on a good, clean portrait will now be worth £150–£200. Signed team souvenirs will also cost a premium.

A replica white England rugby shirt featuring over 20 signatures in bold black felt pen from the 2004 winning squad is up for grabs at the time of writing (late 2008) from autograph specialists Fraser's (www.frasersautographs. com) for £1,250. Signatures include Martin Johnson, Jonny Wilkinson, Iain Balshaw, and Stuart Abbott.

The most cherished item? Film director Mel Smith, at a charity auction in London on the evening of the squad's World Cup win, paid £20,000 for an England rugby shirt signed by the team.

With antique items, it tends to be things which pre-date 1930 that are generally more sought after. If you can find complete and early sets of cigarette cards, then you could be talking big bucks. The same goes for good condition, early photographs. Signed rugby almanacs are a specialist area too. Old programmes are considered most collectable. The one to look for is the Wales v. New Zealand game of 1905. There are plenty of ceramic items to seek out: a fabulous Doulton Lambeth stoneware lemonade jug from 1883 is worth £700+.

To see some of the finest rugby memorabilia in the world, you could visit The Museum of Rugby in Twickenham, London (www.rfu.com/ museum). They display the Webb Ellis Cup from the Rugby World Cup 2003. The original Webb Ellis trophy was returned to the International Rugby Board (IRB) in November 2005. This smaller version pictured was given to the Rugby Football Union (RFU) by the IRB, to be retained permanently.

A replica England rugby shirt featuring over 20 signatures in black felt pen ink from the 2004 winning squad sold, together with a letter of provenance from O₂ (the sponsors of the team) for £1,250 (Image courtesy of Fraser's Autographs)

Webb Ellis Cup, the Rugby World Cup 2003 Trophy (Image courtesy of World Rugby Museum, Twickenham)

The 1985 Sinclair C5 electric vehicle was ahead of its time. Entirely pollution-free, it had a range of 20 miles (40 miles with an optional second battery) (Keystone/Getty Images)

Sinclair C5

The C5 electric car was invented by Sir Clive Sinclair in 1985. Its range was about 20 miles, and it went up to a jaw-dropping 15mph, and you didn't need a licence to drive it. This little gem was only in production for one and a half years, yet they still managed to shift 19,000 of them. Today, mint examples are hard for enthusiasts to find.

Amazingly, they were designed so that the driver's head would be at the same height as a Mini driver's, and higher than a Ferrari! A modified model was once taken up to a world record 150mph! Despite this they didn't require a licence, were charged at home overnight, and were environmentally ahead of their time.

How much?

A basic model C5, in fine condition, might today go for between £400 and £600 to the right, keen buyer. The car, despite the stories at the time, is still considered by some to have been a true attempt at futuristic mass transportation, and is certainly a real icon of the 1980s. A top-notch condition example has proved to be a good investment in the past.

They were sold originally for as little as £200, but now, if boxed, in mint condition and with all the optional accessories (such as wing mirrors, safety flag, and raincover) specialist dealers can ask for £1000+. It is said that a gold-plated one was once created for a wealthy businessman!

Sinclair are still making all sorts of unusual things – a power unit for push bikes, and wheelchairs, etc. Occasionally C5s turn up at car boot sales and in the free ads in the papers. Remember that Sinclair's mint and boxed executive calculators, ZX80s and ZX81s, have all started to become collectable in recent years.

Sindy

Barbie is the doll which most people think of as being the most collectable fashion doll. However, Sindy has started to gain in popularity, and some of the prices for good condition and boxed examples are surprisingly high.

Sindy was first introduced in 1963 by the British Pedigree Company. In 1986 she was sold to Hasbro, but it is the pre-Hasbro items which are most collectable. Sindy had a sister ('Patch'), a boyfriend ('Paul'), and endless costumes and accessories. She even had her own TV studio set.

How much?

There are quite a few dolls which are sought after and attract high amounts. For example, her friend 'Gayle' can make around £150 in top condition, and the doll called 'Spring Time' is considered extremely rare and can make great money if mint. There is even a 'McDonalds Sindy' made in the 1980s.

There are several other gems to look for, though most collectors would say that her French friend 'Mitzi', if found with blonde hair, is the rarest of all. This would be worth hundreds of pounds in mint condition. Look for the number one doll: there are several variations of hair colour. One such early boxed Sindy with auburn hair and real eyelashes realised £160 at Vectis toy auctions in July 2007.

The dolls made by Hasbro mostly make between £20 and £40 if in their box, and the box is in great condition. These might gradually increase in price, though the early examples will always be worth more. Search Internet auction sites and car boot sales, but remember, even a tear in the box's cellophane window can reduce values.

This Pedigree 'Walking Sindy' doll from 1970 realised £820 in July 2004 (Image courtesy of Vectis Auctions)

Smurfs

One of the most collected toys in the 1970s and '80s were the little blue people! Millions and millions were sold to both children and adult collectors. Today there is still a demand, and a trade, in these miniature figures – prices ranging from a few quid to several hundred pounds.

The first appearance of the Smurfs, created by the Belgian illustrator Pierre Culliford – also known as Peyo – came in 1958. They were known originally as Schtroumpfs, and were cast as extra characters in the story *The Flute with the Six Holes*. Interestingly, the tiny figurines were widely collected for years before the creation of the famous cartoon series in 1981. This really put them on the global map, with 256 episodes made. This fever was added to with a number of best-selling records too.

How much?

A typical Smurf sells from 50p to £4. The most desirable figures tend to be the hard-to-find promotional figurines. Around 130 are known of. One such design was a BP promotional Smurf. There are also some rare Jubilee editions out there, and figures which were painted in the wrong colours in the factory. Look out for the ultra-sought-after winged Smurf clutching a gift, and the 'I love New York' Smurf holding a big apple. One to spot now is the limited-edition 40th anniversary boxed set that was released in 1998 and featured the Smurfs as a rock band, together with a stage! 'Smurf Praying' and 'Smurfette Praying' will cost around £125 each from a good dealer.

There are also many variations to look out for, including 'Super Smurfs', and boxed sets made more recently. Smurfs are still made today under the guidance of Peyo's son, and we usually see around five or six new additions each year. They are still a huge business with collectors' clubs all over the world, and in just a three-year period in the late '90s over 10 million copies of Smurf CDs were sold worldwide!

A boxed Smurfs plastic and tinplate drum set.
£50–£60 (Image courtesy of Vectis Auctions)

A late twentieth-century snowglobe featuring the Grimm brothers' Hansel & Gretel story (Getty Images)

Snowglobes

One of the most delightful of all antiques must be a fine glass snowglobe. For some, however, they are more familiar as cheap souvenirs. Also known as 'snowdomes', 'blizzard weights', and 'snowies', collecting really took off in the 1980s. These have a certain fascination for collectors of all ages. The earliest examples may be the rarest, but the multitude of different designs makes them an ideal and affordable collectable.

Did you know that the snow inside the first domes was created using fragments of bone, or even particles of porcelain? These intricate, handmade early versions emerged in France during the 19th century and were a development of the ornate glass paperweight. It wasn't until the 1870s that the business began to take off. They quickly became popular in England, and in the '50s plastic versions appeared and paved the way for mass-produced holiday souvenirs. Possibly the most famous snowglobe is the one dropped by Orson Welles in the opening scene of what some critics regard as the greatest movie of all time – *Citizen Kane*. The actual ones used were made by the top Austrian firm, Perzy. Later they made special domes for the Clinton inauguration, which contained the authentic confetti from the event.

How much?

The prices vary enormously. The German examples made from plastic in the '50s are generally considered the most desirable of the modern types. A 1960s dome featuring 'Raggedy Ann' holding a dome in her lap makes about £60 to £80. Most souvenir and travel-related ones can be picked up for a few pounds. The earlier French designs, such as the one produced to show off the Eiffel Tower in 1889, are worth a few quid, but the handmade true glass examples with ceramic bases can make several hundred pounds if the right collector is interested.

Today, there is a huge array of snowglobes to seek out. Most serious collectors have a dedicated room! They cover every conceivable subject: for example, there is a new *Star Wars* globe to celebrate Episode III. Featuring Darth Vader, it cost about £10 new a few years ago. Snowglobes can also include music boxes, like many of the Disney items (collectable), and even electric motors that make the 'snowstorm'.

Snowman

Our own homegrown animated hero is a timeless classic and a rival to Disney in the nation's hearts. What you may not know is that a collectable that once saw the biggest price rise was one of the wonderful 'Snowman' figurines: their secondary market values literally snowballed – then dipped again.

The enchanting story by author and artist Raymond Briggs was first published in 1978. In 1982 the equally magical short film appeared, introduced by none other than rock legend David Bowie. The figurines sprang from the creative minds of potters extraordinaire – Royal Doulton – and between 1985 and 1994 23 different studies were released to eager fans and collectors alike. They cost just £12 each.

How much?

Prices peaked a few years ago – they couldn't go any higher. The most extraordinary rise was in the hard-to-find 'Snowman Skiing' study. Since 2001 the designers at Coalport have been producing the Snowman range. The 2004 characters were attractive pieces and more affordable, with prices ranging from between £22.50 and £55 new. The early Coalport studies have done a Doulton too: several of the first editions now make good money. Keep your eye out for the limited-edition pieces, as they are probably a better bet if you are buying for a chance to profit down the line.

A Steiff 'The Snowman Dancing with Teddy', one of a limited edition of 1,500, sold for £90 in 2007 (Image courtesy of Vectis Auctions)

Snowman Skiing

The original 'Snowman' series was produced by Royal Doulton. No. DS21 was a delicate figure of the snowman skiing. They didn't survive the firing process very well and then, when bought, were terribly delicate, with the skis breaking quite easily. The Nos 9–23 figures were all modelled by Warren Platt and designed by Graham Tongue. The 'Snowman Skiing' was produced for just two years between 1990 and 1992.

How much?

In March 2007 one good example commanded £300 on eBay – and that was without its box. It didn't sell well when first released, and the undamaged, boxed ones have made £750+ in the past. As time passes, maybe he will make it back up the slope. An auction house might sell a great example today for £150–£250.

As with all such figurines, you need to watch for small hairline cracks. These do occur over time, and collectors will pay over the odds for truly unaffected examples. They should always be cleaned gently with a light washing-up liquid, and keeping the boxes to these collectables really does help when it comes to selling them on.

A pristine example of the Royal Doulton 'Snowman Skiing' figure (Image courtesy of Christie's Images Ltd 2008)

Glossy 19.5inx13in Robert Madden photo on its original mount with the caption 'We Came in Peace For All Mankind', the image depicting the Apollo 11 crew in the quarantine van following the completion of their mission, signed in black felt tip on the mount by Neil Armstrong, M. Collins, and Buzz Aldrin: £9,500 (Image courtesy of Fraser's Autographs)

Space memorabilia

This is a new and exciting field. The big bucks go on the one-off space and lunar used pieces. It's the American items that are rare and more valuable than their Russian counterparts. This is a fascinating and rapidly expanding market. Wise investments now could prove profitable in the future.

The big auction houses showed interest in the 1990s: Sotheby's had their first sale of space memorabilia in New York in November 1993. Christie's also joined the Space Race and had an important sale back in 1999 featuring one of Neil Armstrong's Apollo spacesuits and some very rare items from the Soviet space programme. Collectors are particularly interested in items relating to the ill-fated Challenger mission. Prices for these rarities are often very high. For those on a smaller budget, space toys from the late 1950s and 1960s are a developing area, especially tin plate vintage robots (e.g. 'Robbie the Robot'), ray guns, and spaceships. Boxed and mint is crucial with these items.

How much?

Surprisingly, some of the highest figures paid out have been for replica models of famous craft, some made as movie props. These frequently command more than £10,000. Actual suits worn in space start at tens of thousands because of their historic importance and rarity. Pieces from all the Apollo missions are highly collectable: items from Apollo 9 are Holy Grails for many treasure hunters. The ill-fated Apollo 1, and movie-made-famous 13, are also highly sought after. You don't have to spend a fortune to get in on the action: I've seen a section of Space Shuttle enclosed in plastic sell for £280. Autographed items by any astronaut are accessible, with Neil Armstrong topping many wish lists. Autograph experts suggest a value of £5,500 for a fine signed photograph. There is plenty to see at London's Science Museum (www.sciencemuseum.org.uk), including exciting exhibits of the Apollo missions.

Stamps

Philately, or stamp collecting, is the most popular hobby in the world. Stamps issued before the Second World War are always more likely to increase in value, but it is important to try to find examples in the best condition possible. Collectors tend to develop a good relationship with a dealer and visit auctions to garner knowledge. Joining a monthly club is important, as information is willingly passed around.

Every collector, young or old, aspires to owning an original Penny Black. This was the world's first postage stamp, made in 1840 only, though an amazing 68 million were produced. They are not worth as much as most of us think – starting at £40 and going on up to £10,000+ for mint items. Those in sheets and those with peculiarities are worth the bigger bucks. Look instead for the Twopenny Blue of the same time (worth far more). A stamp on an envelope is usually worth more than a used stamp removed and put in an album.

How much?

There are many highly desirable stamps. A sheet of 25 Chinese stamps, the very first made, were found hidden in a bank vault, and later sold for £374,000. The most sought-after could be the penny or twopenny Mauritian stamp (a British Colony at the time), from 1847. There are around 30 known. The Queen has one, as does the British Library, and they can be worth £500,000.

To get going, decide on either a theme (e.g. birds or cars), or go for a country. Bear in mind that modern commemorative stamps tend not to be worth very much.

This pair of New Zealand One Penny stamps sold for $184,100 in February 2009 (Image courtesy of Spink)

Record-breaking stamps

£5 Stamp makes £15,000

A large orange stamp that cost £5 in 1867, and was used for posting heavy parcels to the furthest reaches of the British Empire, set a new world record price for such a stamp at Bonhams in Knightsbridge a few years ago.

Stamp collecting is a rigorous and thorough pastime, and records are usually excellent. Stamps such as this gem are very rare in tip-top condition. Only 246,826 stamps of this value, with the profile of Queen Victoria, were made.

How much?

This fabulously rare stamp sold for an unheard-of £15,270 at Bonhams in Knightsbridge, at their Great Britain Stamp Sale in December 2006. It made twice its pre-sale estimate. The £5 stamp was incredibly expensive even way back in 1853, being worth £1,000 in today's money. It was often found on sets of accounting books that were posted around Britain or abroad.

According to the top experts in this most specialised of fields, stamps are enjoying a buoyant period, particularly British stamps. The same sale saw a rare mint Penny Black make a mighty £9,500, despite the estimate being £5,000–£5,500. In 2005 a misprinted stamp from 1918 depicting an upside-down airplane was sold at auction for $525,000, the highest-ever price paid for a 20th-century American stamp. The US 1 cent 'Z Grill' stamp, of which only one is known to exist, was once swapped for a block of stamps worth $3 million, thereby making it the world's most expensive single stamp. It remains to be seen whether the credit crunch will affect prices greatly.

A rare US Postal Service stamp from 1918, featuring an inverted Curtis Jenny aircraft, fetched $253,100 at auction in September 2008 (Image courtesy of Spink)

This cover, featuring first issues of an 1858 5k Blue, Large Pearls and 1856 10k Rose, sold for $161,100 in May 2008 (Image courtesy of Spink)

World record stamp

In a packed room in London in February 2009, the audience witnessed the setting of a new world record when a rare Queen Elizabeth II 1960 Republic Issue stamp came up for sale.

The art of philately, or stamp collecting, is the most popular hobby in the world. Stamps issued before World War 2 will always increase in value, but it is important to try and find examples in the best condition possible. Collectors tend to develop a good relationship with a dealer and visit auctions to gather knowledge.

How much?

Spink is the world's leading auctioneer of stamps, as well as medals, banknotes and autographs. It was founded in 1666, and holds three royal warrants and many records for prices achieved at auction. A bidding war for the rare Queen Elizabeth stamp took place and the hammer fell at £31,000 (£35,750 with buyer's premium), creating a world-record price for a British Commonwealth Queen Elizabeth II stamp sold at auction.

This unique control block of six halfpenny 'U34' stamps, with four stamps double printed, sold for £57,600 in October 2008 (Image courtesy of Spink)

This rare Queen Elizabeth II 1960 Republic Issue stamp made a remarkable £31,000 at auction in February 2009 (Image courtesy of Spink)

Starbucks cards

Did you know that one of the newest international collectables is effectively free? Starbucks cards have been changing hands around the world for sometimes silly money. If phonecards are anything to go by, these little bits of plastic may take off in a huge way over here.

The first cards were released in the USA in November 2001. The idea is that customers pick up the card and add any amount of money to them, then use them to speed up their future coffee shop visits. Since then, over 160 million cards have been activated internationally. Look for limited-edition cards and try to get any seasonal items, such as the Christmas stocking, which you could get to go with the free Christmas cards a while back.

How much?

The cards were launched in Britain in November 2006. The very first card is known as the Caribbean Card and was given to regulars and VIPs at stores across the country. It came in attractive packaging. I got lucky and was given one, and they are now being sold online for around £250–£300.

The cards do much better down the line if they remain unused and in any gift packaging. Each country has its own designs, so there is lots of scope for swaps and trades across the world. There are a few dedicated and comprehensive collecting sites, and online auctions are starting to see them being sold too.

The ultra-rare Caribbean Card. This was the first UK card: £250–£300 (Jamie Breese)

A UK Starbucks card (Jamie Breese)

A popular UK Starbucks card (Jamie Breese)

Corgi No. 292 'Starsky & Hutch' Ford Torino (manufactured between 1977 and 1982). This made £180 at Vectis in May 2006 (Image courtesy of Vectis Auctions)

Starsky and Hutch

The classic 1970s cop series has gained cult status over the years, and the movie release featuring Ben Stiller and Owen Wilson added to the hype. The original series ran from September 1975 to August 1979 and, not surprisingly, there's a boost in interest in all things S and H, and there are plenty of affordable collectables out there.

The worldwide success made for a booming merchandise market. You can still find a whole raft of related items: ceramic busts of the crime-busting duo made by Token of Staffordshire, jigsaw puzzles, mirrors, and the famous annuals. Top of the collecting tree is the 'Striped Tomato' 1974 Ford Gran Torino. Ford made a special limited edition of 1,000 cars because of the series, of which it is rumoured only 150 survive. The 'Hero' cars actually driven by the actors are worth a fortune. Corgi brought out a neat, affordable scale model toy version in 2002.

How much?

1970s screen print sewn patches featuring the duo are currently making £20–£30 each. The popular UK-issued original magazines cost 30p new, and today the first issue from way back in December 1976 might set you back £10+. An original 1970s *Starsky and Hutch* Scarf sold on an internet auction site for the very affordable sum of £5.50.

There are some great pieces at great prices. A die-cast Gran Torino can be picked up new for a shade under £30 from toy firm RC2. If you want to splash out a bit, top autograph dealers are currently asking £300–£400 for fine studio stills signed by the original stars, Paul Michael Glaser and David Soul.

Star Trek memorabilia

The cult TV series turned 40 in 2006. It was created by author Gene Roddenberry in the mid-1960s, and the first series was broadcast in 1966. The stories have influenced an army of fans, youngsters, collectors, and even big names in business, from Virgin Galactic founder Sir Richard Branson to Microsoft founders Paul Allen and Bill Gates. Even the NASA space programme was influenced as scientists studied the bridge of the *USS Enterprise*.

Star Trek collecting can be divided into two areas – the TV series and the movies. The toys produced for the series are eternally collectable. Early pieces have risen in value over time. For example, the first action figures appeared late in Britain (1974), long after the first series ended in 1969. Spock is probably the most popular, and worth around £60 with his packaging. Other less well-known characters, also made by Mego, are worth considerably more. There are magazines galore, model kits, figurines, collectors' plates, and board games. Most sought after are authentic and screen-used props and costumes. Many of the first *Star Trek* props were reused, destroyed, or simply disappeared.

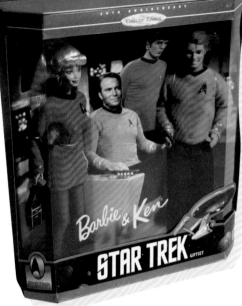

A *Star Trek* 'Barbie and Ken 30th Anniversary' gift set. (Jamie Breese. Item kindly provided by Cream and Chrome Collectables) (Jamie Breese. Item kindly provided by Cream and Chrome Collectables)

How much?

Dinky Toys made several *Star Trek* spaceships. The *Enterprise* was made to fire small plastic discs. In 2008, a Dinky No. 803 *USS Enterprise* and Klingon Battlecruiser – both in mint condition on excellent blister cards – made £70 at Vectis Auctions. The enemy's Bird of Prey battleship toy can make £150. An original movie poster signed by key cast members, on the other hand, can make up to £1,500 at auction. A superb Lonestar *Star Trek* Inter-Space Communicator from 1974 sold at auction in August 2007 for £100. The Playmates range of phasers and communicators are making £50 or so at the moment.

One of the most sought-after gems would have to be the Captain Jean-Luc Picard ceramic figure made by Kevin Francis. This is extremely rare as it was withdrawn from production early. It has a current market value rumoured to be in the early thousands. The other pieces tend to fetch £50–£150 each. In addition look out for the very rare New Force 12in *Star Trek* figures of Spock and Kirk in gangster costumes. Only 1,000 numbered sets were made by the firm Playmates.

Actual screen-used memorabilia is clearly rare. A good example of an affordable item would be Mr Spock's ears, which sold for £1,740 in 2000.

The market for autographs of the stars is huge. They frequently travel the world attending conventions, and sign everything. A William Shatner (Kirk) signed photograph can make £70, while Leonard Nimoy brings in around £50 or so.

In October 2006, the auction house Christie's held a special sale of 1,000 *Star Trek* costumes, props, and other items, from detailed models of the Starship *Enterprise* and phaser guns to outfits worn by Spock, Jean-Luc Picard, and Uhura. The Hero visual effects miniature of the Starship *Enterprise-D* from *Star Trek: The Next Generation*, made an incredible $576,000. The Captain's chair from another episode made $62,400.

Lonestar *Star Trek* 1974 Inter-Space Communicator, inner tray artwork depicting Captain Kirk and Spock: £100 (Image courtesy of Vectis Auctions)

Star Wars figures

In 1977 *Star Wars* redefined the way films were marketed forever more. The first action figures were 3¾in in height and appeared soon after the British release in 1978. They are classified into two groups: 12 and 21. The first 12 figures featured a picture of all the 12 action figures on the back of the backcard – hence the name '12-back'. These came after a huge delay: nobody expected the film to be a hit, and the toy manufacturers simply had nothing to sell for the first Christmas – except for a very rare temporary boxed voucher called the 'Early Bird' gift set. The later series featured 21 figures and these are usually half the price. Values vary according to such tiny details as the colour of the hair ('Ben Kenobi' came with grey or white), the size of head ('Han Solo' had two), to the size of laser sword ('Luke Skywalker' came with a fixed and retractable weapon).

There are many desirable figures from *The Empire Strikes Back* and a handful from the third and final film, *The Return of the Jedi*. Many people have forgotten about the 12in action dolls, which came out at the same time. They were far more expensive to buy and, as a result, boxed examples in mint condition carry premium prices. 'Han Solo' and the 'IG88' dolls are sought after.

A Palitoy *Star Wars* 1978-issue Darth Vader with extending light saber – mint within near mint '12-back' blister pack. He sold for £320 at Vectis Auctions in November 2006 (Image courtesy of Vectis Auctions)

Palitoy Mint 'Han Solo' figure, including first-issue blister card: £400–£500 (left). A full set of mint and carded original *Star Wars* action figures (below) (Images courtesy of Vectis Auctions)

How much?

The much later 'Power of The Force' range of figures (1985) is sometimes just as collectable, with 'Luke' as a Stormtrooper being sought after, and 'Yak Face' who is now worth £1,000+ in near mint condition. The 'Anakin Skywalker' figure (Luke's father) can achieve £3,000+ if together with original packaging.

Boba Fett was also made for release prior to his appearance in *The Empire Strikes Back* in the original

21-figure range. If he is this early figure, with the Kenner company logo (the US manufacturer) and backcard, he can make as much as £1,800 now. An original 12-back R2-D2 in mint shape will cost upwards of £300. Darth Vader, the key focus of the upcoming film, is desperately sought after. If you have the British-made Palitoy figure in top condition packaging, it will cost around £300. The original large-headed vintage Han Solo in similar condition can realise around £1,000 today.

A hot tip would be to look out for some of the figures from the animated TV series spin-off from the mid-1980s, called *Droids*. The Brazilian 'Vlix' action figure sold a few years ago on eBay for over £5,000. Another tip is that the figures with the Palitoy company logo (the British manufacturer) are more desirable than their US-made Kenner counterparts. A few years ago, toy giant Hasbro started to reproduce the vintage figures under the banner of 'The Original Trilogy'. These feature near identical cards and artwork and are affordable alternatives if you look on the web. Remember, with the new films, some speculators were caught out by the over-production of merchandise for *The Phantom Menace*, so pick your new acquisitions wisely.

Luke Skywalker figure

By the mid-1980s, over 300 million *Star Wars* toys had been sold, and it is because of that classic film that there is such a marketing frenzy on any blockbuster today. Against expectations, some of the prequel merchandise/figures are becoming sought after now.

Luke was one of the first 12 action figures. They were 3¾in in height and appeared after the release of *Star Wars* in 1978.

How much?

Luke Skywalker cost just 99 pence when he first landed in toyshops all across the country. In the UK he was made by Palitoy. It is the Palitoy Luke that is incredibly rare. Everybody simply opened up the pack and played with him. Toy auctioneers Vectis (www.vectis.co.uk) have sold a mint, unopened, first issue Luke bearing a yellow light saber for £1,000! The estimate was £200–£300.

A cheaper way to own a slice of toy history is to look out for the US version by Kenner. In near mint condition, unopened, with retractable light saber, you are going to pay £150–£300 at auction.

A mint condition Luke Skywalker figure with yellow light saber sold at Vectis for £1,000 (Image courtesy of Vectis Auctions)

A 1978-issue Denys Fisher Darth Vader figure, with damaged box, made £45 in October 2007 (Image courtesy of Vectis Auctions)

Darth Vader

Darth Vader figures made by Palitoy are also noticeably more valuable than their US-made Kenner counterparts. A Kenner Darth in a fine and unopened state will make £150 or so. A Palitoy '12-back' version in top nick will command upwards of £300.

Darth appears on everything imaginable. He can be snapped up as a tie, as a huge replica model (life-size), as a key fob, or rucksack, or wristwatch. All of these collectables, new or vintage, have a place on the Internet trading sites. There have been many more versions of him as a toy figure, such as the 'Power of the Force' range and the earlier, smaller action figures made to tie in with *The Empire Strikes Back* and *The Return of the Jedi*.

A Star Wars Darth Vader shop promotion unit from Toys 'R Us sold for £60 at Vectis in January 2008 (Image courtesy of Vectis Auctions)

Stylophone

Who would ever have thought that the tiny hand-held Stylophone electronic organ (2008 marked its 40th anniversary) would have started to gain cult status? With the revival of all things kitsch and retro, this little pocket electronic gizmo is perhaps one of the era's greatest icons, along with the Raleigh 'Chopper' bicycle, and flared jeans.

Many people still believe that Aussie wonderman, Rolf Harris, invented the Stylophone. It was actually made by a firm called Dubreq which was founded in 1967, and Rolf was heavily involved in promoting it along with sets of magic markers. There were several different models available; each had its own stylus pen from which the notes could be created when pressing the metallic 'keyboard'. The most popular entry-level model, amazingly, was used by rock and pop legend, David Bowie, on his groundbreaking anthem *Space Oddity*. There are three main colours: white, black, and brown.

How much?

A fine condition, working pocket Stylophone, complete with its box, record and book of songs to play from, usually makes between £50 and £75 at the moment. The mini organ's popularity has rocketed, thanks in part to a celebrity edition of *Stars in their Eyes*, when Pulp's Jarvis Cocker famously became Rolf and played the device to millions at home!

The 350S, developed
as a 'serious' musical instrument
(Image courtesy of www.stylophone.com)

A special 'professional' model was created for true fans: called the model 350S, it boasted an incredible 44 keys instead of the standard 20 and had an array of bizarre features, including not one, but two styli and different paddle switches to recreate new sounds, such as brass and strings! It didn't sell so well at the time and is hard to come by today. It's worth several hundred at present.

The original gems are still quite easy to find at car boot fairs around the country. Recently I was shown one with a genuine signature. This adds around £40 to the value. Why not keep a look out for boxed examples of all those tabletop electronic games and gadgets from the late 1970s – 'Simon', 'Battleships', 'Big Track', etc? All will have a value to somebody, especially if MIB (mint in box).

1 & 2: The first production model made before Rolf's key role in promoting the Stylophone. Note the black spacer keys on this early model (Image courtesy of www.stylophone.com)

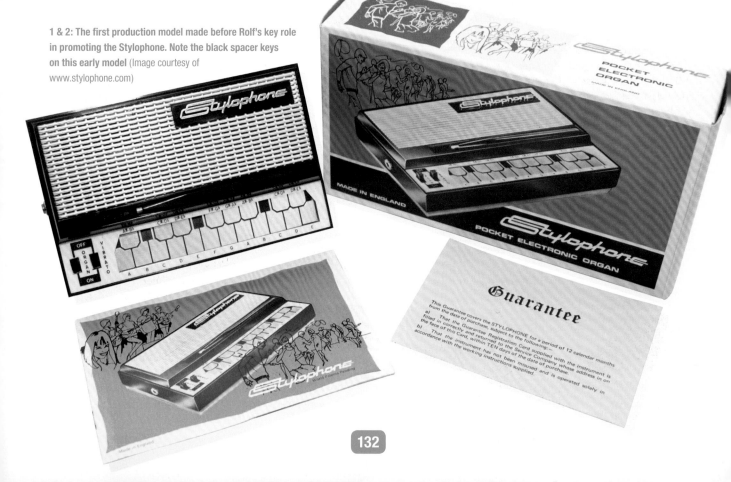

Sunglasses

Commercially produced sunglasses have their origins in the early 1880s, though it wasn't until the 1930s that celebrities took them to their heart and turned them into a must-have item. The 1950s–1980s is now considered to have been the golden age of sunglasses design. Today, some estimates suggest that annual sales have passed the £1.5 billion mark.

Almost all of the key names in fashion have allowed popular access to their designs through more affordable ranges of sunglasses (usually £75–£300). Prada and Chanel are two of the most recent houses to create a less costly range. Other sunglasses are made by Calvin Klein, Gucci, Dolce & Gabbana, and Armani. Celebrities such as Britney Spears and Joan Collins have their own brands of sunglasses for sale – these might increase in value if kept in good condition with original packaging and cases. Ray-Ban shades are perhaps the most famous and have been around since 1937. Robert De Niro wore the 'Outdoorsman' Ray-Ban Aviators in *Meet the Parents* and *Men of Honour*, while Samuel L. Jackson wore the model 3052 in *Shaft*.

How much?

The rock stars make the records: Bono's (from the band U2) famous wraparound 'Fly' shades went for £920 at the Sotheby's Rock 'n' Roll Sale in September 1996. Freddie Mercury's shades sold at Bonhams once for £800. A good bet for the future would be any pair belonging to Robbie Williams: his 'Ace' shades worn in the *Supreme* pop video were sold at auction for £660. They're likely to increase in value if Robbie stays on top.

The ultimate find would be a genuine pair of John Lennon or Elton John sunglasses. In order to achieve a good price, good documentation to provide a solid provenance is required. For example, a pair of Lennon's green-tinted shades from 1966 sold at a Sotheby's sale for £1,955. Christie's sold Elton's orange-tinted glasses for £2,585.

Look out for the Harry Potter themed sunglasses, which were produced by Pan Oceanic Eyewear: there were supposedly an amazing 30 different styles to collect.

Bono's wraparound 'Fly' shades went for £920 at Sotheby's in September 1996 (Image courtesy of Sotheby's Picture Library)

Vivienne Westwood Orb limited-edition Swatch (1990s): £150 (Image courtesy of Metro Retro)

Swatch watches

Made in the early 1980s, the Swatch watch evolved as a reaction to a crisis in the Swiss watchmaking industry. The idea was to encourage people to buy a *second* watch – hence the catchy name Swatch. Their first model, the Delirium, appeared in 1983.

These watches were outrageously collectable. However, the haze of excitement has faded over the last decade, though many watches remain desirable. Collectors, and there are still many, particularly in the Far East, demand perfection. Items must be both boxed, with original paperwork and also in mint, unworn condition. There are several different categories to collect, and these include Art Swatches, Pop Swatches, Chronographs, Christmas and Halloween Specials, Scuba Swatches, and Swatch Automatics.

How much?

The rare Mimmo Paladino Art Swatch was made in the late 1980s and was worth at one point a mighty £11,000–£18,000. The Blow Your Time Away model used to fetch up to £14,000. The exceptionally rare Kiki Picasso Art Swatch is the most fiercely sought-after example and was worth up to £30,000 at one time. These prices are from the peak of excitement and many will now be significantly lower. A limited-edition signed Yoko Ono Swatch wristwatch, numbered 0040 of 499, made just £120 at an auction at Christie's in London in November 2006. The limited-edition Vivienne Westwood Orb design pop Swatch now sells for £150 on eBay.co.uk.

There were several different Swatches made for the Atlanta Olympics. All are collectable. If your watch has a gold strap (GX150), then you have a highly desirable item, as these were given to the athletes.

A SylvaC rabbit (The SylvaC Collectors' Circle)

SylvaC rabbits

The best buys are the hollow china, sitting bunnies with both ears pointing up in different colours and different sizes. What sets these apart from the similar rabbits on the market is that they're by top maker SylvaC – it says so on their bottoms but they're almost instantly recognisable from their matt glaze. Just don't mistake them for very similar Wadeheath – they'll either say Wadeheath or be numbered 509 on the bottom. SylvaC was renamed as such in 1936: the capital C stands for Copestake, one of the original founders of the factory, which began life as Shaw and Copestake back in 1894.

Don't be fooled by pale imitations. The market has been flooded in the past few years by copies of SylvaC bunnies. They're fairly easy to spot: the colours are often too bright and the matt glaze looks dull and feels quite rough to the touch. Another dead giveaway is the mark on the bottom: the back stamp is not very clear.

How much?

There are eight different sizes, starting at 1in and going up to a whopping 10in, and you get a lot of bunny for your money at that size. Expect to pay £30–£40 at auction for a more common 4in bunny, while a 10in pink one could cost you as much as £300. Some are worth more than others, with cottontails (where the tail is replaced by a hole, allowing for cotton wool to be stuck out to form a fluffy tail) being highly desirable, as fewer of them were made. A 7in blue one would set you back about £150_£200 at present.

When it comes to the most popular-shaped bunnies, size and colour are everything – green is the most common, while more unusual colours such as pink and yellow are highly sought after.

SylvaC stopped operating in 1982, and many specialist dealers refuse to sell products from after that time when the factory was taken over by various groups, including Crown Windsor. If you're not sure that the piece feels right, leave it – but genuine SylvaC could be a fun investment, and those rabbits soon multiply! The Collectors' Circle is a superb place for fans to connect – www.sylvacclub.com

Teddy bears

American President Theodore 'Teddy' Roosevelt was the inspiration for the familiar jointed teddy bear. Collecting bears is called arctophily. Since the early 1980s, some very rare bears have fetched enormous sums at auction. One of the first American manufacturers to produce such a teddy was the Michtoms, later to be part of the Ideal Novelty & Toy Company, founded in New York in 1903. Some would argue that this was the firm that produced the very first jointed teddy bear as we know it, based on a cartoon depicting Roosevelt refusing to shoot a bear cub. Others have claimed that it was a Margarete Steiff, a polio sufferer, who exhibited in the same year at the Leipzig Fair.

The most fought-over bears are the examples made by the best manufacturers – Bing, Steiff, and Schuco – particularly the earliest examples (made between 1903 and the start of the First World War). Top British makes include Worthing, Norah Welling, and Ealon Toys. The early bears often feature elongated snouts, are stuffed with woodwool and covered in wool mohair. Early American bears can be spotted by the football shaped body, elongated limbs, and a pronounced back hump.

How much?

More desirable are larger Steiff examples from 1910–1920, which can be found in unusual colours such as grey (worth £7,000 upwards), or black (worth up to £25,000). Value also depends on condition, and without a label or button, prices paid can drop.

In 1989, Sotheby's the auctioneers sold a large-eyed Steiff bear from 1926, called Happy, for £55,000. There must be several more out there, just like him. In December 2006, Christie's sold a very rare Steiff hot-water bottle teddy bear with golden mohair for £31,200. Prior to that, in December 1994, they famously sold a Steiff Teddy Girl from 1905 for an amazing £110,000.

Teddies have been a worldwide craze for nearly 100 years. The market for vintage items has slowed down in the last ten years, and there are some clever fakes. However, why not collect a few limited-edition artists' bears, or buy modern examples and keep them safe and in their packaging, along with any certificate, for future pleasure and investment?

In 1989, Sotheby's sold Happy, a large-eyed Steiff bear from 1926 for £55,000 (Image courtesy of Sotheby's Picture Library)

Josef Pitrmann (Jopi) Musical Teddy Bear, German (1920s): £400-£600 (Image courtesy of Vectis Auctions)

Deans Rag Book/Pastimes Jenny Teddy Bears plus others (1970s/80s). These made £40 in November 2008 at Vectis (Image courtesy of Vectis Auctions)

The world's largest Teddy

Every now and again an auction comes up with some great lots and a great auctioneer behind it. In 2008, a grand collection of Teddy bears went under the hammer, but one lot – the largest teddy in the world – made an extraordinary price.

The auction was made up of former occupants of the award-winning Teddy Bear Museum in Stratford-upon-Avon, which was founded in 1988 by the former Conservative MP Gyles Brandreth. Among the bears offered was Mr Bean's 'Teddy', which was given to the museum by Rowan Atkinson.

How much?

The world's largest teddy bear is over 11ft tall and is unique. It was created for the Teddy Bear Museum and sat at the entrance. According to the auction house, thousands of children have played with him, including two royal princesses. The sale took place at Bonhams, Knowle, and jaws must have hit the floor around the collecting world when they discovered that this fantastic record-breaking bear sold for just £18. I have never quite heard anything like this as a collectables expert. Its sheer size must have put off those present from bidding. Mr Bean's bear 'Teddy' made a respectable £180, though still a steal in my opinion.

Former attractions at the museum included the first Paddington Bear to appear on television, Fozzie Bear from *The Muppets,* and Aloysius from *Brideshead Revisited.* Bears that were loaned to the museum or given on trust were rehoused in the Polka Children's Theatre in Wimbledon, London.

Telephones

Perhaps one of the great inventions of all time is, not surprisingly, quite collectable. There are four different collectable areas. The vintage models from the dawn of telephony (e.g. Gower-Bell types from the 1890s – often worth over £650 if in fine condition). Next are the candlestick types such as the Type 150 from the 1920s (which can make £400+). Then the Bakelite tabletop varieties and, lastly, the more recent retro phones, mobile and novelty phones such as the Plessey Snoopy and Mickey Mouse characters.

How much?

The most cherished phone would be the telephone set which Bell used to demonstrate his new invention to Queen Victoria on the Isle of Wight. It resides in a museum and is impossible to attach a price to.

Blue Target 700 series telephone (1970s): £65 (Jamie Breese. Item kindly provided by Cream and Chrome Collectables)

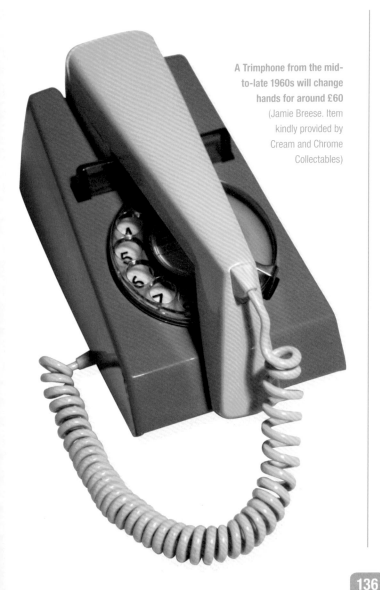

A Trimphone from the mid-to-late 1960s will change hands for around £60 (Jamie Breese. Item kindly provided by Cream and Chrome Collectables)

700 series telephones

Do you remember these? It was known as the 'Modern T', and first introduced in 1959. Made by Ericsson Telephones and the GPO Engineering Department, the design was a big move away from the candlestick or brittle Bakelite handsets, and it proved to be one of the most influential designs of the era. The 700 series continued production until the late 1970s.

They were made from 'Diakon' plastic, which was lighter, less clunky and more colourful than the Bakelite models of the war years. The most familiar colour was the famous two-tone dull grey – this influenced the office look of PCs and filing cabinets! However, there were more vibrant hues available: Ivory and Black for the wall phone, and 'Lacquer Red', 'Topaz Yellow', and 'Blue' for the desk varieties.

How much?

Mint condition 'Modern T' examples are now being sought after for their retro appeal. A black wall phone version, in good condition, can be worth £100+. Lucky finds would include one of the rare coloured examples which were produced as trials or show pieces, such as an 'Ivory and Red' handset, a clear plastic variety, and an experimental 'Tangerine' variation. These can be worth many hundreds to the right person. A 'Cadillac' 700 model was made available in 'Baby Blue and Pink' and can be picked up reconditioned for around £75 in shops. Another funky version is the Blue Target 700 coloured phone – a sort of mod design, which also can be found for about the same price.

These are a household object to watch. I don't think they will ever achieve true cult status, but they are worth picking up at car boots, especially if you spot one of the rare colours.

Red 700 series telephone (1960s): £80 (Jamie Breese. Item kindly provided by Cream and Chrome Collectables)

Black Bakelite telephone

This famous, collectable series of telephones was a huge leap forward in the development of telephony. They were particularly robust, and their streamlined appearance reflected the style of the age. Only available to hire back then, today they are quite collectable and look good in a modern home. These days, it is perhaps more famous for being the set centrepiece in *Deal or No Deal* on British television.

The 300 series phones appeared in 1938 and continued in production until 1959. Look out for those with a 'cheese drawer', which pulls out to reveal a mini address book. This can increase the value slightly, as does the original bell set (which would hold the phone) and the original cloth cord/cables. The earlier models – the 100 and 200 series – are also sought after with the pyramid feel and streamlined design.

A black 300 series telephone with chrome dial: £75–£100 (Image courtesy of Metro Retro)

How much?

The big bucks, however, lay in the rare coloured examples. Look for the upper-class 'Ivory' colour, the emergency 'Chinese Red' phone (worth around £500–£800) and 'Jade Green', which was also made for some government departments (around the same value). The unpopular 'Walnut' models, and 'Gold' and 'Silver' versions, are now worth a premium.

Rumours persist about the 'Royal Blue' examples, supposedly made for the British monarchy. Even rare 300 phones include the metallic 'Explosion-Proof' telephones (made to protect oil refineries), and the clear Lucite examples that were created for one-off shows.

Prices for good-condition 300 phones vary. With a 'cheese drawer', and cloth cord, perhaps £75–£100. The earlier pyramid-shaped black bakelite phones (the 162 made from 1929 and the 232 from 1934) are worth seeking out today. The 232s in 'Chinese Red' or 'Jade Green' are both worth £1,000+ each. If wholly original, a 'Jade Green' can make over £2,000 today.

Look for the 'Jade Green', which was made for some government departments (Image courtesy of Metro Retro)

Cult phone: The Ericofon

This all-in-one telephone set is considered to be a landmark design in plastic. Though it lends itself to the look of the '60s, it was actually created in the '40s and made available to buy in the mid-'50s. Made by L. M. Ericsson of Sweden, this humble handset is one of the true cult collectables.

The banana-shaped gem is also known as the 'Cobra' and was the brainchild of designers Blomberg, Thames and Lysell. It first appeared in 1954, but only found its way into this country, amazingly, in the early '80s. The standard colours are red, green, blue, beige, and grey, but it was available in the USA in an amazing 18 shades. It has become increasingly popular due to its select appearances in cult films and TV shows. More recently it was the phone of choice for Mrs Peel, played by Uma Thurman in the movie version of *The Avengers*.

How much?

The original sets have a timeless quality, and as a result they have steadily increased in value since production ceased in 1982. The rare colours, such as 'Sandalwood', command the most. Always look out for the older, larger-cased dial-operated versions as opposed to the pushbutton models (introduced later in 1967). A standard red model from the 1950s will cost anywhere between £90 and £140 today. The super rare gold-coloured Centenary models (225 made), and the leather model, are worth hundreds of pounds.

If you can't afford an original Ericofon, keep a look out for the low-cost modern reproductions produced by the American company 'Ned & Nora'. These are easy to find, and come in black, ivory, and a few funky metallic colours.

A beige Ericofon telephone (Jamie Breese. Item kindly provided by Cream and Chrome Collectables)

Ivory Bakelite telephone

One of my personal favourites of all, and a collectable household item that has really stood the test of time. The timeless elegance of the ivory-coloured telephone makes it a firm favourite among collectors of vintage communications, but more recently for the discerning individual looking for something radically different for home use. It often stars on *The Dez and Mel* show on British television.

Despite appearing after the peak of the art deco period, the 'Ivory' handset was part of a series of coloured, stylish, deco-influenced telephones known as the 300 series made between 1938–1959 – all in roughly the same shape, and tough enough for prolonged use. The 'Ivory' model was considered the upper-class version of the standard black model. How many phones from today would last for over 70 years?

How much?

If the Bakelite isn't cracked and the colour remains rich and creamy, then you are looking at around £400–£500 or so from a good dealer. Some can be found which have been converted for modern use, but this is still not permitted by BT. If you can find the ivory-coloured pyramid-shaped set (Model 232) then these are often worth more.

Look for posher locations on the stamp in the centre of the chrome dial – Mayfair would win out over Shepherds Bush, for example. As with the black variety, the phone will be worth more if it has the sliding address book, known as the 'cheese drawer', and is in fine condition.

An ivory-coloured 200 series telephone with chrome dial and 'cheese drawer': £500–£700 (Image courtesy of Metro Retro)

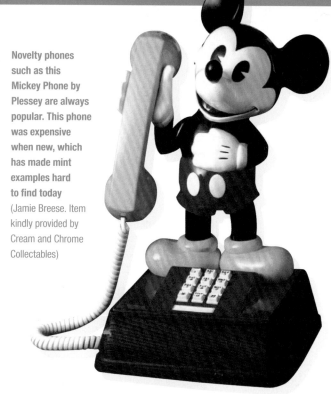

Novelty phones such as this Mickey Phone by Plessey are always popular. This phone was expensive when new, which has made mint examples hard to find today
(Jamie Breese. Item kindly provided by Cream and Chrome Collectables)

Novelty phones

If you remember the late 1970s, you'll probably remember at least one of the two iconic novelty telephones introduced around that time – Mickey Mouse and Snoopy. Mickey appeared in 1978 and was followed by Snoopy in 1981. They were a huge leap forward in telephone design and home communication. Previously, most GPO phones had either been clunky Bakelite or lighter, but often dull, 600 series plastic sets. Both Mickey and Snoopy hold the yellow handset in their hands, and the phone is activated when the user lifts it up. Also, both these sets were fun and extremely colourful – a real talking point for those who could actually afford them at the time.

Both telephones cross-over into two areas of collectables: children's toys and telephony. They were made by Plessey for the GPO, and initially you could only rent Mickey for £3 a quarter. Later, with deregulation, it became possible to buy them from the BT shop for a whopping £120 each! That was serious money back then.

How much?

In top shape, Mickey can be found today for between £75 and £120. Snoopy, being a white beagle, is more prone to discoloration and tends to be harder to find in fine condition. He will make at most between £100 and £140 on a very good day. Phones have consistently proved to be collectable, and these are iconic models.

Today, there are all manner of novelty telephones to look out for. One of the best is the red 'Direct Line' telephone, complete with wheels. Yes, there was actually a telephone that you could buy, and these are very desirable sets to own these days. Quite a few movie tie-in sets have been produced, and my favourite is the Buzz Lightyear set.

Mobile phones

Who keeps their old mobile when they upgrade? Who keeps them packaged with the instructions and in great condition? Here's a tip for the future: mobile phones could well become the next really hot collectable!

Though 'portable' phone technology has been around since the 1940s, it wasn't until 1983 that the first truly portable 'brick' phone went on sale. It was a Yuppie's dream machine! The DynaTAC 8000X was made by Motorola and cost a fortune back then. The real boom came in the mid-1990s with Nokia, Ericsson, Siemens, and other brands also selling feature-packed mobiles to the majority of the population.

How much?

With the incredible array of colours, shapes and sizes; mobiles will make the perfect collectable – much like the early wood and Bakelite land-line phones from the early 1900s to the 1950s. So few have been kept 'mint and boxed' that they are already worth something, to somebody, particularly if they're the early devices with instructions.

A handful of lucky collectors already own one-off or limited-run 'luxury' handsets produced for special events or publicity deals. There is one diamond-encrusted handset knocking about which is supposedly worth £50,000!

As the next generation of phones will one day make today's 3G handsets obsolete, why not keep your eyes peeled for old, classic handsets, and store them away safely (known in the trade as 'stockpiling')? Try looking for the first models in charity shops or car boot sales. Look out also for the very bulky 'transportable' machines: these were huge metal boxes, or contained in shoulder bags, and were used up to the early '90s.

Mobile phones might well be big collectables in a generation's time. Who keeps them in their original packaging? In fact, who keeps them at all! (iStockphoto)

Motorola DynaTAC 8000X

One of the brand leaders, Motorola, got in here at the outset in March 1983 with the revolutionary DynaTAC 8000X – a 1980s Yuppie's dream. This is one to watch. The 8000X didn't arrive in Europe until 1986 where it cost £1,200!

How much?

It was a monster of a 'hand-held', but sparked the communications revolution worldwide. In the US, where it first was in use, it cost a huge $4,000, yet there were still waiting lists. Today, a used grey example will cost around £30–£60, and a beige and white used model will make about the same. Mint and boxed models (with all instructions and batteries) will fetch a premium of £200 from a specialist dealer.

It wasn't an overnight revolution: Motorola invested $150 million and 15 years in the DynaTAC system before its first US sale. These days, no one gives a monkey's if you have a mobile, but back in the glorious '80s it was the last word in business chic, and a real talking point. Remember how popular the radios, home telephones, and TV sets of the past now are. Many of these phones are likely to be the collectables of the *near* future.

Even relatively new phones may well be museum pieces in years to come – think of how early televisions and radios are now collected (iStockphoto)

The DynaTAC phone was a landmark in early mobile phone technology (iStockphoto)

Televisions

John Logie Baird was the first to demonstrate television with his 'Televisor' model in 1926. By the mid-1930s commercial sets had become available, though sales were slow prior to the Second World War as, to begin with, TV transmissions only extended a few miles from Alexandra Palace in north London. After the war, transmissions were resumed, and it was the Coronation in 1953 that persuaded many to buy a television. However, sets remained very expensive until the late 1960s.

Like telephones, vintage TVs are a bit of a secret collectable. Most people will be unaware of how sought after an old wooden box set can be. The sets don't even have to be working! They won't show modern channels, anyway, although specialists are able to modify them – but it is costly.

How much?

Vintage sets, or those from before the Second World War, are the most valuable and will set you back, if in good order, anywhere between £500 and £4,500. Most other examples, from the '50s to the present, are worth far less. An exception would be the groovy space-age JVC Videosphere, or the first ever non-valve set made by Sony in the '60s.

By far the most wonderful TV set ever made is the iconic British-made Bush model TV22. This is the pinnacle in Bakelite plastic design and, though it is not the rarest, it is certainly going that way, as the sets were quite fragile.

Keep your eyes peeled for those early wooden sets. Look for model and manufacturer details on the back saying Marconi 702, HMV 901 or 902 (all from 1936). Cossor also made early sets. Look also for Sony's famous TV8 portable – it was the world's first transistor set – or even Sinclair's groundbreaking MTV1A (the world's first pocket set from 1977).

A Bush TV12 in brown Bakelite cabinet: £300–£400 (Jamie Breese)

The Bush TV12

The Bush TV12 and TV22A appeared around the same time in the early 1950s and remain the most iconic sets ever designed, often seen on TV shows as decoration, and in period dramas.

It stands 16.5cm tall and is made of brown or black Bakelite plastic. The 'de-luxe' wooden version, despite being more expensive at the time, is now only worth £60! This Bush used a different system to create a picture – there were 405 lines on the screens back in those days, as opposed to the 625 standard of today.

How much?

Though this was the cheapest telly in the Bush range, the original cost was an astounding £43 8s, which put it out of reach of most people, as the average weekly take-home pay was around £8. Plenty were made of both models, and today both black and brown versions change hands for around £300–£400, depending on the condition.

Despite rumours that many of these classic sets were taken to Japan and turned into novelty fish tanks in the 1980s, there are still quite a number of them around. Some vintage telly specialists can convert these sets with a kit to allow them to work again, and in glorious colour too. If you want one, try the Internet, local auction houses, or vintage communications dealers. Bush are still manufacturing televisions today.

A GEC BT1091 9-inch Bakelite table-top set made in 1949. Today good examples can make £300–£400 (Image courtesy of On The Air)

JVC Videosphere

This is one of my favourite examples of affordable retro collectables on the market. You may well remember this oddly-shaped television: it was designed and built by JVC in 1970, and had an uncanny similarity to an astronaut's space helmet. Today it is a much-prized retro must-have.

The Victor Company of Japan was established in 1927 and became best known as a leader in consumer electronics. This TV set was revolutionary at the time. Not too big at only 12in tall, but extremely streamlined. As well as a fixed pedestal, it also came with a superbly '70s hanging chain, and it is difficult to find the chain and base together these days. The collectable version has a radio and clock in the base too.

How much?

The production of this great little black-and-white TV set was no doubt inspired by the moon landings of 1969. Today, with their retro charm, they can be found at auction for around £250 to £350: that much will secure you a good example.

The 3250 model Videosphere is a true rarity. It was a later design than the standard 3241 and included a UHF tuner with a separate slide dial scale on the top.

The Videosphere was also produced in an orange cabinet: this is rare, but still harder to find is the black model that was only made for the North American market. If you want to catch a look at one, a Videosphere can often be seen on display at the Design Museum (28 Shad Thames, London SE1 2YD) www.designmuseum.org.

A JVC Videosphere television
(Image courtesy of Metro Retro)

A Bush TV62. These were reasonably common at the time, so look for tidy interiors, and a complete Bakelite cabinet. Mid-1950s. Around £200 (Image courtesy of On The Air)

Sinclair MTV – now a rare example of early Sinclair technology. Late 1970s (Image courtesy of On The Air)

Sinclair pocket televisions

Retro is big right now, especially all things electric. Leading the charge in the '70s and '80s was British wonderman, Sir Clive Sinclair. You may remember his home computers, but did you know Sinclair also created the world's first multistandard 'pocket' TV in 1977?

Born in 1940, Sinclair has enjoyed a remarkable life. He is still working on projects to this day through Sinclair Research. Other achievements include being made Chairman of British Mensa in 1980, and having an IQ of 159! He was a leading innovator in miniaturisation, and is behind many world firsts: pocket calculators, digital watches – and pocket televisions.

How much?

The Microvision MTV1 from 1977 now changes hands for up to £500. A bit later in 1983 he created the flat screen, futuristic looking FTV1, which was a smaller pocket TV and proved quite popular. For some reason, truly portable TV was never a hit – unlike the Walkman. They are now cherished for the future. I have seen a couple of damaged examples at car boot sales for a few quid, but a mint and boxed example could change hands for £100+ on the retro market.

Keep a look out for the rare Executive calculator: this was first introduced in 1972 and was truly a pocket-sized calculator. Now, it can be seen on display at the Museum of Modern Art in New York, and can make £100+. Sinclair also dreamed up one of the first LED digital watches. Called the Sinclair Black Watch, it first appeared in 1975. Sinclair created the smallest monitor in 1977 – the Sinclair Mon1 A. Currently Sinclair Research's miniaturisation continues with their Z1 radio, designed to be the world's smallest AM radio.

Tennis

Lawn tennis was developed in the 1870s by Major Walter Wingfield, and by 1877 the first championship was played at Wimbledon, with Spencer Gore taking the title from 21 other entrants. Ladies soon followed, with Maud Watson winning in 1884. In 1888 the LTA was formed and the rules they made have changed little since.

There is a lot of tennis memorabilia around to collect, and people are after rackets, balls, trophies, books, Wimbledon ephemera, and china decorated with tennis players. Royal Doulton produced some good tennis-related ceramics that sell at a premium.

How much?

The most sought-after rackets are 19th-century wooden ones with a flat top or a tilt-head – rarities can sell at between £1,000 and £2,000. They were often made from different woods – with ash head, walnut throat, and mahogany handle. In general, it is the non-leather-handled versions which tend to be more collectable. Once you get into the 20th century, prices drop rapidly. Early 20th-century boxes of balls can sell for between £50 and £100.

Any racket with a direct connection to an early champion would sell quickly, and anything pre-1880 should serve up a winner too. Hazel's 'Streamline' racket, as used by Bunny Austin, is a very good seller at auction – it has unusual 'wings' near the throat and makes from £300 to £600. It's unusual in that it is a sought-after leather-wrapped handle racket. Bjorn Borg's 1981 Wimbledon Final racket pulled in a stunning £13,200 when it went under the hammer at Christie's in London in July 2007.

Signature or 'Character' rackets are always good to pick up if cheap – these feature images of famous tennis legends. Wooden rackets were still being used in the 1950s and '60s.

Do not get too excited if your old Slazenger or Dunlop is still in its wooden press under the stairs. The most you are likely to get for it is a chuckle on the local court if you use it to play.

10inx8in action shot of Andy Murray on the court: £100
(Image courtesy of Fraser's Autographs)

A signed photograph of Margaret Thatcher (Image courtesy of Fraser's Autographs)

Margaret Thatcher

Baroness Thatcher is one of the most collectable British premiers, second in popularity only to Winston Churchill. Known as 'The Iron Lady', she came to power as Prime Minister in 1979. For 12 years she attracted adoration and controversy, and there was a good deal of memorabilia created at the time.

How much?

Baroness Thatcher items have been steadily rising in value for several years now. The famous character jug (like a Toby Jug) by Kevin Francis was a limited edition of 1,000 and sold ten years ago for £120. It is now worth around £220.

A Margaret Thatcher dog toy will set you back around £25, or you could go for a *Spitting Image* keyring for £10. The folks at *Spitting Image* also had her made into a teapot in 1994, and today this sells for £250+. In 2001, the artist Richard Stone painted her, and the limited-edition lithographic prints of the picture currently sell for around £1,000. The ultimate item would be her black Ferragamo bag, which was used throughout the 1980s. This was auctioned with a handwritten letter of authenticity in 2000 to raise funds for Breast Cancer Care, and it fetched a record-breaking £100,000!

Baroness Thatcher was a generous person with her signature, and because of this examples are not scarce: £300–£400 will secure a classic signed photo. She was always good with correspondence and would often reply in person to letters and gifts. If they reveal any personal or political thoughts, then these are valuable. If you have a standard thank you letter, signed, then it will still be worth £100+.

Thunderbirds

Thunderbirds is not just a BBC series, it is a worldwide phenomenon attracting a huge global audience. There were only 32 one-hour episodes ever made, the first being broadcast in October 1965. The series was named after the US Airforce base where Gerry Anderson's brother learnt to fly. Two feature films, in 1966 and 1967, added to the craze. Prices for many items have grown in the last ten years.

Collecting falls into three areas – the highly-prized original puppets (made from fibreglass and rubber); the props; and the plethora of merchandise, such as books, records, and posters (e.g. 21st Century Toys made purses, rainhats, and sunglasses, while the movie posters are worth £200+).

Thunderbird 2 was used to bring the rescue equipment in. The Dinky Model No. 101 had sprung retractable legs, which were operated by pressing levers. If you have the version with the blue and black base, then it can make £250; if you have the blue and white base version, then around £265. Both need to be in good+ condition in a good+ box. There are two colour types too – a gloss green and a metallic green – to seek out. Model No. 106 was the blue version (1974–1977). One has red legs, and another version has yellow legs.

Many of the actual puppets and sets were tragically destroyed, though amazing finds do come on to the market. The original Lady Penelope puppet sold for £22,000 at a Sotheby's auction in 1995. Like puppets, items of original furniture from the show come up for sale occasionally, and fetch £1,500 upwards for great examples.

After Dinky stopped making these gems, Matchbox toys began releasing their own creations in the early 1990s. All are die-cast. Look for early toys, boxed and mint. There is a wealth of superb-quality brand-new toys and collectors' pieces, which might be worth putting into storage for the future perhaps?

Dinky No. 100 – Lady Penelope's FAB 1. This made £260 in 2008 (Image courtesy of Vectis Auctions)

FAB 1

Lady Penelope's very own FAB 1 car is the most famous pink car of all time. Driven by the trusty ex-convict chauffeur, Parker, FAB 1 is a futuristic, classy limo with some deadly surprises for those who cross her path: namely missiles. It is one of the most enduring images from popular television and has appeared in toy or replica form several times since the first TV series in 1965.

Dinky's FAB 1 (number 100) was made between 1967 and 1975. In March 2008, one fine example sold at Vectis the auctioneers for £260 in its original bubblepack. For the ultimate model version, look out for the 18in model from the 'Supermarionation' range by Product Enterprise. This was a handcrafted prop replica in fibreglass and resin and came with a clear display case with a brass plaque. It was presented with a Certificate of Authenticity – each individually signed by *Thunderbirds* creator Gerry Anderson. It was in a limited edition of just 1,500 and priced originally at just under £300.

Dinky No. 101 – Thunderbird 2 (1968). This achieved £240 at Vectis in October 2008 (Image courtesy of Vectis Auctions)

Tiffany and Co.

Possibly the most famous name in jewellery and silverware, this legendary company was founded by Charles Tiffany, who set up the firm in New York in 1837. Immortalised more recently by the 1960s film *Breakfast at Tiffany's* starring Audrey Hepburn, their wares are considered both romantic and luxurious.

There is a common misconception that Tiffany and Co. were behind the beautiful glassware (including those multi-million pound table lamps) made in the early 1900s. This was, in fact, a separate company established by Charles's son, Louis Comfort Tiffany, which despite enormous success eventually closed in 1932. Charles started out by importing fine commissioned jewellery from Europe and soon became famous for his army of royal fans, including the Russian Tsar and Queen Victoria. Among other advances, he perfected a technique for securing diamonds to rings using prongs, and introduced the Sterling Standard to America.

How much?

The firm still operates today, but there is always substantial interest in their wares of the past. Mostly you find watches, jewellery (usually diamond-based), silverware, and luxury household goods. A good example of a fine household piece might be an inkwell made from sterling silver: today it might cost £1,200. Tiffany doesn't have to be for the super-rich: it is quite easy to buy antique items, such as a silver beaker, for £100–£150 from good dealers. A silver bon-bon dish from the turn of the last century can cost £200 today. If you want to splash out, an eight-piece sterling silver coffee and tea service, from between 1865–1870, realised nearly £10,000 at auction a few years ago.

It is fair to say that any genuine Tiffany and Co. item is going to be worth money. The most valuable pieces tend to be those made for royalty, or those featuring very precious stones. The records are set mostly by Charles's son, Louis: in 1998, two Tiffany lamps made the American top ten of auction prices for decorative arts with a hammer price of nearly $2 million per lamp! An important diamond ring signed Tiffany & Co., set with a circular-cut diamond and weighing approximately 8.23 carats, sold for $962,500 in October 2008 at Christie's New York.

It is always worth looking out for the wares of Tiffany's contemporaries in America of the same era. Quite often, pieces by Gorham, Alvin Corp, Black Star and Frost, and so forth, are cheaper than Tiffany, though still of a high standard of craftsmanship.

An important diamond ring signed Tiffany & Co., Schlumberger, set with a circular-cut diamond and weighing approximately 8.23 carats, sold for $962,500 in October 2008 at Christie's New York (Image courtesy of Christie's Images Ltd 2008)

A Marx Toys (USA) tin plate, clockwork 'Popeye Eccentric Aeroplane' (1950s): £300–£400 (Image courtesy of Vectis Auctions)

Tin toys

Toys always remain popular items when it comes to antiques and collectables as there is so much nostalgia connected to them. Among the most desirable are the tin plate toys of the first half of the 20th century. These are hard to find in pristine condition and, if rare examples, when they come up for sale they often attract international attention.

How much?

One of the highlights of a recent auction was the highly-prized 5403 clockwork Zeppelin by Marklin, painted in cream and silver with side and rear propellers and the German Empire flag. It was estimated to fetch £2,000–£3,000 but realised a mighty £4,560. Originally this was designed to hang from the ceiling in a child's room. Another gem was a Bing three-funnel liner with portholes and masts: this carried an estimate of £2,500–3,000 and made £4,080. The lots appeared at Bonhams' Sale of Toys in May 2008 in London.

This rare, German-manufactured tinplate model U-Boat, circa 1938/39, with clockwork propeller, is worth £600–£800 (Image courtesy of Vectis Auctions)

A tinplate clockwork model railway, from German manufacturer Arnold, sold for £170 in November 2008 (Image courtesy of Vectis Auctions)

Toby jugs

The name comes from an 18th-century song about a man called Toby Philpot called 'The Brown Jug'. They first appeared in about 1760 and were produced in the famous Staffordshire potteries. While being highly collectable and seen frequently on programmes like *The Antiques Roadshow*, more modern versions, called character (or figural) jugs, are becoming ever more popular, and some have proved to be a wise investment.

The first Toby jugs were made by Ralph Wood and Sons – these are incredibly rare antiques and usually have a value to match their scarcity. Purist collectors go for these early examples and look only for those with a tricorne hat and distorted body proportions. Jugs from the 20th century usually fetch less money, but there is far more choice. For example, those in the Wilkinson First World War range of famous admirals and generals frequently fetch £250+ apiece. Look also for Neil Kinnock (made for *Spitting Image*), John Major, and a character jug of Henry Sandon, the famous BBC antiques expert.

Royal Doulton Beatles jugs: a set of all four band members is currently worth £300–£600
(Image courtesy of Sotheby's Picture Library)

A 1990s Royal Doulton Alfred Hitchcock character jug
(Royal Doulton/Wedgwood)

How much?

Most Royal Doulton character jugs can easily be found at specialist auctions. At the close of 2008, many could be picked up on average for £20–£100. There are many, many exceptions of course. Even The Beatles have been immortalised in a range made by Royal Doulton in 1984. They were modelled by Stanley James Taylor, and a set of four currently fetches £400–£500 at auction. They were making several hundred more in the early 2000s. Prices on the newer character jugs vary – for example, Kevin Francis's Maggie Thatcher jug was a limited edition of 1,000 and sold ten years ago for £120. It is now worth around £200. A figural jug featuring a seated Clarice Cliff holding a plate was made seven years ago and sold for £100 – it now can fetch £400+.

Everyone has a Toby or character jug tucked away somewhere, and almost all have a certain value. Potteries Specialist Auctions hold frequent sales and you can take a look at www.potteriesauctions.com Collecting Tobys, modern or antique, is an absorbing hobby and makes for a great display.

'Duchess of Kent', from the LMS 'Princess Royal' class loco, 46212.
£25,000–£30,000 (Image courtesy of Sheffield Railwayana Auctions)

Titanic memorabilia

Since the first annual Onslows auction in 1987, prices have crept upwards for items relating to the ill-fated maiden voyage of the *Titanic* in 1912. The release of the film created enormous interest and prices have increased.

International agreement prevents the sale of items from the seabed, apart from lumps of coal (£1,000). Collections fall into two areas: items that physically came off the ship, e.g. a letter posted (£2,000 to £4,000+) or items produced after the disaster, such as *The Daily Mirror* from 16 April 1912 (£250), or sheet music and 78rpm records with commemorative songs (£30 upwards).

'Lord Rodney', from the SR 'Lord Nelson' class loco, 30863.
£12,000–£15,000 (Image courtesy of Sheffield Railwayana Auctions)

How much?

A very rare poster produced for the return voyage was once found folded in a book, and sold for £10,000. A steward's pocket watch which stopped at 2.14am and went into the sea with him, sold for £15,000. The Chart Room key fetched £12,000. A lifeboat plate went at another sale for over £45,000 in the early 2000s. A sale in America was rumoured to have made several hundred thousand for a handful of Royal Mail bag tags. The prices vary enormously, and an expert's opinion is vital with this subject.

'Hawkins', from the LMS 'Jubilee' class loco, 45649.
£9,000–£12,000 (Image courtesy of Sheffield Railwayana Auctions)

In January 2009, a letter from a first-class passenger onboard the Titanic was sold at auction in New York. The letter, dated April 10th, 1912, was written by passenger George Graham of Harriston in Canada, a sales manager for the Eaton's department store company, to a business colleague in Berlin, Germany. It placed in the mail from Southampton, just prior to the ship's departure for its never-completed trans-Atlantic crossing to New York City. Graham himself sadly did not survive the tragedy. The letter was sold by Spink Smythe in New York City for a $16,200.

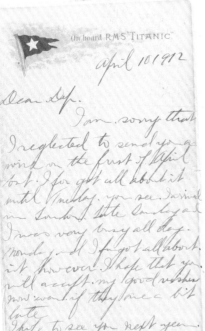

This letter was sold by Spink Smythe in New York City for a considerable amount – $16,200 (Image courtesy of Spink)

Train nameplates

One of the Holy Grails of the antiques world, these iconic examples of railwayana would be the jewel in the crown in any enthusiast's collection. The price paid for a fine nameplate is now almost legendary. Who knows if the credit crunch will affect prices?

There were more than 100 UK operating companies before 1923, so there's a lot to look for. The wish list would be topped by the cast-iron nameplates which adorn British locomotives because for many, the UK is the true home of the railways. Nameplates from the most famous trains will be the most expensive, followed by those from mainline and then industrial trains.

Enthusiasts will collect anything from luggage labels and old staff paycheques, right through to more unusual items such as totems (enamel station signs) and ticket punches. Smaller pieces, such as timetables, early toys, and collectors' cards are more accessible; so are guards' lamps.

How much?

A plate for 'The Duchess of Devonshire' went a few years ago at auction for over £34,200. In December 2004 Sheffield Railwayana Auctions made a world record of £60,000 for a nameplate, beating their previous double world record of £54,000 (www.sheffieldrailwayana.co.uk).

If you are on a real budget there are reproduction nameplates which are quite easy to spot and are relatively affordable. However, you could always invest in a train's number plate (either the cabside plate or the smokebox plates). There is even a nameplate club, and you don't even have to own one. Tickets are also very popular (travel, not platform), and can be worth major bucks if from an early nostalgic route.

Travel posters

Travel in the '20s to the '40s, especially by cruise liner, was a true novelty, and a spectacular dream for most. This was reflected in the bold, colourful, and mostly incredibly striking advertising poster art of the era. Today, these gems are hugely sought after and sometimes fetch significant prices at auction.

Cars, planes, railway, Zeppelin, Underground, and actual destinations are all collectable if vintage. Authentic shipping posters in the art deco style remain the most desirable, and perhaps the most familiar for many. Christie's of South Kensington occasionally hold a dedicated sale of Shipping and Vintage Posters.

How much?

A single poster from 1932 called 'Spidoléine', by A. M. Cassandre, sold a few years back for a jaw-dropping £30,000. A good example of air travel would be an Air France poster from the '40s – they created fine graphic arts posters and are linen backed – you'd pay £500–£700 for a reasonable example. It's not just Continental posters that collect the big money: a North Eastern Railways poster advertising the Yorkshire coast from 1910 can make £10,000, and there is huge demand for posters from GWR in the '30s and '40s. Motoring and cycling subjects, again from the '30s and '40s, are also heavy hitters.

More affordable, and just as colourful, are original travel posters from the 1960s – these, in general, float around the £150–£250 mark if in A1 condition. Fortunately, for the fan, there are plenty of avenues to find high-quality reproduction posters. Of course, they lack the pedigree, but effectively look just as good and can cost as little as £25.

Troika Pottery

Troika was founded in St Ives in 1963 by three talented individuals: a potter, a sculptor, and an architect. Initially, the trio were influenced by artists like Paul Klee. Their rough, textured or plain white ceramics cost a few pounds In the '60s, but today the prices for many of their unusual pieces are quite high.

Many of the items were sold early on to tourists from their own shop at the pottery in Wheal Dream, St Ives. It wasn't long before the heavyweights got wind of them, and mega-trendy stores – Liberty's and Heals – began selling the distinctive ceramic jars, plaques, lamp bases, plates, etc. Later, New York legends Macy's and Bloomingdale's sold Troika too.

How much?

You really want to go for the best-condition pieces, preferably without cracks and with only minimal crazing. An early Troika mug will typically sell for £100–£120 at a shop. The small St Ives cube will cost about £100 today. A chimney vase with an abstract face image on the one side can go for £350–£400+. In November 2008, an ultra-rare 'Aztec Mask' sold on eBay.co.uk, with 21 bids, for a mighty £830. A single 'Love Plaque' changed hands on eBay prior to that for an amazing £3,550!

Sadly, the pottery closed in 1983. That is good news, though, in terms of supply and demand – the new supply dried up and the demand is quite significant today. The publication of several books on the subject, and an important exhibition in the mid-1990s, helped stimulate the new wave of interest. Troika is stylish, idiosyncratic, and previously could be passed over by bargain hunters at car boot fairs. Most pieces are signed by hand, and the roughened surfaces and restrained colours should be easy to spot.

'Zippy'. Part of a group of costumes/puppets from the popular children's series *Rainbow*. These were sold in 2001 at auction (Image courtesy of Christie's Images Ltd 2008)

TV memorabilia

The great thing about TV collectables is the accessibility in terms of price. Unlike movie props, costumes, and merchandise, lots of classic TV memorabilia, particularly from 'cult' favourites such as *Star Trek*, *The Prisoner* or *The Magic Roundabout*, can be found at conventions and fairs across the country for under a tenner.

There are two main approaches. You can buy high-end items, usually props and costumes, and hope they maintain their cult status and increase in value. An example could be the classic *Star Trek* Hand Phaser, many of which were made for the early shows or pilots (these sometimes appear and make £1,500–£2,500 at auction). Alternatively you can buy cheaper toys and merchandise, keep them boxed and your fingers crossed. It usually takes about 20 years for an important or original show to be classed as cult or classic. Oddly, the collecting market for soaps is buoyant, but prices remain low, even for signed memorabilia such as photos, mugs, and beermats.

How much?
One of the popular 'TV Generation' auctions at Christie's in 2001 offered the actual 'Bungle' costume, together with the 'George' and 'Zippy' puppets from the cult kids' show *Rainbow*. They made a superb £7,990. A very rare *Avengers* Dinky toy car (Steed's special metallic turquoise Jag) has been valued at up to £2,500.

Original Thunderbird puppets are probably the most desirable of all TV collectables. Very few come on to the market and they tend to make many thousands of pounds and attract considerable publicity. For example, 'Lady Penelope' was sold by Sylvia Anderson (show creator Gerry's wife), at auction in 1995 for £30,000, and 'Captain Scarlet' went for around £20,000.

Collectors can scour car boot sales and charity events for the jigsaws, annuals, dolls, action toys, comics, and related promotional merchandise. Aim never to spend more than £2, and then see what you can get on Internet auction sites like eBay.co.uk. Why not go for established cult shows, including: *The Persuaders*, *The Avengers*, *Star Trek*, *Lost in Space*, *The Saint*, original *Thunderbirds* and *Space 1999*.

The Sopranos
TV memorabilia is traditionally less popular at auction than the movie items that pop up at sales throughout the year. However, the Emmy-award-winning drama series, *The Sopranos*, proved itself to be a modern-day classic when dozens of items of clothing worn in the show came up for sale in 2008 at an auction house in the US.

Many of the lots were sold with the original production tags attached, and all of the items included a letter of authenticity by James Gandolfini – an important part of the future value for those looking to secure an item which might appreciate in value in time.

How much?
The 25 costumes worn by James Gandolfini as the star, Tony Soprano, sailed past the pre-sale estimate of around $36,500 at the Pop Culture sale at Christie's in New York in June that year. In the end, the collection made a mighty $187,750. The money went on to benefit the Wounded Warrior Project. The top lot of the Gandolfini grouping was a bloody costume worn in a key scene when, in a fit of dementia, Uncle Junior shoots Tony. It sold for $43,750.

Another 37 men's costumes from other main characters in *The Sopranos* also sold. In the packed sale room was Mr Gandolfini himself, who stepped up to the podium next to the auctioneer to greet bidders.

A bloodied costume worn by James Gandolfini in *The Sopranos* sold for $43,750 at Christie's, New York, in 2008 (Image courtesy of Christie's Images Ltd 2008)

Some vintage typewriters are very valuable. Others are not. A specialist knowledge is required to navigate this complex collectable (iStockphoto)

Typewriters

Some of the very first 'typewriter' devices were actually created to help the blind, but in the early 1870s the new demands of Victorian business led the Remington company in the US to begin production of the Sholes and Glidden typewriter. They introduced it as a revolutionary invention to replace pen and ink, and within a few years it had changed the work environment for good.

Rare typewriters now come up for sale at auction and are collected around the world. Prices are improved when the item comes complete with a carrying case or box, when none of the keys are missing, and when the gold-coloured transfers are intact. More affordable names to hunt down include Corona, Imperial, Oliver, and Royal (used by the writer in the film *Misery*).

How much?

One of the most popular collectable typewriters was created by design guru Ettore Sottsass for Olivetti. Called the Valentine, its revolutionary red design appeared in 1969. The oldest machines like the first Crown pointer type model can make several thousand pounds.

There are no true single Holy Grail models: more than 300 different makes were patented in the US alone. Those typewriters that feature finer woods, inlaid with mother of pearl, and the finest boxes like the Kosmopolit, for example, are all desirable. Early machines with names like Hammond, Mercedes, Moya, Blickensderfer, and Franklin are usually making £200+ at auction these days.

Car boot sales are still the best place to pick up these clunky gems on the cheap. Portable typewriters are more practical. Like sewing machines, most mass-produced vintage models, even those from the turn of the last century, are worth less than £50. Top collectors go for 'firsts': the first toy typewriter, the first Braille, etc.

Valentine typewriter

Ettore Sottsass, who died in 2007 aged 90, had been a leading light in world design for many years, and was a founder member of the highly influential design movement known as the Memphis Group. His typewriter was an early work for the giant firm Olivetti and today it is a hard-to-find plastic collectable.

Sottsass's typewriter was called 'Valentine' because it went on sale on St Valentine's Day in 1969. Designed for Olivetti in bright red plastic, the idea was to brighten up the workplace and make the device portable too. Like the Memphis Group, it wasn't around for long – the production period for this award-winning gem was only a year and a half. Now you will have to trawl the web or visit the design museum in London to see this groundbreaking typewriter.

How much?

Despite being mass produced, up to £150–£200 is about right for a good condition Valentine today. For added value down the line, look for models that are sold with the cleaning brushes.

There are many ways to seek one of these '60s style icons, and the best place is holding out for one on one of the Internet auction sites. The Valentine is one of the cheaper classic Sottsass wares: his later 'Tervas' vase can cost much more. Look out, too, for his other office pieces, like the 'Summa 19' calculator and the 'Praxis 48' typewriter.

The Valentine was a breakthrough in office design and is now a museum piece (Wikimedia Commons)

Video games

With the current war between Nintendo's Wii, Microsoft's 'X-Box 360' and Sony's 'Playstation 3' it is just about time to begin to take a look back at the very first video games of the '70s and early '80s – and how they have started to become retro, chic – and collectable.

The first video game is a point for debate. Many agree that the first truly recognisable example was created in 1962 by a student. Called 'Spacewar', it only worked on vast company mainframe computers! The very first home games console was the Magnavox 'Odyssey'. Invented by Ralph Baer; it lasted two years (1972–74), and cost $100 in America. It didn't do that well, oddly, and the games were mind-bendingly crude.

Atari followed soon after with a home version of the legendary 'Pong' (a bat and ball 'game'). Atari later dominated the world market with the 2600 VCS console in the late '70s. All these earlier devices are hard to find in mint condition and are hot collectables today.

How much?

Though Atari and Magnavox led the way, there were many other consoles released over the following few years. All were laughably basic compared to today's supermachines. A mint-condition Vectrex console from 1982 (which came with its own screen) can cost over £200 today. The 1975 Fairchild 'Channel-F' machine was the first cartridge-based device and is quite rare. Other consoles worth a few quid include the ColecoVision system and the Intellivision products. Expect to pay between £55 and £120+ for mint examples in a good box.

Your very best chance of unearthing these up-and-coming retro treasures is to scour boot fairs and charity

Grandstand
'Munch Man' tabletop
electronic game: £30 (Jamie Breese. Item kindly provided by Cream and Chrome Collectables)

Grandstand
'Scramble' tabletop
electronic game: £39, mint in
a box (Jamie Breese. Item kindly provided by Cream and Chrome Collectables)

sales. Failing that, you can try to pick up the smaller, much cheaper, early 1980s tabletop or hand-held games, such as 'Scramble', 'Munch Man', and 'Astro Wars'. These are already collected and can cost £25 to £75 each from a good dealer. See opposite for information about the legendary Game and Watch hand-held LCD games.

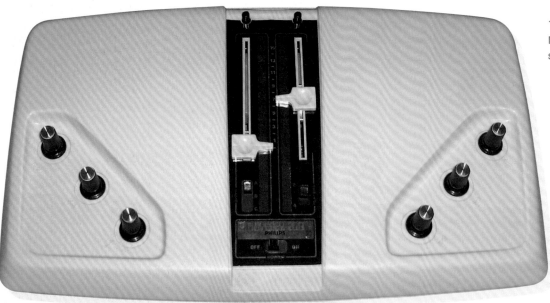

The European version of the Magnavox Odyssey 200 was sold under the Philips brand name (Wikimedia Commons)

Game and Watch

Forget the fact that no kid ever used these for timekeeping; the Game and Watch portable game was the electronic craze that swept us away in the early 1980s. Household names such as 'Mario Brothers' and 'Donkey Kong' all started life here. They sold by the truckload, but really they were setting the path for the monster hit – 'Game Boy'. G&Ws are now keenly collected as retro gems, and some are fetching very good money.

They were made by Nintendo, a Japanese company that started out in 1889 (the name means 'Work hard, but in the end it is in Heaven's hands'), and were designed by Gunpei Yokoi. Altogether 60 different models were made, and these included 'Wide Screens', 'Panoramas', 'Multi Screens', 'Super Colours', and 'Tabletops'. The very first model was part of the Silver series and was imaginatively entitled 'Ball'. This was released in April 1980: one has sold online for £500!

How much?

Any example in a perfect box is sought after. The most desirable are considered to be the second edition of 'Flagman', and 'Mickey Mouse Panorama'. Some companies did deals so they could place their own logo on the games for promotional use. These are scarce too. In short, a complete collection of all 60, mint and boxed, will cost between £11,000 and £13,000.

The most popular G&W ever was 'Donkey Kong', which was introduced in 1982 as part of the 'Multi Screen' series. 'Popeye' and 'Snoopy Tennis' were big sellers too, but are therefore far more common. The craze ended in the mid-1980s, but today there is buoyant trading by completionist collectors. Look out at car boot fairs for these fun collectables. There is some useful info at www.gameandwatchnow.com

Game & Watch 'Mario Brothers':
£30 (Jamie Breese. Item kindly provided by Cream and Chrome Collectables)

Atari Pong was released in 1972, and is now highly collectable
(Wikimedia Commons)

Space Invaders

The first blockbuster video game, 'Space Invaders', was created by Toshihiro Nishikado for Taito of Japan. It was ludicrously simple but totally addictive and was also the first video game to make its presence felt outside arcades, reaching a completely new audience. Hundreds of thousands of arcade machines were produced, yet these are still highly coveted by collectors of iconic objects, as well as gaming enthusiasts.

How much?

It is possible to pick up a reproduction stand-up arcade cabinet version for around £2,000. An original 1970s early-1980s cabinet or cocktail (tabletop) model will cost you anywhere from £500+, depending on condition and year.

You aren't likely to find an arcade cabinet at your local car boot sale, I'm afraid. However, you may wish to consider the investment potential of an original, good-condition machine: this was the groundbreaker, and if computers and consoles keep becoming more and more desirable, it could well appreciate in value. Keep a look out, too, for machines bearing the company name Bally Midway: they made Space Invaders for the US market.

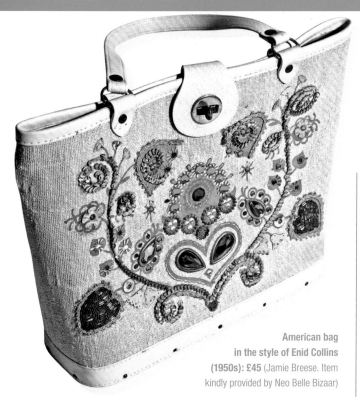

American bag
in the style of Enid Collins
(1950s): £45 (Jamie Breese. Item
kindly provided by Neo Belle Bizaar)

Vintage fashion

Ten years or so ago, the vintage clothing industry had
hit a low. Over the last few years it has picked up and is
undergoing a renaissance, with new shops and fairs opening
up all over the country. Vintage is back with a bang and
prices of good pieces have risen too.

The term 'Vintage Fashion' covers a wide variety of
period items – usually from the Victorian era to the early
'70s. If you attend a fair, you'll find very knowledgeable and
helpful traders selling shoes, sunglasses, travel luggage,
accessories, costume jewellery, hats, bags and, of course,
clothes – lots of them. Top-end 'new' vintage labels, including
Ozzie Clark and Biba, are now fiercely sought after, and
values are high for everything from garments to accessories.

How much?

The fairs are a good indicator of prices. There are 50p
baskets to art deco era dresses at £650+. For example, Ossie
Clark has now got a cult following, so pieces are featuring
far more at auction, and on eBay too. A good corset in great
condition from the 1890s will cost a collector over £200
today, while a top-end set of vintage leather cases from the
'30s or '40s starts at about £400 or so.

Blind Lemon (www.blindlemonvintage.co.uk) run several
superb vintage fairs around the country. Why not have a
rummage around your own home and get on eBay, or if you
have lots of potential stock, you could be a dealer for a day
for £60 at a fair. If you want to buy a few choice pieces, it
could prove a good investment for the future – the vintage
look is currently in, so many items can actually be worn!

Iconic fashion auction

A superb private collection of fashion from the '60s to the '90s
came up for grabs in October 2008. There has been a revival in
interest in fashion's iconic names from the past over recent years,
and this sale in London seems appropriate as many of the lots
were from revolutionary home-grown talent.

With over 250 assembled garments, headwear, and jewellery,
the sale was a vision of the styles and attitudes that defined
international fashion since 1960. Some of the designers included
Ossie Clark, Gianni Versace, Pierre Cardin, Issey Miyake, Vivienne
Westwood, Paco Rabanne, and André Courrèges, among others.

How much?

The auction was entitled 'Resurrection: Avant-Garde Fashion'
and the auctioneers claimed it to be the finest collection of
20th-century fashion in private hands. It was held in London at
Christie's South Kensington saleroom. Estimates ranged from
£500 to £10,000. One of the most prized lots
was an Aluminium Tunic Dress by Paco
Rabane. It sold for £15,000 despite an
estimate of £5,000–£8,000. A World's
End Harris Tweed Collection 'Crown'
from 1987–1988 sold for £2,250.

Many of these lots were limited,
of course, sometimes to one or two
garments even, but it is well known
that many dealers and some
customers have been lucky
enough to find many such gems
in years gone by in some of the
upmarket charity shops and boot
fairs. It might be time to have a
rummage through your attic!

A World's End Harris Tweed
Collection 'Crown' from
1987–1988 sold for £2,250 at
Christie's in 2008 (Image courtesy
of Christie's Images Ltd 2008)

American Lucite bag with
3D butterflies (1950s):
£65 (Jamie Breese.
Item kindly
provided by Neo
Belle Bizaar)

Wade

Despite the wobble in the collectables market of late, one company is pressing ahead and expanding. Wade is perhaps most famous for the NatWest Pigs, Whimsies and decanters. Not a lot of people know that this legendary British pottery actually has its roots back in the early 19th century. They started way back in 1810, and remain based in the potteries.

Wade experienced 10 per cent growth in 2007–2008 and has a completely new factory being built at a cost of £7 million. According to the MD, it will be the most modern manufacturing facility for ceramics in the world. Wade's decanters are still the core business: it is the world's leading manufacturer of ceramic decanters (Bell's, Chivas, etc.) with 2.5 million decanters made a year.

How much?

Wade collectables have often proved to be good investments, especially since the Whimsies arrived in the early 1950s. Over the last few years, they have revived the NatWest Piggies with a stunning range of gold pigs for lucky NatWest competition winners. For Christmas 2008 they produced 2,000 hand-cast Christmas tree decorations called 'Angel Love' to support the Donna Louise Children's Hospice. Anybody who made a donation of £10 or more to the Hospice was entitled to receive one of these limited-edition pieces.

There is a new book out which details Whimsies in great depth – *The World of Wade Whimsies* by Ian Warner and Mike Posgay (published by Schiffer Publishing). The Wade Collectors' Club organises all sorts of meets and events. If you would like to find out more, you can go to the collectors' club website: www.wadecollectorsclub.co.uk

Wade *Snow White* figurines released in early 2009 (Wade Collectors' Club)

A collection of Noah's Ark series Whimsies (Wade Collectors' Club)

Wade Whimsies

'Whimsies' – small, affordable animal figurines, which started a collecting craze. Though they first appeared in 1953, they are still hotly sought after today. They came in boxes of five, were very small indeed, and proved an instant hit. Originally, ten sets of five were created, making a total of 49 Whimsies – one set had only four. Newer sets were produced in the 1960s and '70s right up until their last release in 1984.

How much?

The most common figurines, on their own, usually cost between £1 and £10 each. However, there are probably two Whimsies which beat the others in rarity: the Swan and the Shire Horse. Both figures roughly double the price of a set if they feature in it, to over £100 per set. The Elephant Train set of five from 1957 to 1959 is worth even more today: around £250. The presence of a box in good condition, in particular with the early gems, can add substantially to the value.

There was a second series produced much later, although many collectors agree that the quality was inferior to the earlier figurines. These are accordingly worth less, but more accessible and easier to locate for the novice or younger enthusiast. Whimsies were not just animals: there was a nursery rhyme series and even a Disney tie-in (originally packaged in brightly coloured, round cardboard boxes which looked just like hatboxes). Many of the Whimsies were promotional items linked to products, like tea, and they are of interest to two different types of collector.

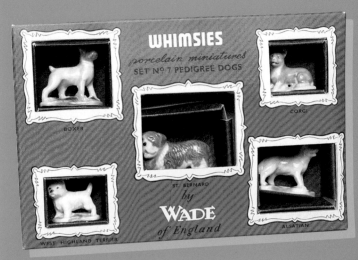

A boxed 'Pedigree Dogs' set No. 7 by Wade (Wade Collectors Club)

The Sony Walkman was a landmark design and a revolution in personal entertainment (Wikimedia)

Walkman

It's amazing to think that the original market research suggested that speakers stuck either side of the head would not be a wise move for Sony. They had been leaders in technology with many world 'firsts' – from home video recorders to floppy disks – but when the little blue machine called the TPS-L2 came out, it proved to be the biggest selling consumer electronic music system of all time!

The first model was going to be named the 'Stowaway' for the UK market. Eventually it was called the 'Walkman' and it was launched on 1 July 1979. It weighed a fairly hefty 390g, but the sound quality was great and it took off. Since then, Sony has made over 300 different models.

How much?

Original examples of the TPS-L2 seem to be few and far between on Internet auction sites worldwide. Maybe owners haven't realised their potential collectability. A truly mint machine in a good box could command £100+ at present, but I expect this to rise steeply in time. Make sure the headphones are included.

Oddly, the first Walkmans had two headphone sockets so friends could share the music, but this was later dropped. Look for the first dual socket machines with the distinctive orange button. For the future, why not keep your Apple iPod's packaging and try to keep it in good condition. The iPod is a stunning design and is changing the music world (and certainly the music business with its iTunes online music store).

Wassily chair

Now considered one of the most important and influential chair designs of all time, the Model B3 chair (later known as the Wassily chair) is a sought-after piece of furniture and can be found in design museums across the globe.

The B3 was created by the legendary designer, Marcel Breuer (1902–1981) in 1925. He later went on to be an influential architect, but this revolutionary chair was designed early on in his career while he was at the famous Bauhaus school in Germany. The Bauhaus was a short-lived but extremely important chapter in the Modernist movement, and it's fair to say that its output affected household object design across the world. Inspired by the design of a bicycle: the Wassily chair was one of the first to make use of tubular steel.

How much?

The original chairs found homes in important offices and celebrities' homes all over the globe. Today, a truly original, very early example in fine condition can sell for thousands of pounds. As it stands, reproductions are quite numerous and can even be bought new today for as little as a hundred or so quid. Almost all reproductions use leather for the seat and arms, instead of the original's canvas.

With these important modernist chairs and other items of furniture, it really pays to research the subject so you know what you are looking for. There are many books to refer to, and you can always visit The Design Museum in London to look at them first hand. It is still worth scanning the free ads, local junk shops, and the Internet to find these treasures. Other top designers of the era, such as Gerrit Rietveld, Mies van der Rohe, and Alvar Aalto, are all worth looking out for, and prices for original pieces remain very high too. All these chairs are unlikely to drop in value, as they are so historically important.

A 1970s reproduction B3 chair (Jamie Breese)

Textured items by Geoffrey
Baxter sold at Christie's
(Image courtesy of Christie's
Images Ltd 2008)

Whitefriars Glass

Studio glass looks great in today's modern homes, and
prices were rising accordingly in the mid-1990s. Once
considered kitsch, you should keep a look out in particular
for Scandinavian pieces, and glassware by the ever-popular
UK studios of Whitefriars.

Whitefriars started out in 1834 as James Powell & Sons.
There had been glassmakers on that very same site since
1680. Though popular manufacturers of church glass (they
even made a series of pieces for the legendary Red House
for William Morris), their big moment came much later, in
the 1960s, with the radical work overseen or created by
Geoffrey Baxter (1926–1995). This is the period that was
undergoing such a revival in the mid-2000s. Sadly, the
company closed down in 1980.

How much?

Larger pieces, say a bowl from around 1965, can command
anywhere from £65–£165 from a good glassware dealer. My
favourites are from the 'Textured Range' that are considered
a must-have by collectors.

It is still quite possible to find good examples of
Whitefriars glass at car boot fairs. Buy a guidebook so you
know your patterns and shapes, and then get out there.
If you have no joy, you can pay between £25 and £60 and
pick up a genuine Baxter item from a dealer or the web.
The 'Nailhead' vase is quite funky and has a very textured
surface. It fits into this price band and makes for a great,
colourful display piece for a shelf or table centrepiece.

Geoffrey Baxter

The Baxter-driven designs by Whitefriars look really great in
the interiors of today's homes, and they have been rising in
value since the early 2000s.

Whitefriars' big moment came in the 1960s with the
radical works by Geoffrey Baxter. He broke new ground with
bold innovations and helped the company recover from the
austerity of post-war Britain and the changes made within
the factory to accommodate the war effort. It was his work in
the 1960s, most notably the very unusual 'Textured Range' of
wares that today are considered a must-have by many studio
glass collectors. These were initially fashioned using all sorts
of raw materials – from barbed wire to tree bark.

How much?

Today, good, undamaged examples of his famous 'Banjo'
Vase are still being sold by top dealers and auction houses.
A tidy example is worth over £600–£800+ in the right colour.
Ten years ago you would have been lucky to have got £100.
Other works which are worth snapping up now, if found
cheap and undamaged, would include the two different
sizes of 'Drunken Bricklayer' vases: they come in several
colours too. Two years ago the large vase in tangerine was
commanding £800+, for example. Now the same vase might
be selling for just over half that. Curiously, the smaller version
of that very vase has crept up in value. In general, a small
orange or blue example cost £200–£300 at auction in 2008.
The same vase in Indigo and Forest Green may make more.

The 'Bark' vases are affordable and range in value from
£30–£100 depending on colour. Once considered kitsch,
now trendy, Baxter designs are great items to keep on
display for the future. The prices started to go a bit crazy in
2003, and have dipped a little
now, but I suspect there is
a good chance that they
will keep as a solid, classic
investment for the future.

A large
Whitefriars
Meadow
Green
'Banjo' vase,
that sold in
June 2005
for £1,380
(Image courtesy
of Sotheby's
Picture Library)

Winnie-the-Pooh

2006 marked the 80th birthday of Pooh. Adored the world over, he has become a true icon of childhood. Though the stories started it, it is the movies and, more recently, the collectable figures that have been keeping Pooh and friends in the limelight. Some of these figures have become quite valuable.

Winnie was actually named after a toy bear that was bought from Harrods for Christopher Robin Milne. Christopher was the son of creator Alan Alexander Milne. The Harrods bear was renamed Winnie after Christopher's favourite bear 'Winnipeg' from London Zoo. Recreations of Pooh have been made by several top names, including Enesco, Beswick, Royal Doulton, Border Fine Arts, Merrythought, Gund, and Halcyon Days.

How much?

Beswick created the first ceramic Poohs in the mid-1960s using the Disney image (with red T-shirt). A set of eight Beswick figures sold for £330 in 2007. Christopher Robin is one of the rarest at £40–£80+ at auction today. Tigger with a brown back stamp can make £60–£80+. In 1996, a range of figures was introduced by Royal Doulton with a 70th anniversary back stamp. These sold for around £20 and now make up to £70. Look out for the earlier plush toys, particularly those made in the '40s and '50s by Agnes Brush before Disney (1964 onwards). These have made several hundred pounds. The only known painting in oil of Winnie-the-Pooh was sold in November 2000 by Sotheby's for the hammer price of £110,000.

The first editions of the first few Pooh books are the real headline-grabbers. *When We Were Very Young* from 1924 is scarce – there were only 5,140 regular copies of the first edition produced – but rarer still was a special limited run of just 110 books printed in the same year. These are worth thousands if in good condition.

A record was made for an A. A. Milne first edition of *Winnie the Pooh* (Methuen, 1926), inscribed by the author 'To Christopher Robin and Winnie-the-Pooh'. It was sold in December 2002 by Sotheby's for £85,000.

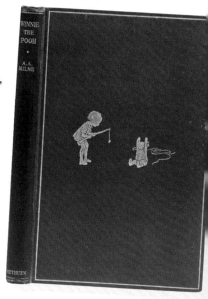

'Christopher Dresses the Tree' (WP57). A current Winnie-the-Pooh piece: £30 (Image courtesy of Royal Doulton/Wedgwood)

Also, for his 80th birthday, several leading manufacturers released new figures: the 'Pooh and Friends' range from Enesco is one example. These pieces are date-limited or limited editions. Previous anniversary items have risen in value – so these might follow suit.

In December 2008, Sotheby's, London, auctioned a set of original drawings by E. H. Shepard, who illustrated the Pooh books. The record for a Shepard drawing was broken at this sale, with one selling for £115,250.

Winnie-the-Pooh (Methuen, 1926), inscribed by the author 'To Christopher Robin and Winnie-the-Pooh'. Sold in December 2002 by Sotheby's for £85,000 (Image courtesy of Sotheby's Picture Library)

This set of Beswick Winnie-the-Pooh figurines (1968–1990) made £100 at auction in November 2008 (Image courtesy of Vectis Auctions)

A 10inx8in black-and-white photograph signed by Ray Bolger. The photograph is a close-up of Bolger in full costume from his famous role as the Scarecrow from *The Wizard of Oz*: £395 (Image courtesy of Fraser's Autographs)

Wizard of Oz

Widely considered to be one of the most popular movies of all time, *The Wizard of Oz* has maintained an astonishing popularity in the memorabilia market. Completed on 16 March 1939 at a then-unheard-of cost of $2,777,000, it raised a fairly paltry $3 million on its initial release. This is not far off what a single costume item later went on to raise at auction!

There have been a number of books and collectables made through the years. The first edition of *The Wonderful Wizard of Oz* written by Frank Baum in 1900 frequently sells for £10,000 or more in good condition. The red slippers from the film version are the real Holy Grail. The House of Winston made a pair of real ruby slippers to mark the flick's 50th anniversary. These were valued at millions.

How much?

In 2005, there was a rare opportunity to own a slice of real film history: Dorothy's dress. The custom-made outfit was designed for the 17-year-old Garland with a 27in waist and her name sewn on the inside hem. Six costumes were made for the film in total, one of which is owned by the actress Debbie Reynolds. It was sold by a British collector, who bought it for just £10,500 at auction in 1989. With an estimate of £35,000, it soared to £140,000! The Cowardly Lion's paw-shaped shoe clawed in £17,500, but the house was blown down when Judy Garland's ruby slippers sold in May 2000. The final price was £450,000.

If you are interested in looking further, then it would be worth picking up a copy of *The Wizard of Oz Collector's Treasury* by Jay Scarfone and William Stillman (Schiffer Publishing). If you are lucky enough to own a Judy Garland autograph then you could afford to travel to Kansas: her signature on a good photo is valued at £2,500 by Fraser's Autographs.

Yellow Submarine

Widely recognised as one of the finest and most influential animated films of all time, this Beatles' landmark picture helped define the late 1960s. The story tells of the Blue Meanies' attack on the kingdom of Pepperland. The Corgi die-cast toy, also released in 1968, has come to be one of the most iconic toys of the 'flower power' era, and is an affordable alternative to the costly animation art from the film itself. It measures around 5in long and has four rotating periscopes and pop-up hatches which reveal the Fab Four in miniature. Perhaps you still have one floating around somewhere in the attic?

How much?

It is vital to have this toy in the best condition to get the best price. The propeller at the rear must be there, and so should the periscopes. The sub also came with a green plastic sea cradle that the toy could be displayed on. The box is important, as the graphics were typical of the era. The top part features John Lennon with a trombone, and three other characters. The cellophane window should be intact too. If you find a mint example of Model 801 or 802, expect to pay up to £400.

Corgi classics released a snazzy reproduction of the original toy in 2002 to tie in with the re-release of the movie and the toy's enduring cult status. There are many other modern associated collectables to look out for: a 'Pepperland' musical globe; a series of seven limited-edition figures; a very cool limited-edition wristwatch made by funky watchmaker Fossil; a Zippo lighter, and even a very special limited-edition (of 5,250) Corgi submarine made in 1998 to celebrate the movie's 30th anniversary.

Corgi Yellow Submarine can cost up to £400 if you have a mint and boxed example (Image courtesy of Vectis Auctions)

Contents by category

If you would like to receive Jamie Breese's newsletter, discover more about his TV shows and find out more about buying collectables, why not visit

www.jamiebreese.co.uk

You can read Jamie's column 'Treasure Hunters' each week only in the *Sunday Mirror*